Betrothed for a

Or, Queenie Trevalyn's love test

Laura Jean Libbey

Alpha Editions

This edition published in 2024

ISBN : 9789367247075

Design and Setting By
Alpha Editions
www.alphaedis.com
Email - info@alphaedis.com

As per information held with us this book is in Public Domain.
This book is a reproduction of an important historical work. Alpha Editions uses the best technology to reproduce historical work in the same manner it was first published to preserve its original nature. Any marks or number seen are left intentionally to preserve its true form.

Contents

CHAPTER I. A STRANGER'S LOVE. ....- 1 -

CHAPTER II. A WORSHIPER OF WEALTH. ....- 6 -

CHAPTER III. THE COURSE OF TRUE LOVE. ....- 12 -

CHAPTER IV. THE MIDNIGHT DUEL. ....- 18 -

CHAPTER V. THE POWER OF GOLD. ....- 23 -

CHAPTER VI. A MAN'S FICKLE HEART. ....- 28 -

CHAPTER VII. A DREAD ALTERNATIVE. ....- 34 -

CHAPTER VIII. WHAT IS LIFE WITHOUT LOVE? ....- 39 -

CHAPTER IX. "A LITTLE ROUGH DIAMOND." ....- 44 -

CHAPTER X. AFTER THIRTEEN YEARS. ....- 49 -

CHAPTER XI. REBUKED BY A GIRL. ....- 54 -

CHAPTER XII. "WHO IS JESS?" ....- 58 -

CHAPTER XIII. LUCK SMILES. ....- 63 -

CHAPTER XIV. A FATEFUL MEETING..- 68 -

CHAPTER XV. THE LOVE THAT IS SURE TO COME. ....- 72 -

CHAPTER XVI. COLD AND HEARTLESS. ....- 77 -

CHAPTER XVII. WAS IT THE DECREE OF FATE? ....- 82 -

CHAPTER XVIII. A PREMONITION OF COMING EVIL. ....- 87 -

CHAPTER XIX. THE BETROTHAL.............................- 92 -

CHAPTER XX. "DO WE EVER LOVE THE WRONG ONE?"..- 97 -

CHAPTER XXI. HOW EASILY THINGS GO WRONG. ....- 102 -

CHAPTER XXII. THE RESCUE..............................- 107 -

CHAPTER XXIII. VAIN REGRETS...............- 112 -

CHAPTER XXIV. ONLY AN IMPULSIVE CHILD. ....- 117 -

CHAPTER XXV. "WILL YOU MARRY ME, LITTLE JESS?"...- 121 -

CHAPTER XXVI. LOVE..- 125 -

CHAPTER XXVII. DECISIONS. ....- 130 -

CHAPTER XXVIII. THE DARKENING CLOUDS....................- 135 -

CHAPTER XXIX. "LEAVE MY HOUSE."...................................- 140 -

CHAPTER XXX. HIS UNCLE'S BRIDE......................................- 145 -

CHAPTER XXXI. IN HIS POWER.............................- 150 -

CHAPTER XXXII. WHAT MIGHT HAVE BEEN. ....- 155 -

CHAPTER XXXIII. TO WRECK A YOUNG GIRL'S LIFE........................- 160 -

CHAPTER XXXIV. UNDER THE MASK OF FRIENDSHIP..................- 165 -

CHAPTER XXXV. HIS STORY. ....- 170 -

CHAPTER XXXVI. THE WEB OF FATE..- 174 -

CHAPTER XXXVII. A GREAT SURPRISE...- 179 -

CHAPTER XXXVIII. AT HIS FEET. ....- 183 -

CHAPTER XXXIX. A TEST OF LOVE. ....- 187 -

CHAPTER XL. THE FIRST LOVE...................- 192 -

CHAPTER XLI. "WAS IT ALL A DREAM?"...- 196 -

CHAPTER XLII. THE PLOT THICKENS. ....- 200 -

CHAPTER XLIII. THE LOVE THAT WILL NOT DIE. ....- 205 -

CHAPTER XLIV. THE WAYS OF PROVIDENCE. ....- 209 -

CHAPTER XLV. NAMING THE DAY. ....- 213 -

CHAPTER XLVI. OLD FRIENDS MEET. ....- 217 -

CHAPTER XLVII. A MOMENT OF TERROR. ....- 221 -

CHAPTER XLVIII. WHAT IS TO BE WILL BE. ....- 226 -

CHAPTER I.
A STRANGER'S LOVE.

"Her lips were silent—scarcely beat her heart,

Her eyes alone proclaimed, 'we must not part;'

Thy hope may perish, or thy friends may flee,

Farewell to life, but not adieu to thee."

It was on the last night of the season at gay Newport; on the morrow, at the noon hour, there was to be a great exodus of the summer guests, and by nightfall the famous Ocean House would be closed.

The brilliant season of 1901 would be but a memory to the merry throng—dancing, laughing, flirting to their hearts' content to-night in the magnificent ballroom; and every one seemed intent upon making the most of the occasion.

As usual, "the beautiful Miss Trevalyn," as every one called her, was the belle of the ball, as she had been the belle of the season, much to the chagrin of a whole set of beauties who had come this summer to take Newport by storm and capture the richest matrimonial prize. Even Miss Queenie Trevalyn's cruelest enemy could not help but admit that she was simply perfect to-night as she floated down the plant-embowered ballroom, a fairy vision in pink tulle, fluttering ribbons and garlands of blush-roses looping back her long jetty curls. Here, there and everywhere flashed that slender pink figure with the lovely face, rosy and radiant with smiles and flushed with excitement, her red lips parted, and those wondrous midnight-black eyes of hers gleaming like stars.

"Who is the gentleman with whom Miss Trevalyn is waltzing?" asked an anxious mother—a guest from one of the cottages—whose four unmarried daughters were at that moment playing the disagreeable part of wall flowers.

Her companion, an old-time guest of the hotel, who kept strict tabs upon the other guests, and prided herself upon knowing pretty thoroughly everybody else's business, leaned forward from her seat on the piazza and raised her lorgnette to her eyes, critically surveying the young lady's partner.

He was a tall, handsome, distinguished man of at least thirty, bronzed and bearded, with a noble bearing that could not fail to attract attention anywhere. He was a man whom men take to on sight, and women adore.

His eyes were deep blue and his hair was a dark, chestnut brown—a shade darker perhaps than the trim beard and mustache were.

"That is just what everybody here has been trying to find out," was the reply, "but no one seems to know; he came here quite a month ago, and the first evening of his arrival proved himself a hero. It happened in this way: The elevator boy, upon reaching the fourth floor, had stepped out of the car for a moment to lift a heavy satchel for a lady who had come up with him, to a room a couple of doors distant, and in that moment two persons had entered the elevator—Miss Queenie Trevalyn and the distinguished-looking new arrival. No one could tell just how the terrible affair occurred, whether one or the other brushed against the lever accidentally or not, but the next instant, with the rapidity of lightning, and without an instant's warning, the car began to shoot downward.

"Wild cries of horror broke from the lips of the guests at each landing as it shot past. They realized what had happened; they could see that there was some one in the car, and they realized that it meant instant death to the occupants when the car reached the flagging below.

"Some one who heard the horrible whizzing sound from below, and knew what had occurred, had the presence of mind to tear aside the wire door. What occurred then even those who witnessed it can scarcely recount, they were so dazeny. Anyhow, seeing the clearing straight ahead, the stranger made the most daring leap for life that was ever chronicled either in tale or history, through it; he had Miss Trevalyn, who was in a deep swoon, clasped tightly in his arms.

"Out from the flying, death-dealing car he shot like an arrow from a bow, landing headforemost among the throng, who fairly held their breath in horror too awful for words.

"The car was wrecked into a thousand fragments.

"By the presence of mind of the heroic stranger Miss Trevalyn's and his own life were spared, and they were little the worse, save from the fright, from their thrilling experience.

"They would have made a great furore over Mr. John Dinsmore at the Ocean Hotel after that, but he would not permit it. He flatly refused to be lionized, which showed Newport society that he was certainly careless about being in the swim, as we call it.

"His heart was not proof against a lovely girl's attractions, however. He finished by falling in love with Miss Trevalyn in the most approved, romantic style, and has been her veritable shadow ever since, despite the fact that there are a score of handsome fellows in the race for her favor, and one in particular, a young man who is heir to the fortune of his uncle, a multi-millionaire, who was supposed to be the lucky winner of the queen's heart up to the day of the thrilling elevator episode."

"I suppose she will marry the fine-looking hero who saved her life," said the mother of the four unwedded maidens.

The other returned significantly:

"If he is rich, it is not unlikely; if he is poor, Queenie Trevalyn will whistle him down the wind, as the old saying goes. Lawrence Trevalyn's daughter is too worldly to make an unsuitable marriage. Her father is one of the ablest lawyers at the New York bar, and makes no end of money, but his extravagant family succeeds splendidly in living up to every dollar of his entire income, and Miss Queenie knows that her only hope is in marrying a fortune; she is quite as ambitious as her parents. With her the head will rule instead of the heart, I promise you; that is, if one can judge from the score of lovers she has sent adrift this season."

"I really thought she cared a little for young Ray Challoner, the millionaire. I confess I had expected to see her pass most of her last evening at Newport dancing with him exclusively; but perhaps she is pursuing this course to pique him into an immediate proposal. A remarkably shrewd and clever girl is Queenie Trevalyn."

"Is this Mr. Challoner deeply in love with her, too?" asked the mother of the four unwedded girls, trying to veil the eagerness in her voice behind a mass of carelessness.

"Hopelessly," returned her informant, "and for that reason I marvel that he is not on hand to sue for every dance and challenge any one to mortal combat who dares seek the beauty's favor."

Meanwhile, the young girl who had been the subject of the above gossip had disappeared through one of the long French windows that opened out upon the piazza, and, leaning upon the arm of her companion, had floated across the white sands to the water's edge.

For a moment they stood thus, in utter silence, while the tide rippled in slowly at their feet, mirroring the thousands of glittering stars in the blue dome above on its pulsing bosom.

Queenie pretends the utmost innocence in regard to the object he has in view in asking her to come down to the water by whose waves they have spent so many happy hours, to say good-by.

A score or more of lovers have stood on the self-same spot with her in the last fortnight, and ere they had turned away from those rippling waves they had laid their hearts and fortunes at her dainty feet, only to be rejected, as only a coquette can reject a suitor.

Yes, she knew what was coming; his troubled face and agitation was a forerunner of that, but her tongue ran on volubly and gayly, of how she had enjoyed Newport, and how sorry she would feel as the train bore her away to her city home.

And as she talked on in her delightful, breezy way, his face grew graver and more troubled.

"He is going to ask me to marry him, and it depends upon his fortune as to whether I say yes or no. He has been wonderfully silent as to what he is, but if I am good at guessing, I should say that he is a Western silver king—he must be worth twice as many millions as Ray Challoner," Queenie said to herself.

She had adroitly led up to a proposal of marriage by knowing just what to say, and how to use her subtly sweet voice in uttering the sentiments low and falteringly, to arouse him to a declaration of the tender passion.

Standing there, he was thinking of the gulf which lay between him and this fair young girl whom he had learned to love, and that he should leave her without revealing one word of what was in his heart; but as he turned to her to make some commonplace remark, and suggest returning to the ballroom, she looked so irresistibly sweet and gracious, his heart seemed swept away from him by storm.

He never knew quite how it came about, but he found himself holding her hands crushed close to his bosom, while his white lips murmured:

"This has been a month in my life which will stand out clear and distinct—forever. In it I have tasted the only happiness which I have ever known; nothing will ever be like it to me again. Will you remember me, I wonder, after you have returned home?"

"Why should I not?" she murmured, shyly. "You have helped me to pass the happiest summer I have ever known."

"Do you really mean that, Miss Trevalyn—Queenie!" he cried, hoarsely, wondering if his ears had not deceived him.

"Yes," she sighed, glancing down with a tenderness in her tone which she intended that he should not mistake.

"I should not speak the words that are trembling on my lips, but your kindness gives courage to my frightened heart, and I will dare incur your displeasure, perhaps, by uttering them; but you must know, you who are so beautiful that all men love you—you whom to gaze upon is to become lost."

"I—I do not know what you mean, Mr. Dinsmore," she murmured, with shy, averted eyes and downcast, blushing face, thinking how different this proposal was to the score of others she had received.

"May I dare tell you? Promise me you will not be very angry," he said, humbly, "and that you will forgive me."

But he did not wait for her answer, he dared not pause to think, lest his courage should fail him, but cried huskily:

"Pardon me if I am brusque and abrupt, sweet girl, but the words are forcing themselves like a torrent from my heart to my lips—ah, Heaven, you must have guessed the truth ere this, Queenie! I love you! I love you with a passion so great it is driving me mad. Let me pray my prayer to you, let me kneel at your feet and utter it. Ah, Heaven! words fail me to tell you how dearly I love you, my darling. My life seems to have merged completely into yours. I love you so dearly and well, if you send me from you, you will wreck my life—break my heart. I cast my life as a die upon your yes or no. Look at me, darling, and answer me—will you be my wife, Queenie. For Heaven's sake say yes and end my agitation and my misery. Is your answer life or death for me, my love?"

CHAPTER II.
A WORSHIPER OF WEALTH.

"I have two lovers, both brave and gay;

And they both have spoken their minds to-day;

They both seem dying for love of me;

Well, if I choose one of them, which shall it be?

One is handsome, and tall, and grand,

With gold in the bank and acres of land,

And he says he will give them all to me

If only I'll promise his wife to be.

The other is bonny, and blithe, and true,

With honest face bronzed, and eyes of blue;

But the wealth of his heart is the only thing

He can give to me with the wedding ring.

Yes, both seem dying for love of me;

Well, if I choose one of them, which shall it be?"

Queenie Trevalyn looked up archly into the handsome, agitated face bending over her, and blushed deeply.

"Before I answer you, let me remind you that you are quite a stranger to us, Mr. Dinsmore; you have not chosen to make a confidant of any one concerning your personal history—from whence you came, or—or—your standing in the community in which you reside," she murmured, sweetly.

"I am aware of that fact," he answered, gloomily, dropping her hands dejectedly, while a heavy sigh trembled over his pale lips. "The truth is, I dreaded telling you, lest I should, perhaps, lose your friendship at first, then, at last, your love; but no! you are too good, too noble, pure and true to let wealth and position weigh—against—love."

His words gave the girl something like a fright. She had counted upon this handsome, bearded adorer being a man of great wealth. She had even fondly hoped that he might be a prince, traveling in disguise—a personage of superior order. No wonder his words—which seemed to bid fair to scatter these delicious hopes—alarmed the girl whose sole ambition was wealth.

She did not answer; for the first time in her life this girl, who was so witty, versatile and brilliant, was at a loss for words.

"It is but right that you should know who and what I am," he pursued, slowly. "Indeed, I should have prefaced my declaration of love with that information. I am but a struggling author, Queenie—a man who is fighting hard to make his way in the crowded field of letters to future great achievements. I might have made money in the past had I grasped the opportunities held out to me. I have been of a roving disposition—nomadic in my tastes, eager to see the whole wide world, and give to the people who stay at home glimpses of foreign lands, through my pen.

"I was prodigal with the money I earned from this source. I gave it freely to the poor and needy, who were everywhere about. On the burning sands of Africa, or on the snowy plains of Russia, when I lay down to sleep, with only the sky above me, I was as happy as men who lie down in palaces. I had no care, I was as free from it as the joyous air that blows. I led a happy enough life of it until I came here and met you; from that hour the world has seemed to change for me. I am no longer the careless, happy-go-lucky fellow of a few short weeks ago, leading a merry, Bohemian existence—just as content without money as with it.

"If you will say that there is hope for me I will remedy all that; I will go to work with a will and make something grand and noble out of my life, with the one thought like a guiding star ever before me: The woman I love shall be proud of me. I——"

The sentence never was finished. Glancing up at that moment he caught sight of her face, which she had turned so that the white, bright moonlight fell full upon it.

The scorn on the beautiful face, the anger that blazed in the dark eyes, the contempt the curling lips revealed, appalled him. He had much more to tell her that was important, but the words fairly froze on his lips, and died away unmuttered.

"Hush! not another word," she cried, quite as soon as she was able to speak, through her intense anger. "You have basely deceived me, as well as every one else. You knew of the current report that you were a man of fabulous wealth and you let it go uncontradicted. You have sailed under false colors to force your way into society. You have cheated and deluded us into believing that you were a gentleman. Being what you are—a nobody—you insult me with your proposal of marriage. Conduct me back to the hotel at once, please."

His face had grown white as marble—even his lips were colorless. His eyes were dim with a sorrow too intense for words, and his strong hands trembled like aspen leaves in the wind, and his bosom heaved. Her cruel, taunting words had struck home to the very core of his heart, and made a cruel wound there, like the stinging cut of a deadly, poisoned dagger.

There was no mistaking the meaning of her words, she spoke plainly enough. If he had been rich he would have stood a fair chance of winning her. The love of a great, strong, honorable heart did not count with her. Her affection was not for exchange, but for sale. The beautiful girl whom he had thought little less than the angels above was but common clay, a mercenary creature, who weighed gold in the scale against marriage, and whose idea of a gentleman, one of nature's noblemen, was measured by his wealth. To her a poor man was less than the dust beneath her dainty feet.

"You have heard what I have said, Mr. Dinsmore," said Queenie Trevalyn, haughtily. "Pray conform with my request by taking me back to the ballroom at once. Were it not for appearances I would leave you and return myself."

Like one dazed he turned slowly around, setting his miserable face toward the lights and the music, but his overwrought nerves could stand no more, strong man though he was, and without a moan or a cry he fell headlong upon the white sands at her feet—like a hero in a great battle falls when he has received his death wound, crying out: "When love has conquered pride and anger, you may call me back again."

"Great heavens! what a dilemma!" cried Queenie Trevalyn, angrily. She did not pause a moment to lave his face with the cooling water so near at hand, or to take the trouble to ascertain if his headlong fall had injured him, so intent was she in hurrying away from the spot before a crowd gathered.

A moment more and she was flying across the white stretch of beach, her pink tulle gossamer robe trailing after her like a sunset cloud which somehow had fallen from heaven to earth.

She gained the hotel by a side entrance, and was soon back into the ballroom. She had been gone so short a time that few had missed her save the partner who was just coming in search of her for his waltz, the first notes of which had just struck up.

"Alone, Miss Trevalyn!" exclaimed Ray Challoner, advancing toward the palm-embowered nook in which she had seated herself. "Why, this is unprecedented. I did not suppose you ever enjoyed the luxury of being alone; such is the penalty of having admirers by the score," bowing low before the beauty, adding: "I beg to remind you that this is our waltz, and it is my favorite music, 'My Queen.'"

Queenie Trevalyn arose graciously, her rosebud lips wreathed in the sweetest of smiles. She danced and laughed, the gayest of the gay, never for an instant did her thoughts revert to the heart that was enduring the agonies of death, for love of her, down upon the cold, white sands.

Ay! There he lay, stunned almost unto death, never caring to arise and face the world again. All he wanted to do was to lie there until the tide would come in and bear him away from life and the love which he had found more cruel than death.

With such a man love, with all the intensity of his grand soul, was only possible. It was not for such a one to worship lightly at a woman's shrine.

How long he lay there he never knew. It was in reality a few moments, but to him it seemed endless centuries. He was startled by the sound of familiar voices.

"It is indeed Dinsmore, by all that is wonderful!" exclaimed a man who bent over him, while his companion said musingly: "What in the world could have happened to have felled him like this, and he strong as an ox!"

"The best and quickest way to find out is to bring him to and see," declared the other, kneeling beside the prostrate form and dashing salt water in the white face, then catching up his hands and beginning to chafe them vigorously.

John Dinsmore opened his eyes slowly and gazed into the two anxious faces bending over him.

"Are you ill, old fellow!" they both cried in a breath. "What in the name of goodness has happened that we find you like this?"

His lips opened to say: "A beautiful woman has broken my heart, and I am lying here for the tide to come in to carry me out—to death," but the words seemed to scorch his lips, he could not utter them. They helped him to his feet, still wondering.

"I was stricken with a pain at my heart," he said. "I shall be better soon."

"Let's hope so, for we have brought the means with us to make you so, if anything on this round earth can. But by the way," went on one of them, "you do not seem the least surprised to find the two chums, poor as church mice, whom you left behind you in broiling New York, apparently 'doing' fashionable Newport, though it is like catching sly old dog Time by the tip

- 9 -

of his tail, coming here on the last evening, when the play is about over, and they are just going to ring down the curtain."

His two companions linked arms with him, one on either side, and drew him along the beach, each waiting for the other to unfold to John Dinsmore the amazing news which had brought them there.

While they hesitated thus you shall learn their identity, reader.

The tall, dark-haired young man on the right was Hazard Ballou, artist; French as to descent, as his name indicated, who was struggling for fame and fortune by painting pictures which nobody seemed to want to buy, and illustrating the joke articles in an evening paper to earn support in the meantime.

His companion was Jerry Gaines, a reporter, that was all, though he did have wonderful ambition and always alluded confidently to the time when he should be the editor of some great New York paper, and when that time arrived, what he should do for the remainder of the trinity, his author and artist friends, who were always ready to share their crust with him when luck went dead against him in being able to gather in good news articles, and getting up acceptable copy. His gains lay all in his name at present, instead of the more practical place—his pocket.

The "Trinity," as the three young men styled themselves, occupied one and the same room in a New York boarding house, each swearing never to sever the bond by marrying, though a veritable Helen of Troy should tempt them.

The three friends had toiled hard, but even in their work they were happy, for they had few cares, and had not been touched by the fever called Love.

"You had better tell him what brings us," whispered Ballou to Gaines, as John Dinsmore seemed in no hurry to question them.

"Reporters are generally chosen to break startling news to people," remarked that young gentleman, dryly. Then, turning to Dinsmore, he began, abruptly: "I say, old fellow, you were a sly dog, when you heard us cussing rich folks in general, never to mention that you had great expectations in that direction, I vow."

"I do not understand you, Jerry," remarked Dinsmore, looking at his friend in puzzled wonder.

"I may as well break headlong into the facts as beat about the bush," laughed Jerry Gaines, adding: "Well, to tell you an amazing truth, we are here to congratulate you upon inheriting a fortune. A pair of English lawyers have just succeeded in ferreting you out and locating you with our aid. They bring the astounding news, and better still, the documents which prove you to be heir to one of the finest estates in Louisiana, an immense tobacco plantation adjoining it, and——"

"My poor old Uncle George!" cut in John Dinsmore, surprised for the moment out of the grief which had taken such a deep hold of him. "And he is dead. I am deeply grieved to hear it. And you say he has left his enormous wealth to me. I can honestly say that I am astounded. He has always given me to understand that I need not expect one cent from him. He was deeply angered at me for my love of roving about the world. There were others nearer and dearer to him who had every right to expect to inherit his fortune. I am bewildered; I cannot understand why he chose to make me his heir.

"If you had brought me this wonderful news yesterday, boys, you would have made me almost insane with joy and gratitude—ay, have made me the happiest of men. Now it is but as dross to me. The gods have sent the golden gift to me too late—too late."

"You did not wait for me to finish, old fellow," said Gaines, coolly. "There is a string tied to the inheritance. If you accept it you must take a girl with it—for your wife, so your uncle's will reads."

CHAPTER III.
THE COURSE OF TRUE LOVE.

"Then let the inheritance go if it be mine only on condition that I take a wife with it," exclaimed John Dinsmore, proudly. "I will have none of it. Never mention it to me again if you are true friends of mine and respect my feelings. I would not marry the loveliest or the richest woman the world holds. I could never look into a woman's face with love in my heart for her, and the man who marries a woman without loving her is a villain, a rascal of the deepest dye. Heaven forbid that I should sell my honor and my manhood for such a price. Say no more about the inheritance, boys, I spurn it."

"You have actually gone mad, Dinsmore," cried Ballou, vehemently. "It would do for an actor on the stage to rant about wealth in that way, but in real life it is quite a different matter. One would think to hear you that you never knew what it was to want a square meal when your stories were returned with thanks, or to borrow enough from your friends to buy a paper dickey and cuffs in which to make a neat show before an editor. Bah!—don't be a fool, I say. Take the goods the gods provide."

"And I echo Ballou's sentiments," declared Jerry Gaines. "No one but a positive madman would let such a chance slip. Money can do anything, old fellow. It can purchase comfort and position, the luxury of idleness, royal good times, every enjoyment—ay, and last but not least, the hand of a beautiful woman in marriage. What more could you want?"

"I should want the heart of the woman I wedded, and money cannot buy the love of a true, good woman's heart," returned John Dinsmore, huskily.

As he spoke he thought of the royally beautiful creature from whom he had so lately parted on those self-same white sands, the girl to whom he had given all the love of his loyal heart, only to be scoffed at and spurned; the girl whom he had blindly believed Providence had especially given to him since the hour he had saved her life so miraculously, risking thereby the loss of his own. He had been so sure of her that he never for one instant doubted fate's intentions, and had given himself up to his idolatrous love for her, body and soul, heart and mind.

"Say no more on the subject, good friends. You both mean well, I know, but it can never be," said Dinsmore, earnestly. "Believe me, I know why I speak thus. Say no more to me of the inheritance. Help me to forget that it was ever in my grasp; that will be true friendship shown to me."

"We must leave you for an hour or so to write up this gay ball and send in the sketch of it," said Gaines, wishing Dinsmore to have plenty of time to think over his good fortune, and not to decide to cast it from him too hastily.

The "Trinity" walked slowly back to the hotel. On the veranda they parted, the two friends going in the direction of the ballroom, while Dinsmore threw himself into a chair in the shadow of one of the great pillars—to think.

How long he sat there he never knew. He was startled at length by the sound of voices. Two people had approached and seated themselves on the rustic bench on the other side of the wide pillar. A massive potted palm screened them from him, performing for him the same service, but he knew well that musical girlish voice which had the power to move his heart at will even yet. It was Queenie Trevalyn, and with her was Raymond Challoner, the handsomest of all the fast, gay set of young millionaires at Newport.

I strictly affirm, dear reader, that it was not Dinsmore's intention to remain there and listen. He would have arisen instantly and quitted the veranda, but fate seemed to decree otherwise. He was unable to raise hand or foot or utter any sound. A terrible numbness seemed to close down upon his every faculty, holding them as in a vise.

Words cannot tell the agonies he suffered there. The tortures of the rack, where he would have been stretched limb from limb, until death relieved him, would not have been harder to endure.

He heard handsome, indolent Raymond Challoner pour into those pretty pink-tinted ears the story of his love, and he heard the lips of the girl who was more to him than life itself accept the young heir of the Challoner millions, in the sweetest of words.

"I have just one odd determination, call it a notion if you will," he heard the young heir of Challoner say, "and that is, never to wed a girl to whom any other man has ever whispered words of love. No man has ever spoken of love to you, Queenie, or ever asked you to be his bride, has there?"

And the girl from whom he had parted on the white sands less than half an hour before steeped her red lips with the horrible falsehood of answering:

"No, Raymond, I have never given any one save yourself encouragement to speak to me of love, believe me."

"I almost believed the bronzed and bearded, mysterious Mr. Dinsmore might take it into his head to try to win you," he remarked, musingly.

Queenie Trevalyn laughed an amused laugh.

"What absurd nonsense," she cried. "Why, he has never been anything more to me than a mere acquaintance," and she polluted her lips with a second lie when she went on smoothly: "Papa paid him for the service he rendered me in that elevator affair, and that ended any obligation on my part. Furthermore, I must say that you do not compliment my taste very highly to imagine for an instant that I could possibly fall in love with such a dark-browed, plebeian-appearing man as Mr. John Dinsmore! The very thought that you could have imagined so mortifies me exceedingly."

"There, there, Queenie, do not take it to heart so. Of course you couldn't; only he followed you about so constantly that I own I was furiously jealous, and thought seriously of calling him out to mortal combat. Now that I do consider it soberly, I agree with you that he is hardly the type of man to inspire love in a young girl's romantic heart, despite his bushy whiskers and melancholy air. But let us waste no more words upon him. We can spend the fleeting hours much more advantageously by talking of love and our future."

They walked away laughing, arm in arm, leaving the man on the other side of the pillar sitting there like one carved in stone. The heart in his bosom had seemed to break with one awful throb, rendering him almost lifeless, and thus his friends found him when they came out to search for him an hour later.

"Did you think our hour an unusually long one?" laughed Gaines, adding, before his friend had time to reply:

"I have now another commission on my hands which is far more important than writing up the grand ball. Shortly after leaving you I received a lengthy telegram from our editor, ordering me to wait over instead of taking the midnight train back to New York, as was first arranged, to meet one of Pinkerton's men, who ought to arrive here at any hour now.

"It seems that he is in search of a young fellow who is giving the police here, there and everywhere no end of trouble. He is a high-flyer with expectations, and taking advantage of future prospects, has gone in heavy—borrowing money, gambling, and even forging for big amounts. He appeared suddenly in Saratoga one day last week, at the races, and was one of the most desperate plungers at the track. The climax to his rapid career is he had a furious encounter with a man that night, who had won large sums on the track, and the upshot of the affair was the man was found murdered in the early dawn of the following morning, and the only clew which could lead to the identity of the perpetrator of the deed is the imprint of a ring of most peculiar design upon the temple of the victim—a triangle, set with stones, diamonds presumably, with a large stone in the center. This is the only clew Pinkerton's man is following, since the descriptions differ so radically."

"This gives an added zest to our trip," laughed Ballou, who was always ready for anything which promised excitement. "Will you walk over to meet the incoming train with us?" addressing Dinsmore.

"No," replied John, almost wearily, "I will sit here and smoke my cigar, as a sort of nerve steadier."

"I advise you strongly to think not twice but a score of times ere you make up your mind to throw up a handsome fortune simply because there is a string tied to it in the shape of a pretty young girl, for no doubt she is pretty. Young girls cannot well help being sweet and comely, I have discovered."

John Dinsmore watched his friends walk away, and as they vanished into the thick, dark gloom he gave himself up to his own dreary thoughts. The story he had just heard, thrilling though it was, quickly vanished from his mind, as did also the fortune that might be his for the claiming. All he could think of was the lovely young girl upon whom he had set his heart and soul—his very life, as it were—who had spurned him so contemptuously and for one whom he could not think worthy of such a treasure, as he still blindly believed Queenie Trevalyn to be.

He had not been thrown into Raymond Challoner's society much, and from what little John Dinsmore did see of him he had not formed a very favorable impression. He had heard that his wine bills were quite a little fortune in themselves, and on several occasions, when in the midst of a crowd of young men in the office, who were as fast and gay as himself, John Dinsmore had heard him boast of his conquests with fair women, and of episodes so rollicking in their nature that John Dinsmore, man of honor as he was, reverencing all womankind, would arise abruptly from his seat, throw down the paper he had been vainly endeavoring to read, and walk away with a frown and unmistakable contempt in his face as he turned away from Challoner's direction, going beyond the hearing of his voice and hilarious tales. If any other man had won the treasure that cruel fate denied to him he could have endured the blow better; but Challoner!

"Ah! Heaven grant that she shall never have cause to rue her choice," he ruminated.

In the midst of his musing he was interrupted by the voice of the very man upon whom his thoughts were bent—Raymond Challoner.

It had been an hour or more since he had parted from the girl who had just promised to be his bride. The lights of the grand ballroom were out, and the greater portion of the great hotel was wrapped in gloom, with but here and there the twinkling light in the windows of some belated guest, and these, too, were rapidly disappearing, leaving the world to darkness and itself.

It was the hour when the sports of Newport banded together to smoke their cigars and talk over their wine, and their revelry usually lasted far into the wee sma' hours. To-night these young men seemed bent upon having a royal good time together, in celebration of their last night at the famous resort.

Half a score of friends were with Challoner. He was always the ringleader among his companions. Just now all seemed highly amused at some anecdote he was relating. His unsteady steps showed John Dinsmore that he was under the influence of wine. He arose and turned away with a sigh, anxious to get out of sight of the sneering, handsome face of his rival and away from the sound of his voice.

At that instant the sound of Miss Trevalyn's name on his rival's lips caught and held his attention. Raymond Challoner was boasting of his conquest over the heart of the belle and beauty of the season. John Dinsmore was rooted to the spot with horror to hear him discuss in the next breath the sweetness of the betrothal kiss he had received from the peerless Queenie.

A general laugh followed and remarks which made the blood boil in John Dinsmore's veins. He was fairly speechless from rage.

"And when do you intend to wed the beautiful Queenie?" asked a dozen or more rollicking voices.

"A month or two later, provided I do not see some bewitching little fairy in the meantime who will suit me better. I———"

The sentence was never finished. With a leap, John Dinsmore was before him, with a face so ghastly with wrath that those who saw it were stricken dumb.

"Take that! for maligning a lady, you dastardly scoundrel!" cried John, in a sonorous voice ringing with passion. And as he uttered the words out flew his strong right arm with the force of a sledge hammer, and in an instant Raymond Challoner was measuring his length before him on the porch.

"So it is you, the unsuccessful wooer, who champions Miss Trevalyn's cause, is it? Well that is indeed rich," he cried, white to the lips, adding: "I am not so good with my fists as you seem to be; however, I insist upon wiping out this insult with your blood or mine, John Dinsmore, ere another day dawns. Here and now I challenge you to a duel on the beach, within an hour's time. I will teach you then that it is folly to interfere in another man's affairs."

As he spoke he raised his hand threateningly, and to John Dinsmore's horror he saw upon it a triangular diamond ring, such as had been described by his friends.

CHAPTER IV.
THE MIDNIGHT DUEL.

The conflict is over, the struggle is past—

I have looked, I have loved, I have worshiped my last—

And now back to the world, and let fate do her worst

On the heart that for thee such devotion has nursed.

For thee its best feelings were wasted away,

And life hath hereafter not one to betray.

Farewell, then, thou loved one—oh, loved but too well,

Too deeply, too blindly for language to tell!

Farewell, thou hast trampled my love's faith in the dust,

Thou hast torn from my bosom my faith and my trust;

But if thy life's current with bliss it would swell,

I would pour out my own in this last fond farewell!

For an instant the lifeblood around John Dinsmore's heart seemed to stand still, and his eyes fairly bulged from their sockets. No, it was no trick of his imagination, the slim, aristocratic hand of his rival, upon which he gazed so breathlessly, bore upon it a ring of curious device—a serpent's body, and deeply imbedded in the flat head was a triangle of diamonds, in the center of which was a large diamond of rare brilliancy and beauty.

It was the identical ring his friends had described as being worn by the man whom they were at that moment hunting down to charge with a terrible crime.

Ere he could utter the words that arose to his lips, Raymond Challoner turned away from him, saying, with a haughty sneer:

"It is well you accept my challenge, John Dinsmore; I will meet you on the spot designated by you upon the beach, at exactly an hour from now. Until then adieu, most worthy champion of the fair sex, adieu!"

Challoner walked down the length of the broad piazza with the easy, graceful swagger peculiar to him, his friends about him, talking in subdued voices, yet anxiously and excitedly, over the event which had just transpired, and discussing in still lower whispers the probable outcome of the meeting, until they were lost alike to sight and sound.

Still John Dinsmore stood there where they had left him, like an image carved in stone, his eyes following the direction in which they had disappeared.

And standing thus, a terrible temptation came to him, a temptation so strong that for a moment it almost overpowered him.

He had only to send quickly for his friends, who had gone to the train to meet the detective, and tell them what he had seen, to bring about the overthrow of his rival in the very hour of his triumph.

The lover who had been accepted by Queenie Trevalyn as her affianced husband, would be taken from the hotel in handcuffs. Ah, what a glorious revenge; sweetened by the thought that Challoner would thus be parted forever from the girl whom he had loved so madly, and lost.

Then the nobler side of John Dinsmore's nature struggled for mastery. Could he, a dismissed suitor, cast the first stone at his successful rival? Would it be manly, or ignoble?

How Queenie Trevalyn would hate him for it! That thought settled the matter, his rival should not come to his downfall through him. Far better that Challoner's bullet should pierce his heart.

He stood quite motionless, leaning heavily against the massive pillar of the piazza, lost in deep reverie, thinking it all over.

What had he to live for, now that Queenie Trevalyn was lost to him forever? Death seemed far more desirable to him than life—without her.

He knew that Raymond Challoner was considered an excellent shot; that every one declared him particularly clever in the use of firearms; but that knowledge did not deter John Dinsmore from his purpose.

When his friends entered the hotel, a little later, they found a summons from him awaiting them, explaining briefly the affair on hand, which was to come off within an hour, and asking them to meet him on the beach, at the place and time indicated.

"Whew!" exclaimed Ballou, with a long, low whistle. "What will Dinsmore be getting into next? Knowing him as well as I do, I realize that it is useless to attempt to talk him out of this affair of honor, as he calls it. Heaven grant that he may not fall a victim of his opponent's superior marksmanship. Of course I don't know what the deadly quarrel between them is about, but——"

His friend, Gaines, cut him short by announcing that they had no time to speculate as to the cause of the contemplated duel, as they had barely time to reach the place described—a sort of cove shut in by high, shelving rocks, fully a mile from the hotel.

"John has given us no time to see him first, and attempt to mediate between him and his antagonist," said Gaines, seizing his hat, which he had but just removed.

"Can nothing be done to prevent the affair from being carried out?" queried Ballou, turning his white, worried, anxious face toward his friend.

"It seems not," returned Gaines, in a voice equally as troubled.

The two friends spoke no other word until they came within sight of the place. Then Ballou whispered:

"Both principals are on the ground, also his opponent's seconds; they are evidently awaiting us."

This proved to be the case. The antagonists were already facing each other, weapons in hand.

Although John Dinsmore had determined that it should not be his lips which should speak proclaiming his rival's suspected guilt of a former crime, he supposed, when his friends came to his aid, their sharp eyes would soon discern the ring. His thoughts carried him no farther than that.

In the excitement attending the meeting of his opponent upon the beach, he failed to notice that Raymond Challoner had removed the ring.

Both friends knew, as they rapidly approached, that it was too late to interfere; the two combatants stood facing each other, fifteen paces apart, weapons in hand.

Challoner's second conferred with Ballou for a moment, then they announced that all was in readiness.

A deathlike silence ensued, broken only by the sobbing of the wind and the dash of the waves, beating a solemn requiem upon the shore. Slowly the command was given:

"One—two—three—fire!"

Simultaneously the report of the two pistol shots rang out upon the midnight air, followed instantly by the sound of a body falling heavily upon the sands.

John Dinsmore had fallen upon his face, the lifeblood from a wound in his breast coloring the white beach crimson about him.

In a trice his two friends were bending over him, beside the doctor, who was making a rapid examination to find out the extent of the wounded man's injuries; believing, however, that Raymond Challoner's opponent was beyond all human aid. He had figured at several of these affairs of honor in which Challoner had been engaged, and had never yet known him to fail to strike the heart at which he aimed.

"He brought it on himself," said Challoner, addressing his second. "He would have it!" and he turned away upon his heel with a mocking sneer curling his cynical lips. Tossing his weapon to his second, he nonchalantly resumed his hat and coat, and walked coolly away toward the hotel, not deigning to cast one glance backward, even to take the trouble to inquire whether his victim was alive, or dead.

Both of the fallen man's friends heard him remark, as a parting shot:

"Such is the fate of any one who attempts to meddle in my affairs."

"Your friend is not dead," said the doctor, hastily, anxious to attract their attention from Challoner, fearing perhaps a double or a triple duel might result from this affair.

"He is badly wounded, there is no doubt about that, but in my opinion the wound is not necessarily fatal. I have every hope that we shall be able to pull him through, with this splendid physique to aid us."

The two friends breathed more freely, and Gaines said, slowly:

"If he were to die, the man who murdered him would have the opportunity to try his hand next on me."

"And after that on me," remarked Ballou, "in case he should escape your bullet."

"The first thing to be attended to is to get him away from here," cut in the doctor, quietly. Adding: "As the hotel is to close within a few short hours, they would not receive him there. I propose removing him at once to a little cottage I know of adjacent to this place, in which lives an old nurse whom I often employ. She will willingly take him in and do her best for him."

The two friends received this suggestion gratefully.

Between the three of them, they succeeded in conveying him to the place indicated, without loss of time, and there the doctor made a further examination of his injuries.

"Mr. Challoner's bullet missed its aim by a single hair's breadth," he said; "but with Mrs. Brent's careful nursing, we may hope for much."

It was with the greatest of regret that the two friends left Newport the next day for New York, leaving John Dinsmore, who had not yet regained consciousness, in the hands of the doctor, who was a resident of the place, and the aged nurse.

Everything had gone wrong with them; they had been unable, even with the aid of the skillful detective, to find the slightest trace of the man for whom they were looking, and concluded that he had left the resort ere they had reached it, having been informed in advance in some mysterious manner of their coming.

Meanwhile, the girl for whom John Dinsmore had risked his noble life a second time, was pacing up and down the floor of her elegant suite of rooms, with a very perturbed countenance, reading for the twentieth time the letter which her mother had but just received, read but half through, and had fainted outright; recovering only to go from one violent fit of hysterics into another.

Queenie Trevalyn had read it slowly through twice, controlling her emotions with a supreme effort.

It was from her father, and announced his utter failure in New York.

He had made an unsuccessful venture in Wall Street, and the result was that every dollar he had on earth had been swept from him.

"When you return to the city," he wrote, "instead of your own home, it will be to a boarding house. For myself I care not; but my heart bleeds for you, my dear wife, and Queenie, knowing full well how much you both love the luxurious trappings of wealth and position! But my grief cannot mend matters. Our only hope of retrieving our fallen fortunes is by Queenie marrying money."

CHAPTER V.
THE POWER OF GOLD.

"The eagle suffers little birds to sing,

And is not careful what they mean thereby,

Knowing that with the shadow of his wing

He can at pleasure stint their melody."

Queenie Trevalyn did not go into hysterics over her father's letter, as her mother had done. Instead, she was very angry.

"How dare a man, who has a family on his hands dependent upon him for support, to risk his fortune in speculation?" she stormed. "The man who is mad enough to do it should be sent to an insane asylum, and confined there for the rest of his natural life!"

"But what are we to do, my dear?" queried the weeping mother, in a sobbing, querulous voice. "I have always lived in elegance; how am I to enter a New York boarding house? I—I should fall down dead on the threshold! I ask you, what are we to do, Queenie!"

And off the poor lady went into another violent spasm of hysterics.

"The genteel poor; how I have always pitied them!" went on the sobbing lady, her tears falling afresh. "Poor people who carry about them traces of former greatness. How our set will comment on our downfall, Queenie, and turn their heads the other way as they pass us by on the street; they riding in their carriages, and we tramping through the dust afoot. Oh, I can never endure it, Queenie! I will take to my bed and remain there until the day I die. I have read of poverty in novels, and always pitied the poor heroine. I never imagined that I should one day be in a similar position myself. Oh, dear, if I could have only died ere this dark dawn fell upon us!"

"If you will only dry your tears long enough to listen to what I have to say, and talk the matter over with me, I may be able to suggest a path out of the labyrinth. You have given me no opportunity to tell you a piece of news that may, in your estimation, offset this dreadful calamity."

Mrs. Trevalyn looked up at her beautiful daughter through her tears.

"Go on, my dear," she said. "I will listen patiently to anything you may have to say; but I think I can tell, by the way in which you have received the distressing news concerning your father's failure, just what it is. Mr. Dinsmore has asked you to be his wife."

"He has, and I have refused him," replied the daughter, laconically.

"Refused him?" echoed Mrs. Trevalyn, looking at the beauty with dilated eyes. "Refused him—while every one is sure that he must be worth barrels of money?"

"Every one is wrong in this instance, as usual. Mr. Dinsmore is only an author; his expectations are in the vapory shape of possible royalties on some future great book which he purposes to astonish the world with. His present income is what little he can earn from writing for magazines and papers; feeling as rich as a lord with twenty-five dollars in his pocket to-day, and to-morrow a beggar, or nearly so."

"Can it be possible?" gasped Mrs. Trevalyn, wondering if she had heard aright. "How did you find it out?"

"From his own lips," replied Queenie; adding impatiently: "But it is not of him I wish to speak; though right here and now, mamma, I frankly admit that I did admire John Dinsmore more than I care to own, and to find out that he was a poor man was a decided shock to me; but I am my mother's daughter, and having a horror of poverty, I threw him over, stifling my regrets with an iron will."

"You are very brave, Queenie darling," murmured Mrs. Trevalyn.

"I had very little time to grieve over having to refuse him," continued Queenie, "for another lover arose instantly upon the horizon of my future, as though to console me. In less than half an hour after I had refused John Dinsmore, I was the affianced bride to be of Mr. Raymond Challoner, heir prospective to all the Challoner millions. I like him in his way amazingly; I think he will make a far more fitting mate for a frivolous girl like me than grave John Dinsmore, had he been worth the same amount of shining gold."

"You have saved us, my dear!" cried Mrs. Trevalyn, dramatically. "You have saved the time-honored name of the Trevalyns. I can hold up my head again and breathe freely once more."

"Mr. Challoner pressed me hard for an immediate marriage, mamma," the daughter went on complacently; "although I told him that it could not possibly be, and that I intended to have a wedding that should astonish all New York society by its elaborateness. Marry like a country maid eloping; ah, no, Queenie Trevalyn must have a magnificent wedding, as befits the station in which she moves."

"After some little demurrer on his part, he yielded gracefully to my wishes. I will see him early to-morrow morning, mamma, and tell him that I have changed my mind as to the date of our marriage; it is a lady's privilege, you know. I will tell him that I am willing that the ceremony shall take place at once, and I will tell him why."

"Have you lost your reason, Queenie?" gasped Mrs. Trevalyn. "If you tell him that, you may lose him, child!"

"I think not," returned Miss Queenie Trevalyn, surveying her rare, lovely face in the mirror. "I should say that he is far too much in love with me for that; in fact, I shall make it a test of his love for me."

"I pray it may come out right," sighed the mother, earnestly; "but if you would listen to me, and be guided by what I think——"

"Leave this affair to me, mamma," cried the imperious young beauty. "What better test can I have of his love than to tell him of our loss of fortune—that in a single day we have been swept by the hand of cruel fate from affluence to pover——"

"Do not utter the word, Queenie. I cannot bear it!" cut in her mother, quickly. "It makes me faint!"

Queenie was headstrong, like all beautiful girls are apt to be, and her mother knew that there was little use attempting to reason with her. She would have her own way when once she had made up her mind upon a course of action, let it cost what it might.

"I only hope you may not rue the telling of it, my dear," she sighed. "My advice is, never to tell your lover anything concerning family affairs which are of a detrimental nature to you or yours; they will find out enough after you marry.

"I thought you were wiser in the ways of the world than most girls, Queenie; but I see you are not when I hear you talking about love-tests, and so on. You can take the plunge, if you cannot be persuaded to hold your silence until after the knot is securely tied; but mind, I, who am for your good, warn you that I do not think it at all wise."

"I am determined to test, as I have said, the strength and depth of Raymond Challoner's love for me, mamma," she declared. "He is so desperately infatuated that I can guarantee that he will sign me over half of his princely fortune on the spot."

"I wish I could be as sanguine concerning the matter as you are, my dear!" sighed Mrs. Trevalyn. "You have made up your mind, and I suppose I shall have to let it rest at that. I say in conclusion, what a man does not know concerning your finances will not hurt, nor worry him. Think twice before you divulge to Mr. Challoner your father's mad move, which has plunged us into beggary."

"I may think twice concerning it, but I shall arrive at the same conclusion, I assure you," replied Queenie.

For an hour after she sought her own apartment, she stood at the window looking afar over the white stretch of beach lying cold and white in the bright moonlight, to the glittering expanse of water beyond.

"Yes, it was really too bad that John Dinsmore turned out to be poor!" she sighed. "He had such a noble bearing, and the head of a king, with a heart as generous, chivalrous and kind as a woman; just such a man as the heroes were in all the books I have read. I hardly think that he is the sort of man to do anything rash, because of my refusal of him—commit suicide, or anything as terrible as that. I could not say the same thing concerning Ray Challoner. Had I said him nay, I am confident that he would have kept his word—that they would have found his body on the sands when the morrow should break, with a bullet wound in his brain; mutely telling the story of his sad taking off."

And the thought of handsome, dashing, debonair Raymond Challoner lying white and lifeless on the beach, and all for love of her, was a gloomy picture which she did not care to dwell upon.

Aside from his enormously reported wealth and splendid appearance, the fact that every marriageable girl at Newport had been head over heels in love with him, and would gladly have been his for the asking, had made him a very desirable *parti* in Queenie Trevalyn's covetous eyes.

In fact, she had been quite live with him until the dark, gloomy, mysterious stranger, whom Newport had known only as Mr. Dinsmore, came upon the scene.

The next morning Queenie heard that Mr. Dinsmore had left the hotel the night before; none seemed to know whence he had gone; he had disappeared as suddenly as he had come.

The fact was, the affair of honor had been kept so profound a secret that even the hotel people had not learned of it, and would certainly have kept it to themselves if they had, being too wise to bruit the sensational story about.

Raymond Challoner appeared at the breakfast table as bright, smiling and gay as usual. He had not seen the doctor as yet, to ascertain the extent of his adversary's injuries; or, indeed, whether or not his aim had proven fatal;

nor did he allow the little affair to trouble him in the least. He did not give it a single thought; it had not cost him an anxious moment, or one hour's loss of sleep.

At his plate he found a dainty note from his *fiancée* awaiting him. Would he join her on the east veranda at ten, that morning, she asked. She had something very particular to tell him.

At ten promptly Raymond Challoner appeared at the place of rendezvous, smiling and debonair, with a white rose in his buttonhole.

Queenie Trevalyn was waiting for him at the other end of the veranda, quite as lovely a picture of girlhood as man's eyes had ever rested upon.

CHAPTER VI.
A MAN'S FICKLE HEART.

"Do not, as some ungracious rascals do,
Show me the steep and thorny way to heaven;
While like a puffed and reckless libertine,
Himself the primrose path of dalliance treads."

Yes, a most beautiful picture of lovely girlhood Queenie Trevalyn appeared in her traveling dress of dove gray, with the crimson rose nestling in her bosom, and her two bright eyes eager with expectancy as he approached.

"Good-morning, my radiant darling!" he cried, availing himself of the opportunity of addressing her as rapturously as he liked, there being no one else on the wide, shady veranda; most every one being busy over the packing of trunks and saying good-by to friends.

"How am I to thank you for giving me the opportunity of a *tête-à-tête* with you, sweet, on this morning of all mornings," he whispered, seizing the two little white hands; and, as there was no one about to witness the gallant, loverlike action, raising them to his lips and kissing them repeatedly.

Before she had time to reply, he went on:

"From the hour we parted last night, sweet, I have done nothing but think of you; I could not sleep until far into the wee, sma' hours, for thinking of you, and wondering over my amazing fortune in winning such a treasure. And when at last sleep did weigh down my eyelids, my dreams were full of you—and, oh, such glorious dreams, my angel! I thought we had just been wedded, and I was bearing you off to some fairy isle——"

"Did you wish it were a reality, Raymond?" she questioned, interrupting him with a little tremor in her voice, which was barely audible.

"How can you ask that, my adored one?" he asked, reproachfully.

"I—I thought if you really cared so much about it, the—the wedding might be arranged to take place this morning, as you pleaded so hard last night that it might."

Girl-like, she dropped her eyes in maidenly confusion as she made this faltering admission.

If she had but glanced up at that moment, she would have beheld a very strange expression on the face of the man bending over her.

Raymond Challoner was wondering if he had heard aright, or if his ears were playing him false. Was it a trick of mistaken hearing, or did he hear her say that she would marry him ere she left Newport that morning? He had expected a hard battle to fight when he asked the astute, wealthy New York lawyer for his lovely young daughter.

It was easy to talk to women of his expectations, etc.; but it was quite another matter to stand before a keen-eyed man of the world, and explain to his satisfaction what he had to support his daughter with. The keen lawyer would want positive proof, in the shape of affirmation from old Mr. Challoner, the wealthy uncle, direct, acknowledging that it was his intention to make his nephew his sole heir. And no one knew better than Raymond Challoner that he was as far away from that old uncle's millions as was the man in the moon, and he well knew why.

Queenie's voice brought back his wandering thoughts.

"I have something to confide to you, Raymond," she whispered in a fluttering voice, "and after you have heard it all, it is for you to decide if you desire the marriage to take place within the hour, or think it best to—to wait."

As she spoke she drew forth the letter from the pocket of her dress and opening it, laid it in his hand, remarking:

"That is the dreadful news which we received from papa last night. It explains itself. Oh, Raymond, in a few short hours we have been hurled down from affluence to—to—— Oh, how shall I say it?—to want!"

He did not even hear her last words. He was so intent upon the perusal of the old lawyer's heartbroken letter to his family.

And as he read a low, incredulous whistle broke from his mustached lips.

"Lost his fortune! That's an amazing piece of business!" he cried. "By George, bad luck seems to follow me like an avenging demon; just as I am about to grasp a big thing, it invariably crumbles to dust in my grasp! Still, it's lucky to find it out in time!"

A ghastly white overspread the girl's face.

"Raymond," she whispered, "does the loss of my fortune make any difference to you? Surely, you were not marrying me for that?"

She spoke in a constrained voice, drawing herself away from his clasp.

"Nonsense, Queenie!" he returned, impatiently. "You know better than that, but it is best to look the present unfortunate difficulty squarely in the face. I am not a very sentimental young man, and I will tell you the plain truth: I do love you, Queenie, better by far than any other girl I have ever met, and I would marry you within the hour, despite the fact of the loss of your fortune, if I could; but the truth of the matter is, I can't!

"You see, it's this way with me, Queenie," he went on. "I am the heir to my uncle's millions, it is true, but he is the most cranky individual that ever lived. If I should marry any one short of an heiress, I have his solemn word for it that he would cut me off; make a new will, leaving me entirely cut out of it, before the next sun rose. It's an ugly hitch, but the hitch is there. I am dependent upon my uncle, and I dare not go against the old curmudgeon's wishes, as unreasonable as they may be."

"You desire to break the engagement, then?" she asked in a husky voice, looking him steadily in the eye.

Her unnatural calm deceived him; he had expected hysterics at this juncture, reproaches, possibly a stormy scene.

His face flushed, and he drew a long breath of relief, telling himself that he was fortunate that she left everything to him.

"I have no wish to say farewell forever, Queenie," he said; "but it would be selfish to keep you bound to me, and away from every one else for perhaps long years. For it might be fully that length of time ere my uncle took a notion to shuffle off this mortal coil. It's a long wait, this waiting for dead men's shoes.

"Your pretty locks as well as my own might turn gray ere we could see our way clear to marry. On the whole, I think it would be cruel to keep you bound by an engagement which might last half a lifetime. I love you, Queenie, but I will not be selfish. I release you from the betrothal we entered into last night, though Heaven knows how bitter it is to say those words—I set you free! You will meet some other man whom you will learn to love, I dare say, and will rejoice then that we were both so sensible as to part when we realized that the stern decree of fate was against us."

The young girl stood looking at him with a fixed, steady gaze; she saw him now as he was, in all his falseness and baseness.

"Good-by," she said, mechanically, turning away from him.

"Let us part as friends, Queenie," he entreated; but she turned on him such a look of utter contempt, that whatever else he was intending to say to her died upon his lips unuttered.

"Friends," she retorted; "I scorn you too much to hold you as a friend! From this hour we are enemies, Mr. Challoner—enemies to the death! You have insulted my pride, and mark me, the day will come when you will bitterly rue it!"

"I could never be an enemy to a fair young girl, let her do what she might, think of me as she may," he returned, with mock gallantry; "and as for your revenge upon me, surely the withdrawing of your sunny face and smile from my dull existence will be a revenge cruel enough to satisfy the one most thirsty after vengeance!"

With one last look, the strangeness of which he never forgot, she turned, and with head proudly erect, walked with haughty step down the length of the cool, shady veranda, and disappeared through the arched doorway.

Raymond Challoner gazed after her with a strange expression on his usually placid countenance, as he remarked to himself:

"It's a very disagreeable procedure. I hope she won't do anything desperate. Those high-spirited girls are apt to kill themselves, or something else equally as terrible. She's tremendously in love with me, poor little girl; and it's flattering, but not at all pleasant under the circumstances."

Queenie Trevalyn walked straight up to her own room with the same proud, measured step.

Her mother, with a newspaper in her hand, was awaiting her in some trepidation. Her keen instinct told her as soon as she beheld her daughter's marble-white face that in this instance surely the course of true love had not run smooth. Had it been as she feared, had the young man not received the story of her father's failure kindly?

Without waiting for her mother to speak, Queenie announced, briefly:

"It's all over between us, mamma; you are right, and I was wrong. It was my fortune that Raymond Challoner wanted, not me! So we parted!"

A shriek from her mother interrupted the recital of what took place.

"And it was for him that you threw over Mr. John Dinsmore!" groaned Mrs. Trevalyn, adding: "Just read that, Queenie! Oh, oh, oh!"

Mechanically the girl took the paper from her; the startling headlines on the first column on which her eyes fell told her of the wonderful news:

A fortune estimated at over three millions of dollars had come to John Dinsmore, the author, through the death of a relative, a London banker of note.

Without waiting for her daughter to read the column through, Mrs. Trevalyn cried, excitedly:

"You must recall him, Queenie; indeed you must, my love!"

"It is too late now, mother," answered Miss Trevalyn, bitterly. "He has gone, left the hotel and Newport last night, so I heard some one remark at the breakfast table this morning."

Mrs. Trevalyn went promptly into hysterics, and then fainted outright.

Queenie uttered no moan, not even a cry.

"Poor mamma," she groaned, "it would be almost better if life ended for her here and now, rather than live to face the future before us!"

In that moment Queenie Trevalyn knew the truth, whatever of love her shallow heart had been capable of feeling, had gone out to the man whose heart the cold hand of her ambition had thrust from her forever. And she had turned from him in such scorn and anger—that was the crudest remembrance of all! But for that she might have recalled him; for the heir of such a fortune could not long hide himself in obscurity. But would he ever forgive her for casting him aside so lightly?

"He loved me—and with such a man, to love once is to love forever!" she told herself, and this thought buoyed up her flagging spirits.

"Yes, I will reclaim him," she ruminated, pressing her hands closely together over her throbbing heart. "He will never know about Ray Challoner, or his proposal. I will tell him a young girl's 'no' always yields to 'yes,' if the wooer is persistent. Yes, I will win him back, and thus avert the poverty that stares us in the face. Of course he has gone directly back to New York, to the address mentioned in this newspaper article."

And to this address Queenie Trevalyn sent the following telegram:

"Love has conquered pride and anger, and I would call you back again."

"That will bring him back to Newport by the next train," she told herself, sitting down by the window to peruse the wonderful newspaper account for the twentieth time.

Strangely enough, no mention was made in the article of the condition attached to the will, that he must wed the girl of his uncle's choosing.

Meanwhile, Mrs. Trevalyn seemed to grow alarmingly worse, much to the annoyance of the hotel management.

By some means they learned of the failure of the lady's husband in New York, and their suave courtesy to the late magnate's wife and daughter changed into positive brusqueness, as they declared to Miss Trevalyn that she would have to remove her mother at once from the Ocean House to some private boarding house, as it was imperative that they should close the hotel by noon.

They condescended, however, to give Queenie a note to a trained nurse, a Mrs. Brent, suggesting that she would in all probability receive her mother and self for a few days, until Mrs. Trevalyn was able to return to New York.

And thither, letter in hand, Queenie turned her steps, murmuring to herself:

"Ah, me! How strange are the tricks fate plays upon us!" little dreaming as she uttered the words of the thrilling event about to transpire.

CHAPTER VII.
A DREAD ALTERNATIVE.

"He said, 'I never can forgive

A wrong so darkly done;

Nor will I ever, as I live,

Regard the faithless one

As erst mine own familiar friend,

Whose fealty was my boast.

Yes, those on whom we most depend

Have power to wound us most.'"

Miss Trevalyn lost no time in applying to the nurse, Mrs. Brent, for admission for her mother and herself for a few days beneath her humble roof; but in this instance fate was unkind to the young lady. Mrs. Brent had no room to spare, she was informed. She returned to the hotel greatly upset, wondering what on earth was to be done now.

As she opened the door of their room, Mrs. Trevalyn flew toward her laughing and crying hysterically by turns.

"We shall not remain in Newport another hour, my love!" she cried. "See, here is another letter from your father, and it has put new life into me. Read it, Queenie."

There were but a few hurried lines this time, and to the effect that his business troubles had been staved off for a period of three months, and that they could therefore return home without any one being the wiser, at present, of the horrible black cloud which hung over their heads.

"Three months' respite, Queenie!" exclaimed Mrs. Trevalyn, clasping and unclasping her bracelets, laughing and crying in the same breath. "Heaven knows what may take place in that length of time; probably you will have made up with the rich Mr. Dinsmore, and—and be married to him; and then we will be saved. Even if you should fail with him," she went on, plaintively, "there is the old Widower Brown——"

"Stop, mother!" cried Queenie Trevalyn, a shudder of horror passing over her slender frame. "I love wealth and position dearly, but I would rather die on the street from starvation than marry a man whom I detest as thoroughly as Hiram Brown, octogenarian, miser, hunchback, and pawnbroker."

As she uttered the words there arose before her mental vision the image of the creature whom her words had described—a shriveled, toothless, horrible being in the shape of a man, who had actually had the audacity to apply to her father for an introduction to his beautiful daughter, "with a view to matrimony," as his terse communication phrased his intentions.

Mr. Trevalyn had put him off with a plausible excuse for not granting his request at the time; but he dared not openly refuse to permit Hiram Brown the meeting with his daughter which he so ardently desired, some time in the future; for the old money-lender held many of his notes, and he told himself discretion in the matter was certainly diplomacy upon his part.

"Let the matter rest until Queenie and her mother return from their summer outing at Newport," Mr. Trevalyn had said, "and then I shall be pleased to present you to my daughter, Mr. Brown."

"What if the girl takes it into her head to fall in love with any of those young bloods there?" the miser had said, in his high-pitched, querulous tones.

"There is not the least fear of that, my dear Brown," Mr. Trevalyn had declared. "Queenie is only twenty, you know; she won't be thinking of love or lovers yet, I assure you. She simply accompanies her mother there, who goes for her health."

But in his secret heart Mr. Trevalyn was only too anxious that his peerless young daughter should capture a wealthy young husband, and save the family from the ruin which he even then saw ahead of them; then he could laugh in old Brown's face, and defy him to do his worst.

He had been rather sorry that he had confided old Brown's ambitions to Queenie and her mother, for the latter ever afterward was wont to declare that Queenie could fall back upon the hunchback miser, rather than not marry at all, much to the girl's disgust, and just anger.

"You have a right to think of your poor mother, even though you do not care for yourself or your father, Queenie," exclaimed Mrs. Trevalyn, hysterically. "Brown is rich, and that covers a multitude of failings."

There was something so utterly heartless in this speech, that the girl's heart sank within her. Since her encounter with Ray Challoner, all her worldliness had disappeared, and she had learned life's sweetest lesson, that it is Love that rules, and that, unless the lover whom she had sent from her for false Ray Challoner's sake returned to her, the future would not be worth living to her.

Then and there she said to herself that she would win back John Dinsmore, and wed him, or go unwedded to the grave.

She had just discovered his worth, as well as the fact that she loved him with all the passionate love of her heart—and would love him to the end of her life.

It was wonderful how Mrs. Trevalyn recovered after the receipt of that letter, and announced herself quite well enough to take the next outgoing train, and insisted upon doing so, much to Queenie's relief.

As the New York express moved out of the Newport depot, Queenie Trevalyn little dreamed that she was leaving all that she held dear behind her.

All the way back to the metropolis her thoughts were upon the lover for whom she now yearned so eagerly.

She was glad that she had had the forethought to put her New York address upon the note she had written him—recalling him; and she did not doubt that he would call upon her quite as soon as she reached home. Indeed, she expected to find a letter from him awaiting her there, and it was with almost feverish eagerness that she counted the miles as the train sped homeward.

There was the usual number of epistles from girl friends and acquaintances, but the one she longed for most was not among them.

"He will be sure to come this evening in person, and that is far better than writing," thought the girl, ordering the servants to unpack her trunks at once.

There were several callers, for the beauty of Newport was a favorite in New York society; but the evening was spoiled for Queenie Trevalyn when John Dinsmore was not among them.

And when a week passed, and there was no sign, no word from him, she began to lose heart altogether.

"I have offended him past all forgiving," she would cry out to herself, in the solitude of her own room; and she would have given all that she held dearest in life, could she have lived over that half hour on the sands at Newport, with that eager, adoring lover at her side, holding her hands clasped closely in his, pouring into her ears the story of his love for her.

Ah, could she live it over again, how different would be her answer!

She had humbled her pride in recalling him, and now he was treating her with ignominious silence. She knew that her heart should have rebelled with the fiercest anger against him for treating her thus; but love conquered pride and anger, all that she ardently hoped for was to meet him once again.

When a fortnight had elapsed, and as yet no word was heard from Mr. John Dinsmore, Mrs. Trevalyn began to renew her entreaties with her daughter to allow Hiram Brown to be presented to her, that he might cease his persistent importunings, not to say threatenings, with her father.

"Wait just a little while longer, mamma," pleaded Queenie, anxiously.

"Well, we will give your Mr. Dinsmore another week in which to show up, and if we do not hear from him in that time, and no other eligible man puts in an appearance, you must accept the introduction to Hiram Brown," declared Mrs. Trevalyn, energetically. "Time is fleeting, we have been home already three weeks, and have but eight or nine weeks left ere we are out of house and home."

Misfortune had not improved Mrs. Trevalyn's temper, and from a plaintive, complaining woman, she had developed into a perfect virago, when she stopped to consider the precipice which they were nearing day by day, and Queenie had to stand the brunt of it, and it was the same old query day after day:

"When are you going to allow Mr. Brown to be introduced to you?" and Queenie, in sheer desperation at length, answered wearily:

"I don't know. If it must be, it might as well be gotten over soon as late!"

After that concession on her daughter's part, Mrs. Trevalyn became more amiable, she did not know that Queenie had resolved to die rather than marry him, if they persisted in pressing her to that point.

"You are becoming sensible at last, my love," said Mrs. Trevalyn, with a beaming smile. Adding: "The woman who marries old Hiram Brown may consider herself very fortunate. He has no end of millions, as every one knows, and his wife can fairly roll in diamonds and point lace, and all the luxuries of a magnificent establishment. He is old, and cannot last many more years, and then his widow would be the most admired, courted and envied woman in all New York."

"For Heaven's sake say no more, mamma!" cried the girl, bitterly. "I cannot endure the thought of marrying Hiram Brown; why, the very mention of his name, which calls up his image before me, makes me almost swoon with horror and disgust!"

"You ought to be grateful and thankful for your good fortune, instead of railing at it!" declared Mrs. Trevalyn, energetically. "Think how many young girls of our set would envy you, if you were to become the wife of so wealthy a man!"

"You mean they would pity me!" cried Queenie, curling her lip scornfully; "for they would know that I had been bartered body and soul for hollow gold. It is positive that no one would dream of calling it a love match, mamma."

CHAPTER VIII.
WHAT IS LIFE WITHOUT LOVE?

"How does a woman love? Once, no more,

Though life forever its loss deplore.

Deep in sorrow, or want, or sin,

One king reigneth her heart within;

One alone by night and day,

Moves her spirit to curse or pray.

Though loves beset her and friends deride;

Yea, when she smileth another's bride;

Still for her love her heart makes moan.

To love once is forever, and once alone!"

"I do hope, Queenie, that you are not commencing to grow sentimental!" cried Mrs. Trevalyn, holding up her hands as though the very idea was a blow which she was warding off.

"Would such a state of affairs surprise you very much, mamma?" retorted the girl, cresting her head defiantly. "Youth is the age of romance, of joy, and—and the mating of true hearts."

"Youth is the age of nonsense!" retorted her mother, spiritedly. "If I had been romantic instead of sensible when I was your age, Queenie, I should have had a sorry enough life of it. I say then, young as I was, that it was wealth that ruled the world, and not love. Why, I threw over a handsome young doctor, whose only wealth was his brains, for your father, who was accounted at that time the best catch of the season at Newport."

"And you married my father for his money, while your heart was the young doctor's?" queried Queenie, gravely.

"That was the way of it," assented her mother, coolly; though she had the grace to flush a little under her daughter's gaze.

"Then I do not wonder that Heaven punished you by causing the man you wedded for his wealth to lose it, at the time in your life when you needed it most; though it is hard lines for poor papa!"

"It is not for you to sit in judgment upon my actions!" cried Mrs. Trevalyn, angrily. "I won't tolerate it. I knew what I was doing. Money is best."

"Love is best!" murmured Queenie, "and without it, all the wealth of the world is but dross," and, as she uttered the words, her thoughts flew back to the lover whom she had left on the white sands, ere she had been taught that pitiful lesson, and she walked slowly from the room. Her mother watched her with darkening brows.

"I thought I had brought that girl up to be sensible," she ruminated; "but I find she is as foolish as the general run of girls. One thing is certain, she must marry rich, and such a marriage cannot take place too soon for my peace of mind! How quickly time flies; we have been home from Newport over a month now, and as yet Hiram Brown is the only wealthy suitor who has come forward for Queenie's hand. The girl has changed, every one notices that; and all on account of that audacious fellow who dared to make love to her at Newport without so much as a dollar in his pocket. He has caught her heart in the rebound, it would seem. One never knows the true inwardness of a girl's heart, anyway.

"Of course, now that he is rich I would be glad enough to have him for a son-in-law; but his pride was cut too deeply when she sent him from her, ever to return to her again, and I now shrewdly suspect that Queenie is breaking her foolish heart in secret over it. And to make the matter worse, that book of his has taken the public like wildfire, and every one is talking of him now. He is not only rich, but famous, and could get his pick of all the society girls in New York, they're so given up to hero worship. And in their eyes the handsome author of 'Life as We Find It' really is a hero.

"But Queenie must not waste her time grieving over him. I must stop that nonsense, and at once; and the best way to accomplish that is to hasten Hiram Brown's proposal—and her acceptance."

And thus she settled the matter in her own mind.

To Queenie the continued silence of John Dinsmore was almost intolerable, but woman-like, her love for him grew under his seeming indifference and neglect, instead of abating.

When the book from which he had hoped so much, and of which he had told her, was launched upon the tide, and instantly met with public favor, and it began to be spoken of everywhere, no one was prouder of it than Queenie.

She longed to say to her girl friends:

"The man who wrote it loves me, and asked me to be his wife," then it suddenly dawned upon her that his love had been but transitory, he no longer loved her, or he would have returned to her at her bidding, and that thought was bitter as death to the proud heart of the girl, who now loved him with so mad and passionate a love.

Meanwhile, the object of her thoughts was still at the Brent cottage, at the now deserted Newport, valiantly fighting his way back to life from the very brink of eternity.

He had had a close call, but his grand physique conquered, and death, which he so longed for, would not come to him then, and he was forced, against his most earnest desires, to take up the tangled thread of life again, and weave it out to the end.

His friends, Hazard Ballou and Jerry Gaines, spent every available hour that they could with him, when it was possible to run up to Newport.

It was they who first carried to him the news of the wonderful success of his book.

To their surprise he turned his head wearily away, asking them to desist from the telling until another time, for he thought he could sleep. They looked at him, then at each other, in blank amazement. Did ever a man take wonderful tidings like this in such a manner before, they queried; and they could not help reproving him on his want of interest in his wonderful success, which would mean a fortune to him.

John Dinsmore turned his head wearily on his pillow.

"Success and wealth have come to me too late!" he said, bitterly. "A month ago I would have gone frantic, I think, at such intelligence; now—well, I can only repeat that, like my uncle's fortune, it has come to me too late, boys—too late!"

"Ah, by the way," cried Jerry Gaines, "speaking of your uncle's fortune reminds me of a letter I have in my pocket for you, which came to your New York address, and instead of forwarding it, waited and brought it, delaying the delivery of it but a day."

"If you will read it, and tell me the contents of it, I shall be obliged to you," said John, wearily.

"By George, now that I come to remember it, there were two letters for you which I slipped into my pocket, and now, as I live, I can find but one of them," declared Jerry Gaines, much perturbed.

"Do not trouble over it, Jerry," said Dinsmore. "If it relates to anything of the least consequence, the writer will be sure to write again."

"You are kind to find pardon for me," returned Gaines, adding, ruefully: "I shall never forgive myself for not taking better care of your mail, old fellow, if it turns out that I have mislaid something of importance to you."

The truth was, fate had taken charge of the letter in question, which was the one from Queenie Trevalyn, recalling him, by causing it to slip through the torn lining of the young reporter's pocket, to be found protruding through the black lining of that self-same coat many a long day later.

Jerry Gaines attended to the commission of opening the remaining letter mechanically, and as he drew the folded sheet of paper from the envelope, lo! a photograph rolled forth from it—the portrait of a very youthful, but a very lovely slip of a girl, and penciled in a scrawling, irregular, schoolgirl hand, was the name Jess, simply that and no more.

He handed the photograph to Dinsmore, while Ballou, with the freedom of an old friend, got up, and coming close to the bedside, looked curiously over John's shoulder.

"If this is the writer of the letter, she is certainly a stranger to me," remarked Dinsmore, slowly, studying curiously the lovely face laughing up at him, for the picture represented a girl, not smiling after the usual fashion, but, indeed, laughing heartily, and with all her might, straight into your eyes, and challenging an amused smile in return from even the gravest lips.

She could not be over fifteen or sixteen. The oval face, with its every dimple displayed, was bewitching, with every promise of future beauty with a year or two added to the girl's years.

The eyes were dark, and deliciously roguish in expression, and she wore the hair which covered the shapely little head in a long braid, tied with a ribbon, wherever the curling tendrils could be ensnared from their persistent effort to break into tiny little curls running riot over the white brow and neck; but the teeth disclosed by that laughing little mouth—were ever teeth so small and white and altogether faultless?

"A lovely girl!" said Hazard Ballou, examining the pictured face with the critical eye of an artist.

"What has this pretty creature to say to me?" said John Dinsmore, breaking through the apathy which had been wrapped about him like a mantle up to the present moment.

"The best way to inform you is to read her letter to you," remarked Gaines, laconically, quite as curious as the recipient to know the import of the missive; for four years of life as a reporter on a daily newspaper, in the metropolis, had stimulated his bump of curiosity, and he was always in the habit of gratifying it, and ever on the lookout for anything which savored of a sensation or a mystery.

"Whew!" he broke forth, whistling as his eyes encountered the first line. "By George, it's the little Louisiana heiress whom your uncle has decided you must wed to become his heir—the girl around whom his fortune is tied, the string to his inheritance, as you phrased it when we first told you about your uncle's strange will, Dinsmore."

"I wouldn't have to think twice in a case like that!" declared Hazard Ballou, still thoughtfully and gravely admiring the pictured, merry, laughing, girlish young face.

"Nor I!" said Jerry Gaines, his whole heart in his eyes. Adding: "Hang it, how can you be so indifferent, you lucky dog?" turning upon Dinsmore excitedly.

CHAPTER IX.
"A LITTLE ROUGH DIAMOND."

"If love should come again, I ask my heart,

In tender tremors not unmixed with pain,

Couldst thou be calm, nor feel the past mad smart,

If love should come again?

"In vain I ask. My heart makes no reply,

But echoes evermore the sweet refrain,

Till, trembling lest it seem a wish, I sigh,

If love should come again!"

"How can a man be so infernally indifferent to so much youth, beauty and innocence?" repeated Jerry Gaines, enthusiastically. "Upon my word, I marvel that you are not jubilant over the prospect fate holds out to you—you are ungrateful, old boy!"

Neither one of his comrades saw the look of pain that gathered for an instant in John Dinsmore's eyes, nor did they see the mobile lips under the heavy mustache quiver for an instant, then draw themselves firmly into a terse straight line.

How could he, whose whole heart's affection had been wasted on the fairest of womankind, look with anything save distrust, nor to say, hatred, on the whole sex, he told himself with a bitter sigh, which he carefully repressed ere it fell from his white lips.

"Love and marriage are not for me, boys—you both know that," he retorted, addressing his words to both his companions. "I shall never love, consequently, never marry," he said, slowly and earnestly.

"Every fellow says that until he meets the right girl," declared the artist, his eyes still fastened upon that lovely pictured face laughing up at him.

"Every one save reporters," laughed Gaines, "and their failure to wed is because no sweet girl in her senses would agree to have one of them if she stops to consider the question of bread and butter," he declared, breaking into a rollicking tune of "How Lonely the Life of a Bachelor Is."

"I beg pardon for this digression, old fellow," he cried, catching up the letter. "Now for letting you know what Mademoiselle Jess has to say to you—in haste—as the lower left hand of the envelope is marked, and underlined with a grand flourish."

The quaint letter, so characteristic of the girl who had written it, ran as follows:

"To MR. JOHN DINSMORE, New York City:

"DEAR MR. DINSMORE: No one knows that I am writing to you, or I should never in the world be allowed to send it. I suppose you are wondering who I am. Well, I am Jess—just Jess.

"I was up in the big apple tree in the orchard when the lawyer from the city came out here, and he not knowing I was up there, sat down on the bench beneath it and told Mrs. Bryson, the housekeeper, of the wonderful will which he said had just been forwarded to him to attend to, by somebody, I forget who; and in it—the will I mean—I was to be a great heiress—the greatest in all Louisiana—if you would marry me, and if you wouldn't, the plantation and all the estate were to be sold, and the money sent to the heathen Chinese, and I was to go out into the world a beggar, as well as yourself, or be a governess, or nursery maid, or kitchen maid maybe.

"I don't know whether it would be nice or not to marry anybody, but I'd rather a million times do that than leave the old plantation, where I know every tree and leaf, and even the wild birds that come and go each season.

"I heard the lawyer say that he had his doubts about whether you would like me or not, and perhaps you'd flatly refuse to comply with your uncle's will when you saw me, for I was so thin and brown, and then my hair was like a tangled mane and looked for all the world, always, as though a comb had never been put to it, and then—a pretty figure I cut in always running about barefoot—though I am within a few days of being sixteen. I wish so much that you would come here and take a look at me, to see if it would be quite convenient for you to marry me, so that I can stay here forever and ever.

"But for fear you haven't time, or something like that, I will send you my picture that you can see if I will suit. It was taken by a traveling photographer who came to take pictures of the old place for a magazine, and he didn't charge me anything for it—I couldn't have taken it if he had. He said, 'Look pleasant, please,' which made me laugh so that the picture was spoiled, he said; but indeed, though, I tried over and over again, I couldn't help laughing to save my life. I never dared show the picture to Mrs. Bryson, for she would have been sure to have raised a terrible time with me for getting it took—taken, I mean. Please answer as soon as you get this, if you will come. Write it to Mrs. Bryson, but don't put in even a hint that I asked you to, or sent the picture, or I would get punished. JESS."

It was little wonder that this straightforward letter, direct from the simple, innocent, girlish heart of the writer, should touch the three masculine hearts most profoundly.

Even John Dinsmore could not help the smile of amusement that came to his lips with the hearing of the first sentence, broadening into a hearty laugh at the conclusion.

"A little rough diamond!" commented Ballou, in a low voice.

"A treasure which almost any man would be proud to win," added Jerry Gaines.

Then, suddenly, he laid his hand on his friend's arm, saying:

"Why don't you take a run down to Louisiana, and look over the ground, and the little maid as well, and then you will be better able to judge whether or not you can afford to throw away the splendid offering which the gods have flung in your way."

John shook his head.

"I shall never marry," he reiterated, "why, then, should I bother about the inheritance which is based upon that contingency? And furthermore, I would be inhuman to take advantage of such a child as this letter shows the girl to be, by tying her to so bitter a fate as being wedded to a man whose only object in marrying her was to secure a fortune. My friends, I am made of different material from that. Of all classes of men, I most despise a fortune hunter—a trader on a woman's heart! There is something sacrilegious, horrible to me, in the thought."

"There will not be the least bit of harm in taking a trip down there, at least," urged Jerry Gaines. "That will not necessarily oblige you to marry against your desire, I'm sure."

Hazard Ballou heartily coincided in this opinion, and between them they were so persistent that he should pursue this course that at last, for the sake of peace, John Dinsmore promised to take the trip, especially as his doctor had suggested that when he was able to leave Newport he should take a trip South, to some mild climate, where his recuperation would be complete.

Neither Ballou nor Gaines would be satisfied until he had answered the child's letter, as they termed Jess.

When he had gotten as far as addressing it, he was met by the fact that Jess had asked him to communicate his response to Mrs. Bryson, instead of herself; therefore he sent the following brief epistle to that worthy woman, whom he remembered, though very indistinctly, as having seen when he was taken on a visit to Blackheath Hall, as the place was called, many years ago, when he was a small lad of five years.

"It makes me feel rather ancient to remember that that was a quarter of a century ago," he remarked, with a smile, as he looked over the brief epistle, which ran as follows:

"To MRS. BRYSON, Blackheath Hall, Greenville, Louisiana:

"MY DEAR MADAM: After many years, I shall be again in your vicinity within the course of a fortnight. May I hope that your hospitality may be extended to me for a few days; I promise not to trespass upon you longer than that.

"With best wishes for the welfare of yourself and all the inmates of Blackheath Hall, I remain,

"Yours very truly,

"JOHN DINSMORE."

"Short, but to the point," remarked Jerry Gaines, as John handed it to him wearily to fold up and place in the envelope.

An hour later the letter was duly on its way toward the sunny South, where it was destined to create such havoc in the old Louisiana home.

"It is best that I should travel about for a little while, at least," ruminated John Dinsmore, long after his tried and true friends had left him; "for the reason that my soul is filled with such bitter unrest that I will find bearing the burden of life more and more intolerable as the weeks roll on.

"Nearly a month has passed, and in a few short weeks more Ray Challoner will lead the only girl I shall ever love to the altar, for I heard her promise to be his bride two months from that day. Those were the cruel words which broke my heart as I listened to them, unable to speak or move, or make my presence known on the other side of those broad palms which screened me from my faithless idol's sight.

"When the marriage occurs, I want to be so far away that no intelligence of it can reach me; for God knows, strong man though I am, I think I should go mad to hear or read of it.

"Heaven pity a man who loves a girl as I have loved, and always will love, Queenie Trevalyn.

"God! why were women made so beautiful, to ensnare the hearts of men, only to cast them aside as playthings of the hour?

"I know her to be a frivolous coquette, a girl without a soul, a girl who loves wealth above everything else earthly; but for all that I worship her still, and her image will be enshrined in my heart until the breath leaves my body, and death ends it all."

And as he uttered the words he meant every one of them, little knowing what fate had in store for him, and it was well that he did not.

A week later John Dinsmore set out on his Southern journey, his two friends accompanying him to the train to see him off.

They would not have said "good-by" so cheerfully, had they known all that was to happen ere they beheld his face again—ay, they would have held him back at any cost.

CHAPTER X.
AFTER THIRTEEN YEARS.

"It is so wide, this great world vaulted o'er

By the blue sky clasping dark shore to shore,

It is too wide—it is too wide for me!

Would God that it were narrowed to a grave,

And I slept quiet, naught hid with me save

The love that was too great—too great for me."

That brief letter from John Dinsmore created no end of excitement at Blackheath Hall. After an absence of five-and-twenty years the heir, whom she well remembered as a handsome, high-spirited, blue-eyed lad, was coming home at last.

All the old family servants were startled out of the lethargy into which they had fallen during the long years since a master had been at the old hall to rule them—most of them but barely recalled the owner, Mr. George Dinsmore, a bachelor, and the most extensive plantation owner in all Louisiana.

Mrs. Bryson, the housekeeper, well remembered a day when he called her to his study and said: "I am going away on a journey. I may return in a month, or it may be a year; perhaps even longer. During my absence, though it be long or short, I want everything at the old plantation to go on the same—you understand?"

The good woman courtesied, and answered: "Everything shall go on the same, sir, though you may be away weeks, months, or years."

Thus he took his departure, and no one knew his destination.

It was five long years ere Mrs. Bryson heard from the master of Blackheath Hall. At that time she received a letter from him bearing the foreign postmark of London.

After giving minute directions concerning the plantation, the letter wound up with this singular postscript:

"My nephew—who will one day be my heir, presumably—together with his tutor, will be at Blackheath Hall for a short stay. I leave it to you to make their stay as pleasant as possible."

Mrs. Bryson carried out her master's wishes to the letter. When the English tutor and the little lad arrived the hospitable doors of Blackheath Hall were thrown open wide to welcome them.

During their short stay they saw but little of the tutor, for he kept to himself much of the time, rarely joining them save at meal times, and even then he had little to say, as though understanding intuitively that they would like to question him as to the identity of the lad—for they knew nothing whatever of the family history of their master, what relatives he had, or where they resided.

Some of the servants began to ply the lad with questions on the first day of his arrival when they had him alone, but they were effectually silenced by the boy replying:

"I will go and ask my tutor and find out for you, telling him that you wish to know."

They stopped him short, covered with confusion. And after that experience, in which they were ignominiously prevented from satisfying their curiosity, they made no attempt to question the boy, and he rode the fat, sleek horses at a mad, breakneck gallop, bareback, down the lane, chased the young lambs over the meadow, and pulled ruthlessly the long, slender leaves of the tobacco plants to his heart's content.

During the short time of his stay beneath that roof every one, from the housekeeper down, loved the gay, rollicking lad who was so full of life and spirit and boyish pranks; and they were sorry enough when the tutor announced that their stay at Blackheath Hall had come to an end, and sorrier still when they saw the lad, who had been the life of the house, ride away—and they always carried the memory in their hearts of how he turned and kissed his little hand to them when he reached the brow of the hill, ere he was lost completely to their sight.

Then, once again, after this short break in their lives, everything settled down to the same dull, monotonous routine at Blackheath Hall—a monotony which was not broken for full many a year. During this time the master of the plantation still continued to reside abroad, giving not the slightest hint or explanation to his wondering household as to the why or wherefore of his strange action.

Thirteen years more rolled slowly by, then came the second break in the dull life of the inmates of the old hall. A second letter was received from the master, this time bearing the postmark of far off Egypt, and announcing that by the time they received his letter a child would be sent to them, who was to make her home at the hall—her name was—Jess.

That was all the information the letter contained. There was not even a word as to what position the child was to occupy in the household—whether she was to be reared to take the place of one of the servants when they should be incapacitated by old age from work, or was to be looked upon as a *protégée* of the master.

In due time the child arrived—an elfish little creature she was—in charge of a woman, a foreigner, who understood no English.

She made no stop whatever, delivering the little one to the inmates of Blackheath Hall and departing immediately, without even partaking of the refreshments which they would have pressed upon her.

They could understand but one thing; she called the little one Jess—just that and nothing more. When they asked her for the little one's other name, she maintained by motions that she could not comprehend their question.

Perhaps this was true, or it might have been feigned; at any rate, she made all haste from the place, seemingly heartily glad to be rid of her charge.

In Mrs. Bryson's opinion, the woman was a French maid—and the child bore such a striking resemblance to her that almost every member of the household remarked it.

Little Jess seemed to take kindly enough to her surroundings. She grew and thrived like a weed, springing up much after the fashion of that uncultivated plant.

She was allowed to roam about as she would—bare of foot and hatless—the great mane of curling hair with which nature had provided her being her only head-covering—lithe and graceful as a young fawn in her brown linsey gown, which barely reached the slender, brown ankles.

Jess was a child of nature—she would have known little enough of books, and cared still less, had not the servants taken pity on her and taught her to read and write, which was quite as much as they knew themselves.

The master of Blackheath Hall never wrote again to ask about the little waif. Except for the brief mention he had made that she was to find shelter beneath his roof, he seemed to forget her entirely.

Therefore the shock of the lawyer's coming, with the sad notice of Mr. George Dinsmore's death, and the will—which was very much stranger still—giving his nephew his entire fortune if he took with it Little Jess—cutting him off entirely if he failed to do so, and cutting the girl off, as well, if she failed to secure his nephew, John Dinsmore, for her husband—was the most mystifying surprise they had ever had.

"It is useless to hope that a fastidious gentleman who has traveled half over the world—as has Mr. John Dinsmore—would take to a wild, half-tamed creature like Jess," Mrs. Bryson said, despairingly, and her heart misgave her that she had not troubled herself to look after the girl better during the years which had come and gone so swiftly. If her late master's plans miscarried, she felt in a vague way that the fault would lie at her door for not looking after the girl better, and making her more of a lady, instead of a lovely little hoydenish savage who would have her own way and knew no will save her own.

For days at a time Jess had been in the habit of wandering about where fancy willed, and no one took the pains to inquire into her coming or going—whether she was in the house or out of it; if she fell asleep from fatigue amid the long grass under the trees when night overtook her, or if she were in her own little room in the servants' quarters under the eaves.

The mistake of years could not be rectified in a day. Mrs. Bryson realized that, and felt, in consequence, deep concern.

For the first time in her life, after the lawyer's visit, she searched for Jess. Through the house and over all the grounds she went, but there were no signs of her.

Jess was like a wild bird ever on the wing; no one knew where she was likely to alight.

Mrs. Bryson was most anxious to have a long and earnest talk with the girl. It never occurred to her for a moment that the girl was evading her for that very reason—that she had heard her tell the lawyer that she meant to have a long and serious talk at once with Jess—but from that hour Jess was nowhere to be found.

It never occurred to the good woman to look up into the magnolia trees which she passed a score of times in her vain search for the girl.

The letter which was received at Blackheath Hall, announcing that the heir would soon arrive there, put Mrs. Bryson in a great state of trepidation. Jess must be found, told the truth and be made to realize that she was to appear before the strange gentleman who was coming, as a young girl of refinement—not a wild, barefooted savage who would not only shock, but horrify him, and shatter at once his uncle's plans of marriage between them.

Clothes would have to be made in a hurry, and lessons given her in deportment; and she would have to be made to understand that her sweetness of demeanor, her behavior and conversational powers would mean wealth or beggary to her.

Every member of the household was sent out in search of the girl, but it was all to no purpose.

Not one of them once dreamed that Jess, up in the tree, was fairly convulsed with laughter at the annoyance she was causing them. She knew their plans, for she heard them discuss them freely as they hurried along, and then and there she determined that she would not take a single step out of her way to please the fastidious heir of Blackheath Hall. It was a matter of little concern to the girl whether he liked her or not.

CHAPTER XI.
REBUKED BY A GIRL.

At this critical point of our story it is necessary that we should return for a brief space to Raymond Challoner, whom we left still at Newport, though the Ocean House was just about closing for the season.

He had not put in an appearance when Queenie Trevalyn and her mother drove to the depot—not even to say good-by to the girl to whom he had been such a devoted lover for the whole season. With the loss of her fortune his interest waned. He did not get up from his comfortable chair as the hotel 'bus whirled past the door, with the girl and her mother as passengers, to take even a last look at the beauty of the season.

"Good-by, sweetheart, good-by!" he murmured, with a grim laugh, as he lighted a fresh Havana—then he proceeded forthwith to forget the Queenie Trevalyn romance and to look forward to conquests in pastures new.

He was terribly short of funds, and concluded that, under the present condition of affairs, he could not afford to settle his board bill just yet. Consequently, when the clerk of the hostelry sent up to the young millionaire's apartments for the trifling amount which was still on the books against Mr. Raymond Challoner, that gentleman was found to be missing, bag and baggage.

Ray Challoner had shaken off the dust of Newport from his heels, and had gone as far away from the scene of his late social triumphs, and failure to secure a matrimonial prize, as possible. Was it fate that he should choose New Orleans as his place of destination? Who shall say?

He was anxious to reach there in time for the races; to recoup, if possible, his dwindling amount of cash. But once again fate seemed determined to balk him.

As they reached a little station the telegraph messenger rushed out and signaled the conductor, and a few hurried words passed between them. The conductor seemed greatly disturbed, and the faces of the trainmen who gathered about them also appeared troubled.

Then came the statement by the conductor that there had been an accident to the mail train just ahead and it would be impossible to proceed. The express was ordered to remain at that station until further orders from the manager of the road.

The uneasiness among the passengers was met with the assurance that they could be transferred to another line, which would bring them into New Orleans some five hours late—that was the best that could be done for them.

Ray Challoner fairly foamed as he cursed his luck—the races would be over by the time he could reach the track—and thus fled his hopes of replenishing his pocketbook with the funds of which he stood so sorely in need.

"Is there no way of reaching there save the one you have mentioned, conductor?" he inquired, pacing nervously up and down.

"Well, there is another way—you might stand a ghost of a chance of finding a horse here that might carry you over to Greenville, a distance of some twenty miles across the roughest road you ever struck; once at Greenville you might get a conveyance to take you the other thirty miles—or a horse, or something of that kind; and if you met no mishaps and pushed rapidly on you might land in New Orleans by noon, or a little after."

"By George! I'll act upon your suggestion," declared Challoner, eagerly. "I cannot more than miss, and that's what I would be doing if——" But here he stopped short, for some one was calling for the conductor, and that functionary was obliged to excuse himself in all haste and hurry away.

Ray Challoner did not wait to see the passengers transferred, but made all haste into the village in which he found himself.

It consisted of a few straggling houses, a blacksmith shop and a couple of general stores, and a farmers' inn.

Toward the latter place Challoner bent his steps, losing no time in making known his wants to his host, but he soon found, to his chagrin, that a horse could not be hired for love nor money.

"Could I buy a cheap animal hereabouts?" he inquired in desperation.

That put a different face on the matter. The man was quite willing to dispose of an ancient animal he owned if the stranger would pay him his price.

"And what is your price?" queried Challoner, impatiently.

"Fifty dollars," answered the man, promptly.

Challoner quickly concluded the bargain, although he had scarcely half that amount left in his purse.

An exclamation of intense wrath, not to say an imprecation, broke from his lips on beholding his purchase; but it did little good to invoke a torrent of anger upon the host of the inn, who already had his money pocketed.

"Why, that animal will not carry me five miles!" he cried, when the horse, already saddled, was led around to the front porch. "He is falling down already, and hasn't a sound leg to stand on; and you could hang your hat on his projecting bones."

"A lean horse for a long race, my friend," remarked his host, sagely; "you'll find that Roger—that's his name—will carry you the twenty miles to Greenville all right."

"And drop down dead when I get there," said Challoner, with still another and more fierce imprecation.

"I didn't agree that he could go much farther than to Greenville," responded the late owner of Roger; "that would depend upon how much rest you gave him when you reach there, friend."

"No doubt I can dispose of him for enough to hire a horse that is a horse to pursue the rest of my journey," declared the disgruntled young man.

"Most likely," remarked his host. But he said to his buxom wife, who stood by, as the stranger mounted the horse and rode off at a rattling pace: "If he keeps that gait up very long, Old Roger will surely rebel and refuse to go a step for him, that's all there is about that. He might lash him to death and he wouldn't stir a leg when the balky notion hits him. He'll be glad enough to swap him for a five-dollar note by the time he gets to Greenville—and Roger will soon be walking home to us again."

Roger had been a profitable animal to mine host. More than once he had sold him, and the new owner was always glad to sell him back to his previous owner at any cost.

Meanwhile the new owner was galloping away at the top of the speed of his new purchase, much to the discomfiture of Roger.

Mile after mile was thus traversed, until, at length, the town he was so anxious to reach loomed up in the distance before him. It was not until then that Roger's impatience began to show itself. When he reached a green lane which led past a grand old place, the animal absolutely refused to go another step forward. This was a dilemma Challoner had not counted upon.

"Besides being as slow as molasses, he's a balker, as well," he muttered, and, taking his whip well in hand, he began to lash the tired beast most inhumanly, a fierce imprecation accompanying each cut of the lash.

One, two, three, four, five strokes of the sizzling rawhide had been brought down upon the quivering flank of the animal, when, forth from the branches of the tree overhead, a blow from a twig fell full upon the face of the startled horseman, a small brown hand was thrust down from among the green branches and a shrill, girlish voice cried, while the blows were rained down faster and faster upon the head of the young man, who was too astounded to make the slightest defense, or make a retreat:

"Take that, and that, and that! you outrageous monster, for lashing a poor, defenseless horse. Oh, I hope that I have hurt you as much as you hurt him—so there!" each word being accompanied by a whack from the stinging twig.

Ray Challoner looked up, as well as his amazement would permit, and saw overhead, sitting on a broad bough, a girl, and surely the angriest creature that he had ever beheld, gazing down at him.

Even in that moment, as he began to dodge the blows, he could not help but notice that the elfish, gypsyish-looking girl had a fine pair of dark eyes, even though they were at that moment blazing with passion, and that the head, crowned with a mass of dark curls, was well set and dainty, the lips were scarlet and curved like Cupid's bow, and the brune face like a picture he had once seen in a foreign art gallery, of a Spanish princess—though, instead of the filmy lace dress of the former, this one wore a brown linsey dress, which made no pretense of covering the brown feet and ankles dangling down from it.

Challoner recovered his usual coolness instantly.

"Ah!" he said, backing away from the reach of that strong, belligerent young arm, that could deal such tremendous blows with the twig, "my assailant is a young girl, it would seem; therefore I am unable to defend myself from this uncalled-for attack."

"Uncalled for!" exclaimed the girl, still more shrilly, for she was thoroughly angry at the stranger; "you provoked it by cruelly abusing your poor horse; I only wish he had reared and thrown you, as you deserved."

"Thank you," remarked Challoner, sneeringly and mockingly, but before he could utter the rest of the sentence which was on his lips, the horse, as though he had heard the suggestion and thought the idea a capital one, immediately reared backward with the quickness of motion that unseated his rider in a single instant, and in the next, Raymond Challoner found himself measuring his full length on the greensward, and the animal, freed from his obnoxious rider, had plunged forward into an adjacent thicket, and was lost to view.

CHAPTER XII.
"WHO IS JESS?"

"But at last there came a day when she gave her heart away—

If that rightly be called giving which is neither choice nor will,

But a charm, a fascination, a wild, sweet exultation—

All the fresh young life outgoing in a strong, ecstatic thrill."

When Raymond Challoner regained his feet he was just in time to see the girl disappearing behind a thicket of alder bushes. To say that he was in a beastly temper by this time but faintly describes the situation—he was furious.

For one moment he paused and pondered as he shook the dust from his eyes, which would pay him best; to search for the horse that had played him so shabby a trick, or make his way on to the village, which was not more than three-quarters of a mile distant at the farthest.

He concluded that the latter course would be best. He would lose more time in trying to dispose of the animal there than the amount received would profit him, if it delayed him on his journey beyond the possibility of being in New Orleans in time for the races.

He was a swift walker, and as he hurried along he beguiled the time by thinking over past events—a thing he rarely allowed himself to do, but somehow he could not get John Dinsmore—Queenie Trevalyn's defender—out of his thoughts.

He had only seen the doctor once since that midnight affair when he had left his adversary lying dying, as he supposed, on the white sands; then, the doctor had come to him, reporting the fact that he had had the injured man conveyed, under an assumed name, to a nearby cottage; but that it was his opinion at the present moment, that the man against whom Ray Challoner had turned his weapon would not live to see another sunrise.

"So much the better," he answered, looking full in the doctor's face, adding: "If he dies, let him be buried under that assumed name, and the world at large will be none the wiser for his taking off."

"You forget that he had two friends who would interest themselves to make inquiry and search for him," the doctor had answered, but Challoner remembered the answer he had made him:

"Tell them that he arose from his bed in his delirium and dashed down upon the sands and threw himself into the breakers, and was never seen again."

"You have a very fertile and imaginative brain, Challoner," the doctor had remarked, dryly; "rather than let this affair come to light, if it should turn out disastrously, I shall act upon your suggestion."

Ray Challoner had little time to ruminate further, for he was already in the streets of the little village of Greenville. The appearance of the handsome, aristocratic young gentleman walking in on foot quite astounded the landlord of the Greenville Hotel, the most pretentious place in the village.

"Could he have a good meal, and after that, engage somebody to take him by carriage on to New Orleans?" queried Challoner.

"The good meal he could have, certainly; but did the stranger know that it was thirty odd miles to the city, and if he was intending to go there, he'd better go by train—they had just finished the new road, and intended to make the initial trip that afternoon."

Raymond Challoner was overjoyed at this piece of news—evidently the conductor of the train he had so lately left did not know of this.

"You will have two good hours to wait here, sir," went on the landlord; "but we can make you comfortable, I reckon."

While Challoner was doing justice to the fried chicken and bacon, the fine mealy potatoes, the gingerbread, honey and home-made bread which was set before him, his curiosity concerning the girl whom he had encountered in the lane a mile up the road got the better of him, and he asked who she was. He also related the story of his experience, which accounted for his appearance there on foot.

The landlord laughed uproariously, as he listened.

"That was Jess you fell in with," he answered, "and bless you, sir, it was as much as your life was worth to abuse—correct, I mean—any animal, from a mouse to a horse, in her presence."

"And who, pray, is Jess?" queried the handsome young stranger, with a cynical smile, as he followed his host from the dining-room out to the barroom, depositing himself in one of the very comfortable rush-bottomed chairs.

It was not every day that the loquacious landlord of the Greenville hostelry had a stranger to gossip with, and he proceeded to unbosom himself at once upon the subject which had always had so much interest for him, because it was shrouded in a mystery.

"Who is Jess?" he repeated, blowing a great puff of smoke from the short corncob pipe he has just lighted; "well, that's what every one around here would like to find out," and then he proceeded to tell the stranger the story of the late owner of Blackheath Hall; of the appearance of the girl Jess there, brought in her infancy one stormy night, and by the master's orders, by the woman who spoke no language save that of a foreign tongue, and she had been allowed to grow up like the weeds about the place—a wild thing, cared for by nobody—and last, but by no means least, of the wonderful will, which the New Orleans lawyer had come up to the village to read to the members of the household of Blackheath Hall, that the great fortune of its owner was to go to the nephew who survived him, on the condition that he marry Jess, and every one was waiting to see what view the heir presumptive, Mr. John Dinsmore, of New York, would take of the matter—whether he would wed the girl for the fortune that would be his with her, or refuse the Dinsmore millions on that account.

His host was so busy with his story that he did not notice the violent start his guest made as the name of John Dinsmore fell upon his amazed ears. He almost wondered if his sense of hearing was playing him false.

Could this be the same John Dinsmore that his bullet had left dying upon the sands of Newport? he wondered, in the greatest of excitement, which he did his best to hide.

"The whole thing came out in a New York paper—which just came in an hour ago. That tells as much about Mr. Dinsmore as they can find out—I mean the people who are looking for him to tell him about his fortune. Would you like to read it while I am attending to other duties which require my presence?" asked the landlord.

"Yes," responded Challoner, and his voice sounded hoarse and unnatural—like nothing human.

He was thankful that he was alone when he read the story of the great fortune which would be John Dinsmore's for the acceptance. He read that he was at the time of writing of the newspaper article a guest of the Ocean Hotel at Newport.

It was the same printed column which Queenie Trevalyn had read—and there followed another column, telling the success of the new book which had just made him world famous.

There was no reason left to doubt the identity of the man, for a fine picture of John Dinsmore—true to life, as he had known him—accompanied the notice, and column of praise.

Ray Challoner laid down the paper with trembling hands.

He stared straight before him, seeing nothing. His thoughts are chaos, his brain whirls, and out of this chaos comes a train of thought that fairly takes his breath away.

He leaps from his seat and begins to pace up and down the floor of the deserted barroom like a madman. The cold perspiration stands out in beads upon his forehead.

"It is a daring scheme, but why should I not accomplish it?" he argues, clinching his hands tightly together. "John Dinsmore is dead; why should not I, with the aid of the doctor at Newport, who would sell his very soul for gold, gain possession of the important papers which were upon his person—and—pass myself off for Dinsmore—gain possession of the fortune—turn it into cash—and then—leave this country forever? There would be but one thing to fear—and that is—coming across any of the fellow's former friends—well I certainly am clever enough to keep out of their way. It is a bold stroke for a fortune, but none but the most daring would ever attempt it—I have nothing to lose and everything to gain; yes, by the eternal! I'll risk it."

He did not like the idea of the girl thrown into the breach, but if he could not gain possession of the fortune without wedding her—the horrible, elfish creature he had encountered—why, wed her he would—and desert her later.

When the landlord returned, he found his guest still pacing restlessly up and down the floor. As he approached, the young man turned to him, saying, hoarsely:

"Landlord, I have a little secret to confide to you; I had thought of not telling it until—well, until I return to Greenville some few days later—but, I fancy that you suspect the truth, and I might as well confess it to you: I am John Dinsmore, the heir of Blackheath Hall."

"Well, well! can it be possible, sir!" cried the landlord, beaming all over with delight; "to tell you the truth, that thought did flash over me when you first came in, inasmuch as they were expecting the heir would come here as soon as he learned the terms of his uncle's will. Welcome to Greenville, Mr. Dinsmore, and long and many a year may you dwell among us. If you hadn't bound me so to secrecy, how I should have liked to have told my wife and daughter that you were here."

"Not just yet," warned the stranger; "wait until I return from New Orleans, which will be two days hence, and then you can spread it about to your heart's content, my good sir."

The old landlord was looking into the handsome, dissipated face with eager scrutiny.

"You do not resemble your uncle, George Dinsmore, whom I remember well," he said, thoughtfully, "and you have changed much since the time when I saw you here before, a little lad."

CHAPTER XIII.
LUCK SMILES.

"A philosopher tells us that free from all care

Is the man who is penniless, homeless and bare;

Unbound by ties of relation or friend,

No position to hold, no rights to defend;

From all common anxieties thus being freed

Having nothing to lose, he is happy indeed.

He may wander at ease through the busiest streets,

With a smile at the care-worried crowd that he meets,

And in thoughts on his neighbors' possessions regale,

With naught to perplex him, by no trouble assailed;

Of all doubt or depression his mind must be clear—

Having nothing to lose, he has nothing to fear."

The landlord of the Greenville Hotel faithfully kept his promise in revealing to no one the secret which his late guest desired him to keep. And in due time, three days later, the false Mr. John Dinsmore returned to the village, and after partaking of one meal at the hotel, for which he paid liberally from a large roll of bills, he set out at once on foot for Blackheath Hall, which lay on the outskirts of the town.

For once fate had been exceedingly kind to the daring adventurer—his hasty letter to the doctor in Newport had come in the nick of time. In John Dinsmore's haste away from the place where he had so nearly lost his life he had accidentally left behind him a satchel which contained all of his valuable papers. These were handed to the doctor by the nurse at whose cottage the sick man had been stopping.

He was just on the point of advertising it—not knowing where his patient was bound for when he left—when two things happened at one and the same time: the total wreck of the train on which he was believed to have been a passenger; and the second, the receipt of the letter, in which Raymond Challoner laid his daring scheme of the winning of a fortune—if he had his co-operation—before him, offering him a goodly share of the Dinsmore millions if he would but help him to obtain them.

The doctor was poor; everything had been going against him of late, and he needed money badly. The battle between his will and his conscience was sharp but decisive—his will had won.

Lest he should change his mind, the doctor had shipped the satchel containing John Dinsmore's important papers to Challoner, at New Orleans, in accordance with his request, and eagerly awaited results, for he had misgivings as to how it would turn out.

Armed with the needed credentials, the fraudulent Dinsmore proceeded at once to present himself to the New Orleans lawyer who had the settlement of the Dinsmore estate in charge.

It was no easy ordeal to pass muster with the astute old man of law, but Challoner accomplished it.

The important documents he brought with him for that gentleman's inspection proved satisfactory upon examination, leaving no room for doubt—there being a letter among them from the deceased George Dinsmore, written fully twenty-five years before to his nephew—for the postmarked envelope bore that date—stating if he grew up to be a good boy he should one day inherit Blackheath Hall, to which he was invited on a visit.

The old lawyer did not fancy the young heir particularly—there was something about him that seemed to grate harshly upon him.

"If I mistake not, I saw him betting at the races when I went there to find an important witness yesterday," he ruminated, "and if that is the kind of life he leads, poor George Dinsmore's wealth will flow like water through those white, slim, idle hands of his.

"There is but one formula necessary now to be gone through with ere the fortune can be made over to you, Mr. Dinsmore," remarked the old lawyer, with a grim smile, "and that is to wed the—Miss Jess," he said, hurriedly, changing the words that had been almost on his lips.

"If I do not like the young girl, I shall not marry her—not for all the fortunes that were ever made!" cried the false Dinsmore, dramatically, and the lawyer liked him the better for that dash of spirit.

"The estate is a fine one, young man, and it would be a pity for you not to inherit it, as you are next of kin to the deceased Mr. Dinsmore. It was a great mistake, in my opinion, to tie it up as he did."

Armed with the lawyer's letters of introduction, it was an easy matter for the daring, fraudulent heir to gain an entrance to Blackheath Hall.

Mrs. Bryson, the old housekeeper, looked with unfeigned astonishment at the handsome young man who soon afterward presented himself at the hall as Mr. John Dinsmore.

"I—I beg your pardon for staring at you so hard," she said, apologetically, as she bade him enter; "you are changed so much from the boy that it is hard to look at you and believe you to be one and the same. Your eyes were quite blue as a boy, I remember; now they are positively black—and you look so very young. The years have rested lightly on you, sir; I should scarcely take you for two-and-twenty, let alone thirty, which you must surely be."

"You are inclined to be complimentary, my dear madam," remarked the young man, with a covert sneer in his tone and a curl of his lips which the black mustache, luckily for him, covered. "I try to take good care of myself, and do not dissipate, which may, in a measure, account for my youthful appearance, as you are pleased to term it; but, as to changing the color of my eyes, that, my dear madam, would be quite beyond my humble power. I would say that your memory has been playing you a trick if you ever imagined them blue."

Mrs. Bryson was certainly bewildered. She must certainly have been laboring under a most decided blunder in believing them blue all these years, she told herself.

"Come right in, sir," she said, holding the great oaken door wide open for him. "Welcome to Blackheath Hall."

Mr. Dinsmore lost no time in accepting her invitation, and looked around in considerable satisfaction at the handsome suite of rooms which had been prepared for him.

"What an unlucky dog my rival was to kick the bucket and leave all this good fortune behind him," he thought, as he gazed about him; "but still, what was his loss is my gain."

"I will inform Miss Jess that you are here, sir," remarked the housekeeper, with a courtesy, as she turned and left the room. Like all women, she was attracted to him because of his singularly handsome face, and she was wondering what the fastidious young gentleman would think when he beheld the incorrigible Jess—who was a child of nature still, though she had done her utmost during the last few days to revolutionize the girl's appearance.

The thin pink and white mull dress, with its soft, fluttering pink ribbons, became her dark, gypsyish beauty as nothing else could have done, but Jess declared that she would a thousand times over wear her brown linsey gown, that bade defiance to briar and bush as she sprang like a wild deer through them.

Mrs. Bryson had had a severe and trying ordeal in bending the will of Jess to her own, in submitting to the transformation; but at last the good woman accomplished her purpose, and when at last the young girl stood before her, gowned as a young girl should be, she could not repress her exclamation of great satisfaction.

"If your manners but correspond with your looks, Jess," she said, "you would be simply irresistible, and would be sure to capture the heir for a husband."

"It seems that my tastes and inclinations in the matter are not to be considered at all!" cried the girl, with flashing eyes; "he is to come here and look me over quite the same as though I was a filly he wished to purchase, and if I suit, he will take me; if not, he will coolly refuse to conclude the bargain."

"My dear—my dear—do not look upon the matter in such a horribly straightforward light—of course, he must be pleased with you to want to marry you—and——"

"I don't want to marry your Mr. John Dinsmore! I hate him!" cried Jess, stamping her tiny little foot angrily.

"How can you say that you hate him when you have not even seen him, child?" argued the old housekeeper.

"But I have seen him," replied the girl, with a toss of her jetty curls; "I was in the hay field when he came along the road, and I had a very good look at him."

Jess did not add that she was surprised beyond all words to behold in him the ill-tempered stranger with whom she had had the encounter a few days before.

She wisely refrained from mentioning anything concerning the affair to Mrs. Bryson, in anticipation of the scolding she would be sure to receive. Perhaps Mr. John Dinsmore would fail to recognize in her the assailant who had given him a little of his own medicine for abusing the old horse that was fairly staggering under him.

"There isn't a young girl in all Louisiana who would not be delighted to stand in your shoes," declared the old housekeeper, energetically; "he is well worth the winning, and as handsome as a prince. And remember, besides all that, your benefactor, Mr. Dinsmore, who kept this roof over your head for so many years, set his heart and soul upon your fancying each other."

"Would they be glad to stand in the slippers I am wearing at the present time, as well as in my shoes?" queried Jess, with a flippant laugh. "And as to the last part of your remark, Mrs. Bryson, a girl can't like a young man simply because he has been picked out for her by somebody who has no idea of her likes and dislikes. Kissing goes by favor, you know."

"You would exasperate a saint, girl," cried the housekeeper, "do not fly in the face of your good fortune, but make the most of such a grand opportunity of winning a handsome young husband, and a fine fortune, at one and the same time."

CHAPTER XIV.
A FATEFUL MEETING.

It was with evident satisfaction that the false John Dinsmore looked about the elegantly appointed suite of rooms when he found himself alone in them. The open windows looked out upon the eastern terrace, which was delightfully cool and shady this warm afternoon, with the odor of the tall pines and of the great beds of flowers floating in on the breeze.

He threw himself down in a cushioned chair by the window; and as he sat there, quietly reflecting for an hour or more, he could not make out why the elder Dinsmore had made it imperative in his will that his nephew must marry that freak of a girl, Jess, if he would inherit his millions.

He was aroused from his meditations by the sound of the dinner bell.

"There's not a particle of use in making any change in my toilet because of the freak, or the old housekeeper—these backwoods people would not know the difference between a *négligée* and a regulation dinner costume, I'll be bound."

He had a good appetite, and responded to the summons with alacrity. He was not surprised to find Mrs. Bryson only in the great paneled dining-room.

She greeted him with stately courtesy, remarking, as she assigned him a seat on her right at the table, that Miss Jess would be with them directly.

And the good lady felt called upon to tell the young man then and there that the girl had no other name, at least they knew of none; observing that this incident concerning the past showed how easy it was to cloud the future by carelessness in determining anything so important at the right time.

Mr. Dinsmore made some light, conciliatory reply, inwardly congratulating himself that the impish freak, as he styled the girl, had not put in an appearance, for the sight of her would not improve his digestion, rather it would nauseate him if she came to the table garbed in body as he had last seen her and minus any foot covering.

Five minutes passed, in which Mrs. Bryson vainly attempted to keep up the conversation, while the dinner waited for the truant Jess, much to the housekeeper's annoyance and that of the handsome guest, for the odor of well-cooked viands sent his appetite up to almost a ravenous pitch.

"I think we will be forced to dine without Jess," she began, apologetically, but the words were scarcely out of her mouth ere the sound of ear-splitting whistling, sweet, even though its shrillness fell upon their ears.

"Jess is coming," murmured Mrs. Bryson, flushing hotly, for she was ashamed beyond all words that their guest should hear her actually whistling, and she added, apologetically, "the child is something of a tomboy, Mr. Dinsmore, having no little girl companions must surely account for that"—she looked anxiously at the door as she spoke, and the guest's eyes naturally followed in the same direction.

He was prepared to see a wild, gypsyish creature, more fitted for wild camp life than life at stately Blackheath Hall, where the grand old dining-room, with its service of solid silver, might have satisfied a princess.

As the fluttering steps drew nearer, the young man smiled a sneering, satirical smile beneath his dark mustache.

He was wondering if the girl would recognize him on sight as the stranger with whom she had had the angry encounter in the lane a few days before.

As she neared the great doorway the whistling suddenly ceased, and almost simultaneously the girl appeared in sight, and it was no wonder that the elegant stranger forgot himself so much as to actually stare—for the vision that suddenly appeared before his sight haunted him to the end of his life.

Instead of the hoydenish creature he expected to see, he beheld a tall young girl, in a pink and white flowered dress, which became her dark beauty as no Parisian robe could have done; the jetty curls were tied back by a simple pink ribbon, and a knot of pink held the white lace bertha on her white breast.

She advanced with the haughty step of a young empress and took her seat opposite Mr. Dinsmore.

He never afterward clearly remembered in what words the presentation was made.

He was clearly taken aback, and he showed it plainly.

Not one feature of the girl's proud, beautiful face moved, but there was a subtle gleam in the bright, dark eyes which made the handsome stranger feel uncomfortable. He knew that she had recognized him at the first glance, and was secretly laughing at that memory—a fact which he resented.

She took but one glance at him, but in that one, instantaneous glance she had read not only the face, but the heart and soul, of the man sitting opposite her, and her first impression of dislike of him was strengthened.

He was quick to see that this little Southern beauty did not go in raptures over him, as almost every other girl whom he had ever met had seemed to do; in fact, he felt that she disliked him, and he was sure that it was on account of the episode with the horse.

"I will change all that," he promised himself confidently. He would not notice that the girl acknowledged the introduction curtly, if not brusquely; a fact which quite horrified good Mrs. Bryson, who remembered full well her words:

"If I like the paragon who is coming I will be as amiable as I can to him; if I dislike him, no power on earth can compel me to pretend that I do. I will be as civil as I can to him, do not expect any more from me, Mrs. Bryson. I have heard all that you have to say about this strange young man's taking a fancy to me—which is the peg upon which riches in the future or beggary are hung—but I do not care a fillip of my finger for all that. I would never marry him unless I liked him, though a score of fortunes hung in the balance. If I ever marry, I want a lover like the heroes I have read of—a——"

Mrs. Bryson held up her hands in horror, exclaiming:

"Again, in after years, I behold the fruits of my folly. I allowed you to read what you would in master's library, forgetting there were sentimental books there; and no young girl should read that kind. They have filled your foolish little head with all sorts of wild notions."

"I shall know when I meet my hero, thanks to them," declared Jess, with a toss of the curls and a defiant expression of her dark eyes, which had a habit of speaking volumes from their wonderful dark depth.

And looking at her, Mrs. Bryson knew from her indifferent manner that handsome Mr. Dinsmore had not made a favorable impression upon the girl—he was not her ideal—not her hero, evidently.

Mr. Dinsmore noticed that she made no attempt to entertain him or to be anything more than civilly indifferent.

He was annoyed, but he would not notice it. The elegantly appointed table, the excellent dinner, and the fine old wines made an impression upon him.

He set himself to work with a will which was new to him to overcome the girl's prejudice. He was all animation, vivacity and high spirits, literally charming the old housekeeper with his flow of wit and collection of anecdotes.

Glancing now and then to the lovely girl opposite him, he saw that she was bored instead of being amused by them.

Her indifference piqued him, she aroused his interest, and that was more than any other girl had done—and he had traveled the wide world over, and had seen the beauties of every clime.

"I almost believe I have lost my heart to the girl," he muttered, as he arose from the table, and at Mrs. Bryson's suggestion, followed her out into the grounds.

"Jess, will you show Mr. Dinsmore the rose gardens?" she asked of the girl, adding, "he was very fond of them when he was a child." Suddenly she asked: "Do you remember gathering roses from a bush when you were stung by a bee?"

"I remember the incident well," he remarked, with a laugh, looking the good woman straight in the eye, as he uttered the glib falsehood unflinchingly, adding: "I believe I could go straight to that very bush now."

"You have a wonderful memory," declared the good woman, admiringly. She managed to whisper to Jess, as the girl passed her, to be more civil to their guest, and to pretend to take more interest in him for hospitality's sake, if for nothing else—a remark to which Jess deigned no reply.

To tell the truth, she was rebelling in her innermost soul at her restraint in being gowned in a dress in which she could not do as she pleased without getting it ruined. Better a thousand times were she in her brown linsey dress, in which she could climb into her old seat in the apple tree if she liked, or roam over the dew-wet grass, with her dogs for companions, to her heart's content.

Try as she would, she could not forget this handsome young man's cruelty to his poor horse; how fearfully he had lashed him, every stroke being accompanied by a curse.

CHAPTER XV.
THE LOVE THAT IS SURE TO COME.

"What is love, that all the world
Talks so much about it?
What is love, that neither you
Nor I can do without it?"

The hour which followed in the old garden sealed the fate of the false heir—he was hopelessly head over heels in love with the girl whom he had come to Blackheath Hall determined to hate. He was frightened at the vehemence of his mad passion.

What if she should not return it and refuse to obey the conditions of the will?

"I will not think of such a possibility," he told himself, setting his handsome, white teeth hard together.

He felt that the first thing to be done to get on an amiable footing with her and remove her prejudice—for he felt reasonably sure that she recognized him—was to apologize for his seeming harshness to his horse on that memorable occasion when the girl had encountered him.

He got around the point most admirably, in his opinion, when he turned lightly and said to Jess:

"I have been trying to think, ever since I beheld you to-day, of whom you remind me. I have it now, your face is very similar to that of a young girl whom I met in this vicinity a few days ago as——"

"I am that girl, Mr. Dinsmore," cut in Jess, icily, and with more dignity of manner than good Mrs. Bryson would ever have dreamed that she possessed, adding: "Your conduct exasperated me, and I administered to you what I considered a lesson and a rebuke in one. I know you are intending to tell Mrs. Bryson about it to get me into trouble, but I do not care; I would do the same thing over again under the same provocation, Mr. Dinsmore!" she cried, with flashing eyes.

"You mistake my intentions," he hastened to reply; "I have no wish to ever mention it after this conversation, believe me. Instead, I wish to explain my actions to you, that I may not seem quite such an ogre in your sight as I must at present. Remember, I asked you to hear me then and you refused; surely you will not judge me too harshly until you have heard what I have to say upon the subject?" he said, eagerly.

"I would rather try to forget it," retorted Jess, her slender, dark, jetty eyebrows meeting in a decided frown.

He would take no notice of her remark, but went on, quickly:

"You shall hear my reason for my actions, which will, I am sure, excuse them——"

"Nothing will ever excuse a man for lashing a poor dumb brute!" cried Jess, trembling with indignation. "Spare your words, sir!"

Without noticing the interruption he went on, in a low, injured voice:

"Some five minutes ere you saw me I had been taken with an attack of my old enemy—acute gastritis—and I knew that my only hope of not falling dead in the saddle was to reach a place where I could summon assistance, for in five minutes more I would be in spasms. In moments like that one uses every means within one's grasp to reach safety and succor. I realized dimly that the animal was tired, but it was his life or mine, and the latter, of course, was the one to be saved. In my excruciating pain I know not what words I used—I never will know. My brain seemed on fire and whirling about; my only thought was to reach the village beyond, and with all possible speed, while I was able to control the lines and keep my seat. The terrible fall which the animal gave me had its good effects; it restored the circulation of blood as nothing else could have done, and probably saved my life then and there. That is all I have to say; surely, after knowing the truth, you cannot withhold your pardon from me, Miss Jess?"

"Not if your statement is true," replied the girl, with terrible straightforwardness. "I did you two injuries: the first, in believing you unmercifully wicked and cruel; the second, in reaching out from the limb of the tree on which I was seated and striking you. It is I who should sue for your pardon, sir, and pray that you might forget it."

"I beg you to believe that my pardon is fully and freely granted," he replied, eagerly. "And now, may I hope that we shall be friends, Miss Jess?" and, emboldened by her forgiving mood, he caught the little brown hand that was hanging by her side ere she could know what he was about to do, and began kissing it rapturously.

With an angry gesture Jess quickly drew her hand from his clasp.

"You ask for my friendship," she said, "that is quite another matter; you will have to deserve it. And I shall not know whether you are worthy of it until I know you better, and have learned your good traits, and your bad ones."

The young man laughed outright, highly amused. Was there ever such an original girl as this Jess? he asked himself.

"I shall strive for it as man never strove for a girl's friendship before," he declared. "Now that I have removed your distrust—nay, even your hatred—I may hope to gain your good will—which is so much to me."

She looked at him in unfeigned astonishment.

"Why should you care whether I like or hate you, Mr. Dinsmore?" she asked, looking straight into his face with her dark, childish eyes.

Had he chosen to utter the truth he might have responded:

"For two reasons: first, because I have taken a fancy to you; and second, because you must marry me, whether you will or not, that I may secure the Dinsmore fortune."

But he only responded, quietly:

"Why should one wish for an enemy when that enemy can be made a friend of, Miss Jessie?"

"Do not call me Jessie!" cried the girl; "I detest it. I am simply Jess—nothing but that."

"Jess, then," he said, laughingly. "It shall be as the queen wills."

"I shall be sure not to like you if you go on making speeches like that!" declared the girl. "I don't like queens, they are not my style; I have read all about them. I'd rather be a plain American girl than be the grandest queen in the world."

"You are enthusiastically patriotic," he said, admiringly. "I quite honor you for that sentiment," and he drew nearer, that he might look more closely into the beautiful face, whose expression varied with every passing thought.

And Mrs. Bryson, watching them eagerly from behind the screening vines of the porch, said to herself that they were getting on famously together.

It was a difficult matter, during the week which followed, to keep Jess within the prescribed bounds of civilization which Mrs. Bryson had laid out for her.

But that the brown linsey dress was destroyed, literally torn to pieces before her very eyes, Jess would have donned it, and taken to her old life again, roaming barefooted through the woods and dales, with never a care.

She chafed like an untamed cub at the confinement she was now undergoing, and of being thrust into stays and dainty dresses, and her feet into slippers, even though they were of a size the far-famed Cinderella herself might have envied. And the curls, which had always been allowed to blow about as they would, free from restraint as the breeze itself, did not take kindly to the jailer of a ribbon, and were constantly breaking forth in crinkling rings here and there, utterly defying detention.

"I was in great fear that he would not take to Jess," mused Mrs. Bryson, anxiously; "but now I know that that fear is groundless; she can be mistress of Blackheath Hall if she so wills it; and, no matter how obstinate she may be, I will see to it that she marries the young heir when he asks her. Dear, dear! what a wonderful difference fine clothes do make in the girl. I never knew before that she was positively beautiful; but such is actually the case. 'Fine feathers make fine birds,' most truly."

Mrs. Bryson had too much tact to ask Jess what she thought of the handsome young stranger, even when she found herself alone with the girl that night. Instead, she said, with a sigh:

"Mr. Dinsmore is far more elegant than I thought he would be. I have little hope that you will ever reign mistress of this vast estate, for he would never think of falling in love with you, poor child."

"Nor would I ever fall in love with him," retorted Jess, spiritedly; but all the same the words of the housekeeper rankled in her girlish heart for an hour or more after Mrs. Bryson had left her; in fact, until her dark, bright eyes closed in dreams. It was the first thought that occurred to Jess when she opened her eyes at the dawn of day the following morning.

"If it were not for the trouble I would show Mrs. Bryson how mistaken she is," Jess ruminated, as she made her simple toilet and hurried down into the grounds.

Early as she was, to her great amazement she found Mr. Dinsmore already in the grounds, smoking a cigar as he paced restlessly to and fro.

"What an unexpected pleasure, Miss Jess," he cried, throwing away his cigar at once and advancing toward her. "I hardly hoped for so agreeable a surprise. Usually young girls are not visible much before noon—those whom I have met in the world of fashion."

"Then I should not like to belong to the world of fashion," declared Jess, "for the early morning has a charm for me which no other part of the day can equal. I had almost forgotten to give you the letter which Toby just brought up from the village post office for you, Mr. Dinsmore."

As he took it from her hand, and his eye fell upon the chirography, a chalky, ashen color overspread his face, and he started violently. Even before he opened it, he had an intuition of what it contained, and he muttered to himself:

"I have not time to waste—I must marry this girl and collect all the funds possible without delay. And after that—well, let the future look out for itself!"

CHAPTER XVI.
COLD AND HEARTLESS.

Once only, love, may love's sweet song be sung;
But once, love, at our feet, love's flower is flung;
Once, love—only once—can we be young;
Say, shall we love, dear love, or shall we hate?

Once only, love, will burn the blood-red fire;
But once awaketh the wild desire;
Love pleadeth long, but what if love should tire?
Now shall we love, dear love, or shall we wait?

The day is short, the evening cometh fast;
The time of choosing, love, will soon be past;
The outer darkness falleth, love—at last.
Love, let us love ere it be late—too late.

After hastily perusing the letter which he had received, Ray Challoner thrust it quickly into his pocket, muttering hoarsely to himself that there was little time to lose. He must propose to Jess as expeditiously as possible.

He would not trust himself to figure on the result further than to assure himself that the marriage ceremony should be consummated by fair means or foul, and that, too, without delay.

That evening, when he followed Jess to the drawing-room he primed himself for the coming ordeal, for he felt that it would amount to simply that.

She was advancing toward the open window, and he hastened to her side, saying:

"I know you were just about to step out on the porch. You love the outdoor air so well that I am sorry to inform you that it is raining heavily."

"What difference will that make to me, Mr. Dinsmore?" exclaimed the girl, cresting her dark, curly head. "I love the rain and the warring of the elements. I am at home among them. They will not harm me; I am not sugar, nor salt; therefore the rain will not spoil me nor make havoc of my complexion." And she laughed airily as she uttered the words.

"But the rain will make havoc of that lovely costume you have on," he declared, biting his lips with vexation.

"I shall throw my waterproof cloak about me, and put on my rubbers," she retorted, nonchalantly.

"But what is the use of venturing out on to the porch in a driving gale like this?" he cried. "You will take your death of cold." Adding: "Besides, I am not so fortunate as to be equipped to accompany you."

"Indeed, I did not expect you to do so," retorted the girl, quickly. "And you are mistaken about my intending to stop on the porch. Why, I'm going out into the very teeth of the storm—out into the grounds—possibly farther down the road. There is a miniature cataract in the woods about half a mile from here. I always go there to watch the swirling, angry water in a storm. It is simply grand, especially when the lightning strikes and fells some of the giant trees, which it is nearly always sure to do."

Challoner looked at the girl in dismay, wondering what sort of a creature she could be. She was so vastly different from the rest of the girls he had known. Silks and laces could not make her different from what nature had intended her—a veritable tomboy, and a heathenish one at that.

No matter where she went, he was determined to accompany her and propose to her, that very evening, come what might.

He swallowed his chagrin in the most amiable manner possible, remarking with apparent calmness:

"As the queen wills, I suppose. Here is an umbrella close at hand, fortunately," and as he stepped out of the long French window after the bounding figure of the girl who preceded him, he comforted himself with the thought that the stake he must win that night was worth a thousand times more than his evening suit and new patent leather ties, which would, of course, be ruined by this mad escapade.

In that moment he fairly hated this girl whom he had come there to win at all hazards—playing such a daring game for the great fortune involved. He would soon stop such mad freaks as this, after the knot was tied, even though he crushed her spirit, and broke her heart to accomplish it—he promised himself with a good deal of inward satisfaction.

He wondered if there was ever a man on earth who proposed marriage under such trying circumstances.

Jess scorned the use of his umbrella, and his arm, but ran on before him at a breakneck pace, and it was all that he could do to keep up with her and manage to keep the umbrella from turning inside out in the mad gale and torrents of downpouring rain.

He even had the uncomfortable feeling that the girl was laughing at his plight and enjoying his discomfiture hugely.

There was clearly not the slightest use, or opportunity, as for that matter, of uttering one word of the declaration he had prepared with such care, for he could scarcely catch his breath as it was. He must wait until they reached their destination, the cascade, and had time to recover himself after so swift a race at the girl's heels.

The half mile she had spoken of seemed three times that length to him, and he was nearly dropping with exhaustion when at last the welcome sound of the dashing of the water fell upon his ears.

"Here we are, Mr. Dinsmore. I hope you are not tired," said Jess, and if they had not been standing in the shadow of the trees he would have seen the amused sparkle in her eyes as she heard him actually panting for breath.

"Not at all," he remarked, grimly. But she noticed that he made all haste to throw himself down upon a fallen log to rest.

"The rain will soon cease, for it is only a shower, then the moon will come forth from behind the clouds in a flood of silvery brightness, but the wind will take up the battle, and uproot the trees that the lightning failed to find."

"For Heaven's sake, why should you elect to remain where there is so much danger?" he cried, as her words were verified at that very instant by the crashing down of a giant oak almost at his feet.

"Because I love danger!" answered the girl, musingly. "I think if I had been born a boy instead of a girl, I should have gone on the high seas, and perhaps turned out a pirate captain, or something equally as romantic. I crave a life filled with excitement. I cannot understand how young girls can sit in parlors dressed up as puppets and crochet, and talk by rule. Such restraint would be simply unendurable to me. I should feel like a wild bird who has been captured from his nest in some grand old tree in a deep green wood and thrust into a gilded cage. He sees not the gilding, nor the food and drink placed in it; he sees only the cruel iron bars that hold him back from freedom and its joyousness."

This was the very opening which Challoner desired, and he was quick to take advantage of it.

"Marry me, little Jess, and you shall live just the life you crave," he cried, falling dramatically on his knees at her feet, and at the same instant seizing both her little clasped hands in his and covering them with hot, passionate kisses.

"You shall go where you will, do as you like. Your caprices shall be as law to me. I—I——"

"Stop!" cried Jess, drawing her hands away from him angrily. "You are cruel to spoil the beauty of the scene and the night."

"My heart compels me to speak," he answered, hoarsely, "the words force themselves from my heart to my lips. I can no more keep them back than I could withhold the mad torrent of waters that are dashing down the bed of yonder cataract. Listen to the story of my love, little Jess, and then blame me if you can find it in your heart to do so."

"I do not want to hear about it now," persisted Jess, impatiently.

He drew away from her and leaned against a tree with his arms folded across his chest and a decidedly queer expression on his face. He was struggling hard with himself to keep down his anger. Such a declaration as he had just uttered had never been known to fail in winning a feminine heart, and the idea of this girl "calling him down," as he phrased it, for declaring himself, filled him with rage which he found difficult to master.

It was not the first time she had snubbed him during their short acquaintance, and then and there he told himself that he had a long score to settle with this girl, and he would settle it with a vengeance some day, but he had yet his game to win, and for the present he must play the part of an adoring lover, which was very repugnant to his feelings.

He looked at the slim slip of a girl the winning of whom meant a fortune to him, if she could be won quickly, and commenced the attack in another way, and more adroitly.

"So fair, so cold and so heartless," he murmured. "Cold as yonder lady moon breaking away from the clouds that would fain clasp her and hold her; but the moon has not so true a lover in the clouds as you have in me, little Jess. I pray you listen to me, for I must speak and tell you all that is in my heart—or die!" he added, dramatically.

An amused laugh broke from the girl's fresh red lips as she looked up into the handsome, cynical face.

"Ah, if you were less heartless, Jess," he sighed. "But even the hardest heart may sometimes suffer, and your day may come. Perhaps you may experience some day the love that I feel now, and if the object of your affection laughs at you in your face for your folly in loving, then you will know what I am suffering to-night."

"I did not mean to do anything so positively rude as that!" declared Jess, "but somehow this whole transaction seems so very ridiculous to me, just as if I were a bale of tobacco put up for a purchaser. You were to come here and look me over, and if I half suited you, you would marry me, because that was the condition of that dreadful will. But I tell you here and now that I have something to say in the matter—a voice to raise—since my future happiness is at stake. All the money your uncle left could not make me marry a man I did not love. And I do not love you, that is certain, Mr. Dinsmore. And what's more, I never will. Marriage between us is, therefore, impossible. Speak no more of it, for it can never be, I tell you."

He was silent from sheer rage. He knew if he opened his lips to speak he would curse her as she stood there before him in the bright, white moonlight. Was ever so splendid a fortune lost! and all through the willful caprice of a girl. It fairly drove him mad to think of it—ay, mad—and desperate.

CHAPTER XVII.
WAS IT THE DECREE OF FATE?

"Mark well, who wed should give the hand

With undivided heart, and stand

In single purpose true to one;

Or else the loving soul's undone,

And, like the curse which blights the land,

The heart's in variance with the hand,

And found, alas! too late—too late,

Fate linked them to a faithless mate,

They thought the flower of chivalry."

Even in that moment of fierce anger, this man, who had so much at stake, did not give way to his feelings. Instead he sought to use every persuasion, every argument possible to dispel her prejudice, and then win her heart. But it seemed a useless attempt. She simply grew more and more annoyed with him for his persistence; was actually bored by his eloquent avowal of love.

It was to be a long and laborious task, awakening her interest, to say nothing of hoping for a tenderer regard, he could plainly foresee, and when she turned away from him, with never a word of answer in response to his passionate appeal, he determined upon a clever maneuver to bring her to accepting him.

"You have spoiled my hour at the cataract," she said, pouting like a spoiled child, "and now I am going back to the house. You shall not accompany me the next time."

If she had looked at him she would have seen that his face wore a dull red flush in the white moonlight.

"You shall never leave this spot until you have promised to marry me, Jess, or have looked upon your work, if you persist in refusing me."

And as he spoke, he sprang into the path before her, barring her exit to the main road, and at the same time seizing her wrist in a steel-like grasp.

Jess was no coward. This action aroused all the girl's spirit of angry resentment.

"Stand aside and allow me to pass, Mr. Dinsmore!" she cried. "How dare you attempt to bar my way! Another moment of this, and I shall hate you instead of being merely indifferent to you."

For answer he drew from his breast pocket a small, silver-mounted revolver and placed the muzzle of it against his temple.

"Is your answer to be yes or no, Jess?" he said, hoarsely. "Promise to marry me and you save my life; refuse, and I fire. I love you too well to lose you. I give you while I count five to reach a conclusion."

"How dare you threaten me in this way?" panted the girl.

"Is it yes—or—no?" he questioned, stolidly.

Terror, for the first time in her young life, robbed Jess of all power of speech, and like one in a trance she heard him call out hoarsely:

"One—two—three—four——"

"Speak! Is it yes, or no?" he cried, bending toward her, his fiery eyes and breath scorching her face.

But Jess could make him no answer, her lips were stricken dumb.

"Five!" he shouted, and simultaneously with the word the deafening report of the revolver rang out on the stillness of the night air in that lonely spot.

Even as he had uttered the word, Jess sprang forward to wrench the revolver from his grasp and prevent the tragedy, if indeed he really meant to carry out his threat of blowing his brains out. But in her excitement she forgot that he was standing on the very brink of the precipice which overlooked the cataract, and in her intense horror she forgot that the tree which had so recently blown down lay directly across the path, and her foot caught on the up-standing roots, and in less time than it takes to tell it, she had fallen across it, her head hanging over the very edge of the precipice.

If her foot had not been so securely fastened in the intertwining roots, she would surely have gone over it; as it was, she was held fast.

But Jess did not know that, for, with that plunge forward, when her terrified gaze encountered the foaming waters dashing below her into which she was falling headlong, consciousness left her.

For an instant Challoner contemplated the girl and her perilous position with darkening brows.

"If I served her right, I would give her a push which would send her down to the bottom of the falls," he muttered. "She sprang for me to wrest the weapon from me; I saw that in her eyes, and outstretched hands. The little fool never dreamed that the weapon contained only blank cartridges. I'm not so fond of shuffling off this mortal coil as I led her to believe. In the first place, I think too much of my precious head, and in the second, I intend to remain on this terrestrial sphere long enough to win the Dinsmore millions, if it be within man's power."

Very coolly he replaced the revolver in his breast pocket, then set about to release the girl from her uncomfortable position, telling himself that he ought to let her remain there until her senses returned, to see how brave she would be when she found herself hanging head downward over the chasm.

Then another idea occurred to him, which he proceeded to put into execution. Laying Jess hurriedly down, he dragged the tree by main force forward, and hurled it across the yawning space. A cry of delight broke from his lips as it lodged securely upon a jutting point of rock some ten feet below, making a bridge, which spanned the chasm, quite as completely as though it had been fashioned by the hand of man.

"Excellent!" cried Challoner. "Affairs could not have been adjusted more to my liking. I will win the girl through her love for romantic chivalry. By the means of this I have not the slightest doubt."

Coolly lifting the slight figure in his arms, he proceeded to convey her by way of a short cut through the grounds back to Blackheath Hall.

The old housekeeper was on the porch when he reached the outer gate with his burden, and when he staggered up the broad walk and laid Jess at her feet, her cry of terror brought the household to the scene at once.

To them Challoner, or John Dinsmore, as they called him, told the story which he had prepared for their ears, to the effect that as they were standing on the precipice, looking down on the foaming waters, as Jess had insisted upon doing, the girl had lost her balance, and had fallen over headforemost into the chasm.

For an instant he had thought it was all over with her. Then, to his intense joy, he discovered her hanging by her skirts to a tree which had blown down and was lodged fully ten feet below. He had not waited an instant to consider what was best to be done, but, with the fixed determination to save Jess or die with her, he had plunged down to her rescue, succeeding in grasping her just as her garments were giving way.

Then followed his recital of his terrible climb up that ten feet of slippery rock with his burden clasped close in his arms. One slip meant certain death for both, and, hardly realizing how he had accomplished it, he at last, by an almost superhuman effort, had succeeded in pulling himself and Jess up, thanking Heaven that the girl was unconscious, and had not realized the frightful danger through which she had passed.

Mrs. Bryson, the old housekeeper, trembled like an aspen leaf as she listened; then her pent-up feelings broke forth into hysterical sobbing.

"Little Jess owes her life to you, Mr. Dinsmore," she cried. "She should adore the very ground you walk on for it to the day she dies, and I shall impress that upon her mind," she added. "Perhaps it would be best never to let her know of her danger," he suggested, suavely, but Mrs. Bryson would not hear to any such arrangement. "It was but just that Jess should know how he had saved her life at the risk of his own," she declared.

And this was the story which was told to Jess when she regained consciousness under Mrs. Bryson's skillful treatment some half an hour later.

The girl listened with eyes opened wide with amazement. She recollected hearing the report of the revolver as she sprang forward to dash it from his hand, and missing her foothold, stumbling over the fallen tree, and going over the precipice, as she imagined, and a shudder of terror swept over her.

"Then he did not kill himself, after all!" she faltered, and Mrs. Bryson, who imagined that she referred to the perilous descending and rescuing of herself, knowing nothing about the episode in which the revolver played a part, answered:

"Heaven saved him to rescue you in the most miraculous manner, and you should fairly worship such a grand hero as he has proven himself to be, Jess."

Jess could not bring herself to explain to Mrs. Bryson the cause which had brought the accident about. She merely closed her eyes, wondering how it happened that he had missed his aim, and failed to shoot himself when he held the revolver close to his temple, and she echoed the old housekeeper's observation that it must indeed have been a miracle.

The fright through which Jess had gone did not affect her much, and she was as good as new, and up with the birds, and out in the grounds, the next morning.

But early as she was, "her hero," as Mrs. Bryson declared she was going to designate him forever after, was out before her.

Jess never remembered in what words she attempted to thank him for the service he had rendered her in saving her life.

He put up his white hand with a quick, impatient sigh, saying, softly:

"It was to be, that is why I missed my aim; that much I owe to you, for, as you brushed past me, you turned my hand aside, and my bullet went wide of its mark. I owe my life as much to you therefore, little Jess, as you owe yours to me."

CHAPTER XVIII.
A PREMONITION OF COMING EVIL.

"I am really glad if I was the cause of preventing you from committing so terrible an act as suicide," said the girl, solemnly, "for that would have been very wicked."

"If you have lost all that makes life worth the living, you care little enough how soon existence ends for you," he replied, artfully; and with a well-simulated heartbroken sigh, which caused little Jess to begin for the first time to pity him.

He saw her softened mood in her eyes, and followed up his advantage with adroit skill, and, ere Jess was quite aware of it, he was proposing to her for the second time.

"I do not want your answer to-day, little girl," he went on. "Take a week to consider it, if you require that length of time, and in the meantime, talk it over with Mrs. Bryson, or any one else who has your true interest at heart. Will you do this?"

Jess could not find it in her heart to refuse this request to the man who had risked his own life to save hers.

"I am going to run down to New Orleans for a few days," he continued, "and when I return you can have your answer ready for me."

Early that forenoon he took his leave, promising Mrs. Bryson that he would be back by the end of the week.

After he had gone, Jess made a clean breast of what had occurred, and the fact that she was to give Mr. Dinsmore his answer when he returned as to whether she would marry him or not, to Mrs. Bryson, who expressed herself as delighted that he had thought so well of her as to propose, a remark which Jess did not relish, as it savored of the idea in her mind that the old housekeeper considered the handsome Mr. Dinsmore very much above her—a thought which she greatly resented.

From the moment in which she divulged the secret which she had concluded at first not to tell to any one, Mrs. Bryson gave her no peace. Every hour in the day she dinned into the girl's ears the practicability of her union with Mr. Dinsmore, which her benefactor, the young man's uncle, had foreseen, and so earnestly desired.

It was all Jess heard from morning until night; she had it for breakfast, luncheon and dinner, until she fairly grew irritable at the sound of the name of Dinsmore, and hated the bearer of it, despite the fact that he had rendered her so valuable a service. She could find no peace until she had in a fit of desperation promised Mrs. Bryson that it should be as she wished— she would say yes to Mr. Dinsmore when he returned, and that the wedding should take place whenever he desired.

"I knew you could not be so insane as to throw over such a fortune, together with such a nice young husband," declared the housekeeper, with a sigh of great relief, "for few young girls would have been mad enough to refuse him. I shudder to think what the result would have been had he taken you at your word and committed suicide, or gone off and married somebody else. Why, you would simply have been a beggar, Jess; thrust out at once upon the cold mercies of the world; for, according to the will, Blackheath Hall, and all of his other possessions, would have been sold within a few months, and the great fortune would have gone to charities."

"I see how it is," said Jess, dryly; "you would lose a good home and fine income—that is where your great interest lies, Mrs. Bryson."

The old housekeeper flushed a fiery red: she knew what Jess said was quite true. She was considering her own interests when she urged this marriage, but it was not pleasant to hear the truth dragged unmercifully forward, and when it was just as well that it should be hidden.

"Very well, I'm going to marry this man just because you insist upon it," said Jess, bitterly. "I do not love him, and never will; and I shall do quite well if I do not hate him outright."

"You will learn to care for him in time, my dear child," declared Mrs. Bryson, who was in no way disconcerted by the girl's outburst. She was used to Jess' fiery temper, as she phrased it. She lost no time in communicating the act to Lawyer Abbot, who came to the village to congratulate the girl in person, and to assure her that she had taken an eminently proper course in looking with favor upon the young man whom her benefactor had selected for her husband.

He was considerably flustered by the girl answering in her terribly straightforward manner:

"Perhaps I have, and perhaps I haven't. All the books that I have ever read have been unanimous in the opinion that a girl should not marry a man unless she loves him."

"Tut, tut, my dear child; those were only love stories—romances, and people are not romantic in real life, you know," declared the astute lawyer.

"Then I pity the people in real life, and I wish I were the heroine in a romance," replied Jess, tossing her dark, curly head defiantly, "for they are the only ones who live ideal lives."

The lawyer looked as he felt, bewildered, and he could see dimly outlined in the future, breakers ahead for the young man—if she married him.

"She would be as likely as not to fall headlong in love with the first strolling gypsy that crossed her path," he ruminated as he looked at her critically, "and then it would end in a divorce suit, or worse, if anything could be worse. I almost believe the girl is right. A creature of her fiery disposition should not have her hands tied in matrimony without her heart has been won by the man she marries. I hope all will be well; I can only hope it." And as he looked thoughtfully out of the window, a premonition of coming evil seemed to sweep over his heart.

Suddenly he joined Mrs. Bryson, saying:

"I have a plan to suggest which I think you will approve of. Jess ought to be sent away for a few weeks where she will see something of the world, and when she sees how well Mr. Dinsmore compares with the generality of men, and learns by meeting them that they are not such heroes as her vivid, romantic imagination has caused her to believe them to be, she will be more—well, more satisfied with the future a kind fate has laid out for her."

"Your plan is a capital one, sir," replied Mrs. Bryson, "but I know of no place that I could send her to."

"While we have been on this subject, the very place, an ideal home, has occurred to me. Some few years ago, when I lived in New York, I had a partner, a Mr. Trevalyn, who would be glad to receive her beneath his roof on a visit, if I requested the favor. He has a charming wife, and a daughter, Queenie, who cannot be so very much older than Jess. Would you like to go and visit this New York family, my dear?" he asked, turning to Jess.

"Oh, yes, indeed!" exclaimed the girl, eagerly, her face dimpling over with an eager smile. "All my life I have wanted to see what New York was like. I'd love to go under one condition."

"You must let me know what it is before I can decide as to that," said Mr. Abbot, quietly.

"Well, I wouldn't like them to know that I was an engaged girl if I went there. I wouldn't like them to know there was such a man as Mr. Dinsmore; nor one word of that crazy will."

"Why should you wish to conceal the fact of your betrothal?" asked the old lawyer, wonderingly; adding: "Most young girls are more than eager to proclaim such a fact, my dear."

Jess laughed, saying:

"If you really want to know, I don't mind telling you. They make all sorts of fun down in the village of engaged girls. I shouldn't want any one to make that sort of fun of me; I wouldn't bear it."

"Life in the city, and city manners, you would find quite different," replied Lawyer Abbot, quietly; adding: "But if you do not wish the engagement known, I see of no reason to tell it. Mr. Dinsmore need not be mentioned in any way, or even known there."

"Then I'll go, Mr. Abbot. And, oh, I'll be so glad to get away from Blackheath Hall for ever so short a time," cried Jess, dancing around the room and clapping her hands in joy like a veritable child over the promise of a holiday.

Mrs. Bryson flushed a dull red. She had the very guilty and uncomfortable feeling and knowledge that the grand, old place had never been a home to the child any more than it had been to the wild birds that were sheltered there at night under the broad eaves. Her existence had been like theirs; she roamed where she would by day, until darkness drove her back to the shelter of its roof; and so matters would have continued to have gone on had it not been for that death abroad, and the strange will which was the result of it, and which had named the little Bohemian will-o'-the-wisp as one of the heirs of the vast estate, providing the conditions contained therein were carried out.

It had not been until then that Mrs. Bryson had taken the trouble to cultivate Jess' acquaintance, as it were, and now she felt keen shame as she reviewed the past, and the little care she had expended upon the girl who had been left in her charge.

If the girl had grown up wild as a deer, and untamable as a young lioness, she was to blame for it, she well knew.

The wonder to her was that matters adjusted themselves by the young nephew proposing to Jess at all. She realized that it would never have been if the girl had not grown up as beautiful as a wild rose; and Jess had no one to thank for her wondrous beauty but nature, which had made her as perfect as it is given mortals to be.

"All's well that ends well," said Lawyer Abbot to Mrs. Bryson, as he was taking his leave.

"But has it ended?" asked his companion, anxiously. "I shall always be looking for something to happen to prevent it, until the girl actually stands at the altar. Even then she is as likely as not to back out. Jess does not realize the value of money, nor the fortune which hangs in the balance, or what its loss would mean to her. All that she is thinking about is that she does not love the man she is so soon to marry. I repeat—how will it end?"

CHAPTER XIX.
THE BETROTHAL.

"It is not much the world can give,

With all its subtle art;

And gold and gems are not the thing

To satisfy the heart.

But gentle words and a loving heart,

And hands to clasp my own,

Are better than the fairest flowers

Or stars that ever shone."

For the next few days there was great bustle and excitement at Blackheath Hall over the expected departure of Jess.

"She might as well begin her preparations at once," Lawyer Abbot had said, as he left, "for I feel sure there will be no doubt as to the Trevalyn family receiving her. I will write at once, and have a reply to that effect in the course of two or three days. In the meantime, Jess can make her preparations to be ready to start on the next northern-bound express after I have heard from my old friend."

Accordingly, Mrs. Bryson went at once to the nearest town and purchased all that was needful for the journey, opening her purse-strings so far as to procure a creditable outfit for the girl. She was determined that Jess should not look like a veritable dowdy before the New York people, whom Lawyer Abbot assured her were millionaires.

But, alas for hopes which are perched too high! Quite as soon as the mail could bring it, a reply was received from Lawyer Trevalyn, saying that his wife and daughter, Queenie, were away from home, and would not return for a month, possibly not for six weeks, later; and at that time he would be more than pleased to receive as his guest the young girl of whom his friend had written to him.

Jess' disappointment was intense when the lawyer brought the letter over to Blackheath Hall and made known its contents to them.

"I ought to have known how it would be," sobbed Jess, throwing herself downward, face forward, on the carpet, and weeping as though her heart would break.

"My dear child, don't do that!" exclaimed Mr. Abbot, nervously. "You try my nerves terribly—you do, indeed. Stop that crying, and we will see if we cannot discover some loophole out of the difficulty. I have it!" he cried, in the next breath. "I wonder that it did not occur to me before. I have a brother, a farmer, living at the junction of the roads a little over a hundred miles north of here. He has a daughter, Lucy, and you can go there, if you like, and pass the time until the Trevalyns, of New York, are home, and ready to receive you. It will be exchanging one farm, as it were, for another. Still, it will be a little change."

Jess dried her eyes at once.

"I don't like a farm," she declared, ruefully. "Still, anything will be better than humdrum life at Blackheath Hall."

"I need not accompany you there, my dear child, as I would have done had you gone on to New York. I can simply place you in charge of the conductor, whom I know quite well. My letter, explaining matters, will have arrived a few hours in advance, and they will be down to the station to meet you. Will that arrangement meet with your approval, little Jess?"

"Yes, sir," responded the girl, quickly, smiling up at him like a rift of April sunshine through her tears.

"I am glad that we have found a way out of the dilemma," he said, heaving a sigh of relief, for the care of Jess, who was so suddenly thrust upon his guardianship, was a sore trial to him.

The next morning, bright and early, saw Jess taking her departure from Blackheath Hall.

"There is no one here who will miss me much—except the birds and squirrels about the place, and the stray dogs," and a very bitter little smile crept up about her mouth, to note how much Mrs. Bryson and all the servants were making of her now, after neglecting her so pitifully during all the long years of the past in which she roamed about as uncared-for as the stray dogs that crept there when the wildness of the night forced them to seek shelter.

Jess had left no one behind her who loved her, or whom she loved.

As the train moved away from the station, the girl's new life began. Surely, the strangest fate that any young girl was ever to know. Who shall say after that that the hand of fate does not guide us along the path which destiny has marked out for us to follow at the time of our birth?

Jess paid strict heed to Mrs. Bryson's warning to keep her veil drawn carefully over her face; but through its heavy folds she could see the green fields and silvery streams, the villas and towns, as the lightning express whirled by them, and she was lost in wonder at the great world that lay beyond Blackheath Hall.

In her wildest imagination, she had never pictured the world so wide as this. The hours flew by as quickly as the miles did, it seemed to her, and her daydreaming came to a sudden end by the appearance of the conductor, who began gathering up her bag and parcels.

"This is your station, miss," he said. "I am going to place you in charge of Mr. Abbot's brother-in-law, a Mr. Caldwell, who telegraphed me to the station below that he was already at the station to meet you."

It was like a dream to Jess, she was so little used to traveling, and was so bewildered, of being bustled out of the train, and led toward a portly, old gentleman, who was advancing in all haste to meet the conductor and herself.

"Is this the little girl, Jess, whom my brother-in-law placed in your charge, conductor?" she heard him ask, in a hale, hearty voice.

She was too dazed to hear the reply.

The next instant she was standing alone with the old gentleman on the platform of the station, the train having suddenly dashed away and hidden itself behind a curve in the road.

"Come right this way to the carriage, my dear," he said, wondering why the girl trembled so, and why her little hands were as cold as ice on this glorious October day.

"See, there is the carriage, and there is my daughter, Lucy," he said, and glancing in the direction in which he was pointing, Jess saw a roomy, old vehicle, and in the front seat, holding the reins over a restless horse, a young girl of about her own age—a buxom, rosy-cheeked girl, whom she liked immensely—on sight.

The girl handed the lines to her father, and sprang out of the carriage to meet the newcomer, saying:

"We received uncle's letter only this morning. I am Lucy Caldwell; and you are Jess—Jess what?" she queried, in the same breath. "Uncle forgot to tell us that. But, dear me, I must not stand talking. Jump right into the back seat, and we can talk away to our hearts' content as we ride home. We haven't far to go, and we wouldn't have thought about hitching up if it hadn't been for your trunk."

Miss Lucy had been so busy rattling on in her voluble fashion that she did not notice the flush that stained her companion's face from neck to brow as she questioned her concerning her name, which poor Jess had none to give. Nor did she note that her query remained unanswered.

"I am so glad to have a girl companion of my age," declared Lucy, settling herself back among the cushions. "Ma has settled it that you are to share my room with me. I hope you won't object to that?" she rattled on, adding:

"We have a spare room, as uncle knew, but he did not know that there was one in it just now; not a visitor, oh, no, though he is ever so much nicer than any visitor that comes here. To make a long story short, he was one of the passengers who was on that train which met with the terrible accident a few weeks ago, and was brought to us to care for, more dead than alive. He progressed wonderfully, however, and is nearly well now. I shall feel very sorry when he goes," she added, her voice dropping to a low key and faltering ever so slightly. "His name is Moore, and, oh, he is so nice. See," she cried, as they neared the farmhouse, "there he stands at the gate, waiting for us, and to see what you are like, most probably, for he heard uncle's letter read aloud at the breakfast table, and he, who has seemed so little interested in anything, immediately took the liveliest kind of an interest in your coming."

Jess' eye followed the direction in which Lucy's finger pointed, and beheld a picture which was to be engraven on her memory while life lasted; and this is what she saw:

A tall, graceful figure leaning against the gatepost, his folded arms resting upon it, his face, pale through illness, turned expectantly in the direction in which they were advancing.

"Odd," he was muttering, between his compressed, mustached lips, "that this girl, above all others, is coming here.

"I suppose she is like the rest of her sex, false and fickle as she is fair. It is well that I gave the name of Moore to these quiet farm people, when consciousness after the railway accident returned to me, in order that the affair might not get into the New York newspapers.

"Unknown to her, I will study this girl, whom I was going down to Greenville to see; ay, study her at my leisure, and find her—like all the rest." And he heaved a sigh which told plainly that he was bored with life, its failures and regrets.

"I suppose it is fate that I am to meet this girl whom my uncle was so desirous that I should wed that he cuts me off in case I refuse to comply with his insane wishes; otherwise, I would have fallen a victim to Ray Challoner's bullet, which came near enough to plowing my heart, or to death in this railroad wreck, from which I was saved, by almost a miracle. It would seem that my time has not yet come. It is strange, when life has no gladness left in it for a man, that he should still be compelled to live on. When I lost all hope of calling Queenie Trevalyn my bride, I lost all that was dear in this world to me. I have hated all womankind because of her falsity ever since. Even the farmer's daughter, Miss Lucy, bores me terribly with her many kindnesses."

CHAPTER XX.
"DO WE EVER LOVE THE WRONG ONE?"

"If love should come again, I ask my heart,

In tender tremors, not unmixed with pain,

Couldst thou be calm, nor feel thy ancient smart,

If love should come again?

"Would Fate, relenting, sheathe the cruel blade

Whereby the angel of thy youth was slain,

That thou might all possess him unafraid,

If love should come again?

"In vain I ask. My heart makes no reply,

But echoes evermore that sweet refrain:

If love should come again!"

"Yes, the loss of Queenie Trevalyn was a blow which I can never get over, though I believed myself a strong man," he mused, the hard, bitter lines of disappointment and pain deepening on his face, and painting shadows in his troubled eyes.

"And what a surprise it was to me to hear that letter read which the farmer received from his brother-in-law down in New Orleans, which so vitally interested me. How strange it is that this girl was to be sent to the home of Queenie, in New York, and fate interposed in sending her here where I am instead. But she shall not know me. I will take care of that."

He had no opportunity to cogitate further, for the carriage by this time had reached the gate where he stood.

Lucy Caldwell did not wait for him to approach to assist her from the vehicle, but sprang out with the nimbleness of foot which characterized her.

He looked rather eagerly for the second figure in the old carryall to step forth, as he advanced. He was thinking of the letter which he had received from his little Jess when he was at Newport, in which she had described herself, and he wondered vaguely if the description she gave him was true or false. He paused for an instant as he beheld the lithe, slender, girlish figure seated within. He could not see her features, for, contrary to his expectations, her face was concealed by a heavy veil.

Like her companion, she sprang from the carriage ere he could take another step forward to proffer his assistance.

"A society girl and belle," he muttered, frowning darkly as his quick glance took in every detail of her stylish traveling dress. "Now, why under heaven did she give me such a false description of herself in that letter she wrote me?"

"I want to introduce you to Mr. Moore, Jess," said Lucy, catching her by the arm.

A little, brown hand swept aside the heavy folds of tulle that covered the girl's face, and then Jess, with the same face as the picture he had received from her, stood before him. He knew that she had not misrepresented her character in her letter, when, the next instant, the little, brown, warm hand was extended to him in greeting, and she said, eagerly:

"I know all about you and your awful mishap, Mr. Moore, and I am quite as glad as Lucy is that you are getting well."

The impulsive action, and the straightforward words that accompanied it, softened his heart in a measure toward her, although she was of the sex whom he had sworn to himself that he should evermore detest with the deadliest of hatred.

"You are very kind, Miss—Miss——" he returned, with a low bow, raising his hat with a gallantry which surprised Lucy, who was looking on a little jealously, as she wondered if Mr. Moore thought the stranger pretty.

"Your sympathy is very pleasing, believe me," he added, continuing: "I suppose we cannot shuffle off this mortal coil, no matter what good opportunities seem to be thrown in our way, until our time comes; at least, it would seem so in my case, Miss—Miss——"

"My name is simply Jess—nothing more," said the girl, looking up into his face with just the faintest suspicion of tears in her big, dark eyes. "When names were given out, whoever was responsible for the giving of them in my case, passed me by, it appears, either by accident or design, so ever afterward I was known by the simple cognomen of Jess—just Jess."

Somehow, as he looked into the lovely, young face, his resentment against one of the sex which he had sworn to hate seemed to be melting away, although he would have scoffed at the idea had any one told him that an interest had sprung up in his heart toward the girl in the first moment they had met.

"Come," said Lucy, "we will go to the house. We can talk afterward. Mother and dinner await us."

And as the two girls got beyond the sight and hearing of Mr. Moore, Lucy turned to her companion, saying:

"What do you think of our invalid, as we often laughingly call him when we want to tease him? Do you think him good-looking?"

"He is more than that, Lucy," returned Jess, gravely. "He is simply splendid! I know of no word which will express it. We have just such a pictured face hanging up in the library of Blackheath Hall, and it is named 'Apollo Belvidere,' who is supposed to be the perfection of manly beauty, so the legend runs which tells about him in old books."

"You have fallen in love with him at first sight!" cried Lucy, in terror, her heart sinking and a stifling sensation creeping up to her throat.

Jess laughed a strange, little laugh. Stopping short in the path, she suddenly threw her arms about Lucy's neck, saying, with a laugh which was almost a sob:

"I never had a girl friend or a girl companion to make a confidant of in all my life, and I would so love to make a confidant of you, Lucy; may I? There's something that I would love to tell you, if you would never, never tell—never breathe one word of it to any living soul in the whole wide world."

"Of course you can make a confidant of me, and tell me all the secrets you have, and I'll never tell them," declared Lucy, solemnly. "You can depend upon me. I've kept lots of girls' secrets, and never told one of them yet; I would not be so mean."

"Well, then, Lucy," cried Jess, half laughing, half sobbing, "I couldn't fall in love with your Mr. Moore if I liked him ever so much, for I'm engaged to be married to another gentleman, and—and it's to take place—the wedding, I mean—just as soon as I come back from the visit to the Trevalyns, of New York. I never intended to tell anybody that I was an engaged girl, but, somehow, Lucy, you have wrung the truth from me in spite of myself, it seems."

"How delightful, and how romantic!" exclaimed Lucy, clapping her hands. "You must confide to me just how it seems to be—engaged. I've wondered about it so much."

Jess determined to tell her new-found friend all about her betrothal, and how it came about, and also to confide to her the terrible secret that was gnawing her heart out, like a worm in the bud; that she hated the man, handsome though he was, to whom she had sent the note of acceptance just before she had started away on her trip, in accordance with the wishes of Mrs. Bryson, who had concluded that it was wisest and best to nail Jess down with a solemn promise, by post, which had been duly forwarded to the expectant lover at New Orleans on the morning on which Jess had left Blackheath Hall.

Yes, Jess concluded to tell Lucy all about it, but that could wait until after she had her bonnet off and had been in the house an hour, at least.

"Her coming is not so much to be feared, after all," breathed Lucy, growing more amiable instantly. "I feared she would be trying to lure Mr. Moore, whom I have set my heart upon winning, away from me. He has not said so much as a word to me yet, but I am sure he intends to, else why is he lingering here when the doctor said that he could go his way, almost a week ago, if he so desired?

"His waiting to recuperate still further, as he called it, was merely an excuse to linger where I am, and he would not do that unless he was in love with me, and meant to propose to me, Ma says."

For an hour or more, Mr. Moore lingered in the old garden, lost in deep thought. At length he retraced his steps slowly to the old farmhouse. Lucy was standing on the steps which led into the wide, cool kitchen.

"What do you think of our guest, Miss Jess?" she asked, displaying more anxiety in her tone than she was aware of.

"She impressed me very favorably at first sight," he answered, adding: "I imagine she would wear well in a long and close acquaintance."

"Do you think her pretty?" persisted Lucy, eagerly.

"Well, no, not as artists and critics define beauty. Still, she is scarcely more than a child at present. She may become, in the years to come, a girl who might be termed unusually handsome. Father Time is so prodigal in his gifts in the flower of youth. And then, again, she might develop into a—well, comparisons are odious, they say, and we will make none in this instance, content to let time do his best or his worst, as fate decrees."

He did not see a young face, half screened by the climbing rose branches at the window directly overhead, nor did he, therefore, know that the young person under discussion—Jess herself—had heard every word of the conversation.

Jess had drawn hastily back, her face as red as the great, dewy roses that nodded to her from outside the window.

From the first moment her eyes had met those of the handsome stranger at the gate, the old life had seemed to fall suddenly from her. She had said to herself: "Surely, this is the hero of my daydreams; the face, come to life, of the Romeo whom Juliet loved, whose picture hangs on the walls of Blackheath Hall, and like the boyish face, too, of John Dinsmore, when he was a little lad, and came there to visit; and like the bust of Apollo, too; and the knight's pictures in the old books." And he did not think her fair: probably, on the contrary, he considered her homely; he had said as much, and tears of wounded pride welled up to the girl's eyes. She never realized until that moment that she had so much vanity to hurt.

CHAPTER XXI.
HOW EASILY THINGS GO WRONG.

For the first time in her young life, Jess lies awake through all the long, dark, cool hours of the night. As a rule, her senses droop swiftly into the lands of dreams quite as soon as her dark, curly head touches the pillow. To-night the sweet boon of sleep is denied her for the first time.

She believes it is the great event of the journey which has unsettled her, for it is the first time in her young life, that she can remember, that she has been away from Blackheath Hall. Then she drifts into thinking of the handsome stranger whom she met at the gate, and still thinking of him, the long hours wear away at last, and morning breaks.

It is a hardship for Jess to lie in bed after the pink dawn has ushered in a glorious day, and, creeping silently out of her white nest, in which Lucy is still sleeping soundly, she is soon dressed and out of the house, exploring the grounds.

There is another one beneath that roof who is an early riser, and that one Mr. Moore, as he has permitted himself to be called.

Looking out from his window, in the dewy light of the early morning, he is amazed to see the lithe, slim figure of Jess gliding like a fairy vision among the great rosebuds of the old-fashioned garden.

And, furthermore, he is still more amazed to see her running over the diamond-incrusted grass bare of foot, swinging her shoes and stockings in her right hand as she hurries along.

Last night he had formed the opinion of the girl—that she had deceived him, when he had beheld her in all the furbelows of fashionable attire in which she had made her appearance at the farmhouse; now he realized that she was indeed a child of nature, with a heart as light and free as a bird's.

He made haste to join her.

Jess was not aware of his presence, for she had not heard his step on the thick, green carpet of grass until a voice beside her said:

"Permit me to gather those roses for you, Miss Jess. The thorns on that bush are long and sharp; you will never be able to manage them, I am sure."

A cry of dismay broke from the girl's lips; down went the shoes and stockings all in a heap in the dew-wet grass.

For the first time in her life, Jess wished that the earth could open and swallow her, for, standing directly in the path before her, was the object of her thoughts, and he was looking amusedly down at the bare, brown feet, which the green grass seemed to part wide to display, instead of bending over and pityingly covering them from his sight.

For the first time in her life, Jess was covered with a strange, hitherto unknown, unexperienced, bashful confusion.

"I did not know that any one would be up for hours yet," she stammered, gaspingly, thinking, shudderingly, of the awful bareness of those feet, and that she would give anything that she possessed on earth if she could cover them from his gaze—only cover them. A new, sweet shyness was coming over her. It was the dawning of womanhood breaking through the childish existence she had led up to the hour when she had first met the gaze of the man standing before her.

"Farm life means a life of early rising," he returned. "They are astir in the house, all save Miss Lucy. She is rarely visible before eight, when half of the morning is spent, as I often tell her."

To the last day of her life, Jess is thankful to him that he turned to the rosebush and began gathering roses, cutting them off with his silver penknife; and, as he cut each one, slitting off the thorns.

Jess never knew how she seized upon that moment of time to replace her shoes and stockings, wet though they were, and the next moment, when he faced about, instead of seeing the slender, brown feet among the green grasses, which he had been so eagerly admiring, he noted that they were now clothed; and he noted, too, that the girl's face, as her eyes followed the direction of his gaze, was covered with confused blushes.

Handing her the roses, he said:

"Shall we saunter over the hills, or shall I take you for a little sail on a miniature lake which lies down in yonder valley?"

"Neither. I—I am going back to the house," she answered, a little hesitatingly, "to—to unpack some books which I promised Mrs. Bryson I would read a little of every morning."

"The books and reading can wait for an hour or two," he urged. "This is too fine a morning to waste indoors. This is October, you know, and even in this sunny, Southern clime, it will not remain for long as delightful as it is to-day."

The quiet mastery in his voice seemed to exercise a spell over her which she was powerless to shake off or combat, and when he led the way down the path, her feet involuntarily led her along in his wake.

It was but a short walk to the lake, and when they reached it, bathed as it was in the crimson light of the rising sun, Jess was enraptured at the beautiful sight which it presented, and with the glorious white water lilies which swayed to and fro on its glassy bosom, and the tiny, white boats moored here and there along its flower-bordered banks.

"I will go out for a row with you, if I may gather some of the lilies!" cried Jess, enthusiastically. "Oh, how beautiful they are—and, see, there is a bed of pink ones farther out."

"The lilies are fair to look upon, but they are unattainable," her companion answered, gravely. "They have cost every one who ventures near enough to lay hands on them their life. It appears that in their vicinity is an underground whirlpool, which draws down beneath the water's surface, and probably far down into the depths of the lake, all who come within its reach. Therefore, I repeat, that one can admire the lilies, but they cannot be gathered."

"The longing for them, while they are in my sight, and so near, will spoil the pleasure of the row on the water," said Jess.

"You are like the moth who would flutter around the flame, although it knows that therein lies danger, a singed wing, perhaps death," he said, slowly. "The lilies are not worth such a sacrifice."

"I should not mind making it to possess them," declared Jess, very coolly. "I should like to gather them, and surprise the folks at the farmhouse by wearing them in to breakfast in my hair and in my belt."

An expression of deep annoyance crossed his fine face.

"Vain, and proud of adornment—at any cost," was his mental comment, as he looked down at the eager, flushed face coldly.

"I dare you to row me out to them, Mr. Moore!" she cried, shrilly. "What do you say?"

Without a word, he commenced to untie the boat.

"You—consent!" cried Jess, excitedly, and with shining eyes.

"I will go for them, alone," he replied, quietly, stepping into the boat, and with a dexterous movement pushing away from the shore almost before she could divine his intention.

"Oh, Mr. Moore, let me go with you, to manage the boat if—if it become unmanageable!" she cried, her face blanched to a whiteness rivaling the leaves of the snow-white lilies.

He shook his head emphatically.

"Can you swim?" called out the girl, as the little, rocking boat shot out farther from her over the glassy waves.

"No," he answered, and that one brief word seemed to stifle and kill the beating heart in her bosom as it fell upon her ears.

Her great, dark eyes opened to their widest limit in horror too great for words.

"You cannot swim!" she gasped, faintly; then, in a fervor of frenzied terror, she called to him:

"Then come back. I do not want the lilies, indeed I do not."

But if he heard, he did not heed her words, nor the gasping words which accompanied them.

Out over the water sped the tiny boat, with almost the swiftness of an arrow, under the measured strokes of his arms, while the girl stood on the green, mossy bank, with locked hands and beating heart, watching his every movement with terror-stricken conscience.

"What if I have sent him to his death!" she whispered, hoarsely, and in that moment the truth came to her—that this man, whose acquaintance she could count by a few, fleeting hours, was more to her than life itself. She had done as the heroine in the greatest book she had read had done—fallen in love; lost her heart to this handsome stranger at first sight.

"Oh, Mr. Moore, come back! Come back!" she called, shrilly, repeating: "I do not want the lilies; it was only a thoughtless, girlish caprice which prompted me to dare you to get them for me. Can you hear me?" And now her voice was raised shrilly in the most piteous agony.

But he never once turned back toward her, and the echo of her wild cries came back to her from over the dimpling waters and the forest trees that lay beyond.

On and on shot the little skiff over the sun-kissed waves, heading toward the fatal spot where the alluring lilies lay so white and pure on the bosom of the lake.

"Oh, merciful God! if he would but hear, and heed me!" sobbed Jess, wildly. "Why will he not?"

But the waves that babbled on the green, mossy bank at her feet, and the wind sighing among the boughs of the trees over her head had no answer for her.

Another moment and he would be within reach of the lilies. The girl's brain reeled and a deathly faintness stole over her, as she watched every motion of the oars as they rose and fell, catching the gold of the sunshine and carrying it down with them into the water's dark depth.

Standing there, with strained eyes, she saw him reach for the lilies: then—all in an instant—boat and boatman were suddenly swallowed up in the seething underground whirlpool, disappearing from sight, and not even a ripple marred the spot to show where he had gone down—down to death among the beautiful, shining, white water lilies that he had risked sweet life for at her command!

CHAPTER XXII.
THE RESCUE.

"The dream is over, and I stand
Alone upon the sun-kissed shore;
My heart is lone—empty each hand;
My love comes here no more.
Oh, hush! ye waves; dance not in play
When I am waiting here;
Ye breezes, pass upon your way,
There is no pastime here.

"Oh, love, lost love, the world shall know
No more of this unfinished tale;
It shall not taunt with laughter low
Because I chance to fail.
And so, I stand alone and mute
Upon the bare, forsaken shore,
And broken is Love's fairy lute.
I hear its notes no more."

For an instant, that seemed the length of eternity, Jess stood on the bank, watching, with strained eyes, the spot where the boat and its occupant had gone down to death among the treacherous lilies that floated to and fro on the bosom of the waters.

In all the after years of her life she could never fully explain just how it was accomplished. The girl was only conscious of seizing a little skiff that floated idly near at hand, and rowing for dear life to the scene of the catastrophe. She was indifferent to the awful danger, though she had just witnessed a cruel example of it. Her one thought was to seek death in the same spot where the victim of her foolish caprice had gone down to his untimely fate.

In that moment her athletic powers stood the girl in good stead, for the arms that wielded the oars were like steel, which told in the powerful strokes with which she sent the little skiff fairly flying over the placid water.

In less time than it takes to describe it, Jess had reached the spot; but her weight was too slight to capsize the boat, though she could feel it being drawn down—down—down.

She reached out and grasped the lilies, and as she did so, the boat disappeared, and she was left struggling in the water, with apparently the same fate which her hapless companion met awaiting her.

And as she realized this, she realized also that her hands were grasping something else beside the slimy stems of the lilies. One glance, and the heart in her bosom seemed to fairly leap with wild exultation and joy. Her fingers were clutching tightly the hand of the man whom she had told herself that she would rescue, or she would meet the same fate which had befallen him.

By the strange ministration of Providence, in reaching out for the lilies, he had fallen among them, and the thick network of stems had borne him up, despite the underground springs which would have carried him down had he not fallen in just the spot where fate had placed him.

He had not lost consciousness, but was struggling with might and main to keep his head above water.

A cry broke from Jess' lips, and her grasp tightened on his hand.

"Courage!" cried the girl. "I will save you! Keep still and let me float you along. I—I am an expert swimmer."

"No, no! Save yourself!" he cried, white to the lips. "I would only hamper you. I have nothing left in life worth the effort of living for. To you life is sweet; life is everything. Save yourself, girl—never mind me."

If the girl heard, she did not heed his words, but grasping him the more firmly with one hand, with the other she struck out into the stream again, dragging him with her by main force.

He was sorry that she had undertaken such an herculean task—this slender child—yet he dared not struggle to free himself from her grasp, knowing that it would not only retard her progress, but make it doubly hard for her.

With a courage that was almost superhuman, Jess struck out, dragging her living burden after her.

And with the strength of an Amazon, strength which had been developed by her out-of-door life and daring exploits, the girl passed safely over the mouth of the underground current, which yawned wide to swallow her, and struck out valiantly for the shore.

When she was within a rod or so of the bank, her splendid strength and heroic courage seemed suddenly to fail her, and when within reach of safety by but a few more strokes, she suddenly sank back.

It was at this critical moment that he whom she had thus far brought from a watery grave came to the rescue.

The water was up as far as his neck, but he knew that the danger was past. Catching the lithe form in his arms as she sank backward in the water, he succeeded in bringing her quickly to the shore.

When Jess returned to consciousness, she found herself back in the old Caldwell farmhouse, in her own bed-chamber, with Lucy bending over her.

"What is the matter? What has happened?" she exclaimed, with wide-open eyes staring into Lucy's white face. But before a reply could be given, she cried out, shrilly:

"Oh, I remember it all—the water lilies, and Mr. Moore going for them because I dared him to—the accident, and how I tried to save him, for he could not swim—and how everything grew black around me when within but a few yards of the bank!"

"Mr. Moore turned the tables then, and saved you," said Lucy. "You had brought him to wading depths; the rest was easy. It gave us all a terrible scare when he brought you in, dripping wet and white in the face as one drowned! And then he explained, in a word, almost, how it had all come about."

"It was all my fault!" sobbed Jess. "Will he ever forgive me? I deserve that he should despise me to the end of his life. If he had died! Oh! oh! oh!"

"Never mind conjuring up such a possibility," declared Lucy. "Be glad that he did not, and never send any human being into such danger again. I hope this will be a warning."

"Don't say any more," sobbed Jess, pitifully. "Indeed, I feel bad enough over it. Will you tell him that for me, Lucy?"

The farmer's daughter shrugged her shoulders. The turn affairs had taken was not at all to her liking. Jess and Mr. Moore were getting along altogether too famously in their friendship to suit her. They had not known each other twenty-four hours, and now Mr. Moore owed his life to the girl, and she, in turn, owed hers to him.

It was with some little trepidation that Jess entered the presence of Mr. Moore, late that afternoon. The feeling was so strong within her breast that he would hate her for sending him to the death which he missed so narrowly.

He held out his strong, white hand to her, with a grave smile which disarmed her fears at once.

"I am so sorry it happened," she faltered. "Do you forgive me?"

"Certainly," he responded. "That should go without saying. I may also add, but for that affair I should never have known what a brave and daring little girl you are, I have to thank you profoundly for the life you have saved to me, useless though I find it, and wish also to add that hereafter it is to be devoted to you and your interests, if you will allow it to be so. If life and living were sweet to me, I should thank you for giving me a chance to continue them."

Jess was puzzled at his words. She was too young, and had too little experience with the world, to comprehend them fully.

The entrance of the family interrupted the reply she would have made him.

But from that hour the friendship between the two ripened wonderfully. Each hour little Jess fell deeper and deeper under the glamour of a spell which she could not cast off—the glamour of a young girl's awakened heart, with its sweet throbbings, proclaiming that it had learned its first lesson from the book of love, and the lesson enthraled her.

What Mr. Moore's feelings were it was hard to conjecture.

One moment he hated all womankind, for the sake of the one he had found so fair and so false—beautiful Queenie Trevalyn, whom he had loved too well, and to his bitter cost.

Then he found himself softening toward one of the hated sex—little Jess, whose heart was as innocent and pure as a little babe's.

He wondered if she would ever have the heart to draw a man on to declare his love, and then, when she found that he was not possessed of wealth, discard him as unconcernedly as she would a withered flower of which she had grown tired.

Had it not been for his cruel lesson in that unhappy past, he might have looked with favor upon the girl whom his uncle picked out for him to wed—might even have learned to care for her, though she was little more than a child, while he was a man of the world, too used to finding all things different from what they appeared on the surface.

A week passed, and during that time he was thrown constantly into the companionship of Jess.

To him she was nothing more than an innocent, young girl, a very happy, thoughtless child; one who would grow, perhaps, in the years to come, into a very interesting woman. Further than that, his thoughts regarding Jess never traveled.

He remained at the farm simply because the cause which would have taken him down to Louisiana—to see this selfsame little Jess—was now removed.

He had now no need to go to the mountain, as it were, for the mountain had come to him.

He wondered idly at the interest the girl seemed to take in his society, with never a thought as to whether he was rich or poor. But, then, she was very young; all such worldly knowledge as to the importance of making a good match—that is, marrying a man who had money—would come to her later.

And at the thought a bitter smile curved his lips, a smile accompanied by a heavy sigh.

CHAPTER XXIII.
VAIN REGRETS.

"Ah, they know not heart

Of man or woman who declare

That love needs time to do or dare.

His altars wait—not day nor name—

Only the touch of sacred flame."

The week which follows the advent of Jess to the old farmhouse Mr. Moore will never forget. It is a changed place.

Lucy Caldwell, the farmer's daughter, is a quiet girl, quite as ladylike as many a city-bred, boarding-school miss. But Jess is decidedly the reverse.

She bounds up and down the carpetless stairs, three steps at a time, whistles ear-splitting snatches of coon songs, as she describes them to Lucy, bangs doors and romps about to her heart's content, all of which indicates that she is perfectly happy. She is so content in the old farmhouse that she does not care if the Trevalyns never return to their home. She could stay at the farm forever; yes, forever.

She does not realize, child that she is, what causes her exuberance of spirits, what is it that makes her so wondrously joyous and contented. She only realizes that every hour of her life is filled with a new, sweet pleasure—the pleasure of being so much in the company of Mr. Moore.

Jess' first thought in the morning, upon waking, is of him, and her last thought at night, until she trails off into deep, healthful slumber, is of the handsome, kingly man who makes the days pass so delightfully for her.

Mrs. Caldwell and her daughter note with alarm Jess' fondness for Mr. Moore's society, and comment on it in no kindly manner.

"She behaves most outrageously for an engaged girl," declared Lucy. "Her betrothed ought to know how she is flirting with another man when out of his sight, and Mr. Moore ought to be advised that she is not fancy free. Oh, dear! Oh, dear! why did I allow myself to become pledged to silence in regard to the matter? But for that I could tell him. She cares so little for her *fiancé* that she has not even written him a line since she has been here—which is quite a week now. Why, every other young girl who is engaged, and who is away from the man she is to marry, writes to him every day of her life, I am sure. I know that is the way that I should do." Lucy even ventured to drop a hint to Jess regarding this matter, and she never forgot the effect which it produced upon her, to the last day of her life.

They were standing together out on the porch. Jess was watching eagerly down the road, in the direction Mr. Moore was sauntering, her cheeks slightly flushed, and her eyes full of a bright light which Lucy had not seen there before.

"I can guess of whom you are thinking, Jess," she says, lightly.

A great flood of crimson stains Jess' cheeks, quickly extending from chin to brow, as she wheels about and catches Lucy's gray eyes, which have a malicious gleam in them. But this she does not note.

Before she has time to utter the words that rise to her lips, Lucy adds, smoothly:

"Of course, you were thinking of the young man whom you are soon to marry. How strange it is that you have not heard from him since you have been here. Now, were I in your place, I should feel worried, to say the least."

Jess throws herself face downward on the red-painted bench of the porch, sobbing as though her heart would break.

All in an instant she had been hurled from the heights of bliss down to the very depths of dark despair. She had forgotten Mr. Dinsmore completely for one short, happy week, as completely as though he had never existed.

"Oh, how cruel of you to remind me, Lucy," she sobbed, bitterly. "You have brought me from heaven back to earth."

"You are talking wildly, and in riddles," remarked Lucy, sharply. "Why should you not be pleased to hear of the man whom you are soon to marry? Yours is a strange sort of love, I should say."

Then the truth came out. Jess could keep it back no longer.

"I do not love him. I—I fairly hate him," she sobbed, vehemently. "I wrote to him in accordance with—with—the expressed desire of one who is dead—that I would marry him, and I have been regretting it every hour of my life since."

"You ought to be ashamed to acknowledge such a state of heart," returned Lucy, indignantly. "It is sinful!"

"I cannot help it. That is just how I feel," cried Jess, great sighs welling up from her heart to her lips.

"You have promised to marry a young man whom you do not love!" repeats Lucy, for the first time realizing that part of Jess' excited remarks. She was about to add: "How could you do it?" Then she thinks better of what she was about to say, and goes on: "Mother says the greatest love has often commenced with a very decided aversion."

"I must marry John Dinsmore, but I shall hate him till the day I die!" sobbed Jess, vehemently.

They have been so absorbed in their conversation that neither of the girls noted that Mr. Moore had made a tour of the grounds and entered the best room by the side door, and stood by the open window, looking out at them, screened by the heavy, white curtains.

He had heard the last words of that conversation, and stepped back from the open window, with a very strange pallor upon his face, but it soon gave place to the cynical smile that played about his lips.

"Woman-like, she is not disposed to lose the Dinsmore fortune," he muttered. "She is worldly enough for that, childlike though she appears," and he turns on his heel and walks as noiselessly out of the room and out of the house as he has entered.

There is a sneering expression on his handsome, cold face.

"Yes, she is like that other one," he thinks, "willing to barter herself for glittering gold and the pleasures it may bring," and he thinks of the lines which he applies to all womankind:

"Away, away; you're all the same,

A flattering, smiling, jilting throng!

Oh, by my soul! I burn with shame

To think I've been your slave so long!

Away, away! Your smile's a curse;

Oh! blot me from the race of men,

Kind, pitying Heaven, by death or worse,

Before I love such things again."

And as he walks quickly along, smoking the cigar which he has lighted, he thinks, amusedly, that the girl's resolve to marry him is like the old quotation of counting chickens before they are hatched; for he has not as yet asked her hand in marriage—that marriage which is so distasteful to both of them—and then he falls to abusing the will which would tie them together for life—two who had not the slightest affection for each other.

He wondered, as he smoked, what Jess would think if she knew that he was the obnoxious person whom that will had dealt with. He regarded her with a glance of keen scrutiny as she hurried down the walk and up to the rustic bench where he was seated an hour later.

"I—I want to ask you a question, Mr. Moore!" she cried, breathlessly. "Will you answer it?"

"If I can," he responded, gravely, as he tossed aside his cigar, and made way for her on the rustic bench. But, instead of accepting the seat, she threw herself, with childish abandon, in the long grass at his feet, looking up at him with those great, dark, limpid eyes, which reminded him of a young gazelle.

He leans back and watches her.

She seems in no hurry to unbosom herself as to the question she has intimated that she is so eager to ask.

He looks at her curiously. He does not understand this queer child—for woman she certainly is not—and before he knows it, he is drawing a comparison between her and the girl who jilted him so cruelly because he was not rich—beautiful Queenie Trevalyn, and at the thought of his lost love, his brows contract with a spasm of pain, and a stifled groan breaks from his lips. Yes, he was comparing Queenie and Jess. That cruel wound is still gaping open, and every thought of Queenie gives his heart a stab of the keenest pain, and for the instant he forgets the girl at his feet, remembering only that summer and the beautiful, false face that drew him on like a lodestar, only to wreck his heart on the bitter rock of disappointment.

And at the memory of it all, he covered his face with his hands and groaned aloud.

Jess was a child of impulse. With no thought of the imprudence of her action, in an instant she was on her feet, and in the next a pair of warm arms were thrown about his neck, two terror-stricken, childish eyes were looking into his, a soft face was close to his, and Jess was crying, excitedly:

"Oh, Mr. Moore, are you sick? I'm so sorry. I wish it were I instead of you. No, that is not just what I want to say. What I mean is that I wish that I could take it from you, or suffer it in your stead, that you might be free from it."

And the young voice which utters the words quivers with emotion, and a little gust of tears, wrung from an anguished, little heart, fall upon his face.

He is so startled for a moment he is fairly speechless—struck dumb with astonishment. If a thunderbolt had fallen from a clear sky, or the ground had suddenly opened beneath his feet, he could not have been more astounded.

The touch of those soft arms about his neck fairly electrifies him. He starts back, turns a dull red, then flushes hotly, as he looks at her and tries to answer.

"Ill! No," he replies. "I am not ill, thank you, Miss Jess," he says, at length, and he laughs a little, forced laugh, as she stands and looks at him in wonder, her arms having fallen at her side.

She is dimly conscious that she has made herself ridiculous in his eyes by her solicitude, and that her impulsive action throwing her arms about him had greatly offended him, and she wondered vaguely, as she stands before him covered with confusion, how she ever dared do it.

CHAPTER XXIV.
ONLY AN IMPULSIVE CHILD.

Mr. Moore looks at the girl standing before him long and earnestly; then, reaching forward, he catches her hands in one of his own, asking, slowly:

"Why should it matter to you, little one, whether I was ill or well? Why should you care?"

"Because I like you so much," answered the girl, unconscious of what her words implied. "I should not be quite happy unless you were happy, too." And she looked up, with those frank, childish eyes of hers, directly into his face.

"Why do you like me, little Jess?" he queried, somewhat huskily.

"Because you have been so kind and gentle with me, and I am little used to either; and, then, you have never censured me, as I had every reason to believe you would do, for being the cause of you nearly losing your life. If you had let me drown, when it was in your power to do so, it would have been serving me exactly right, you know."

He looked down into the childish face, with strange emotions throbbing in his breast. Of all people the world held, not one of them had ever told him, up to the present hour, that they liked him, or cared to see him happy. On the contrary, the great, cruel world had hustled him about sharply, and every one had been only too eager to trample him down, utterly regardless of his feelings, whether he was doomed to misery or not.

Long and earnestly he debated with himself as to whether he should tell her that he was John Dinsmore, instead of Mr. Moore, as she thought him, the hated being whom the elder Dinsmore had stipulated in that ridiculous will that she should wed, or lose a princely fortune.

But at last he decided that it would not be amiss to sound her in regard to her feelings first, before disclosing his identity to her. But ere he could proceed to do this, fate, in the shape of Lucy Caldwell, the farmer's daughter, intervened.

She was hastening toward him, with a paper in her hand.

From the house she had seen him grasp and hold Jess' little hand, and, fearful that he was growing overfond of her pretty visitor, joined them hurriedly, to prevent the attempt at sentimentalism, telling herself that Jess should never have the opportunity of being alone with Mr. Moore again if she could prevent it, and she would certainly be ingenious enough to head off any *tête-à-têtes*, with her mother's aid.

Down the path came Lucy, with a haste unusual to her, and at her approach the gentleman dropped Jess' hand, not altogether displeased at the interruption which had caused the words he was about to utter to remain unsaid for the present.

"Your New York papers, which you are always so anxious about, have come, and here they are, Mr. Moore," she said, handing them to him, the heightened color flaming up into her face as he thanked her, expressing the regret that she should put herself to so much trouble as to bring them out to him.

"There is a letter for you inside the house, Jess," she said, turning to his companion. "Uncle Abbot wrote to papa from New Orleans, and a Mrs. Bryson—I think he said she was the housekeeper at Blackheath Hall—incloses one for you, which, he wrote, was of the greatest importance, and must be delivered to you at once."

Reluctantly, Jess followed Lucy to the farmhouse. She had little curiosity to read Mrs. Bryson's letter. She would rather have remained outside in the golden sunshine talking to and worshiping her hero under the great oak trees.

Meanwhile, the hero in question was following the forms of the two girls with a troubled glance.

"If she knew who I was, she would hate me," he mused, "but, not knowing, I have the deepest, truest and warmest friendship that young, girlish heart is capable of giving."

He thought of the words he had somewhere read, "that the love which is tenderest and sweetest in a woman's breast has its birth in friendship, gradually growing into a deeper passion." Then again his eyes took on the look of cynical coldness so habitual to them.

"Bah!" he cried; "what man is mad enough to trust the happiness of his future in the hands of a girl of sixteen, when he has passed the boundary line of thirty? She might like me in her childish way now, but at five-and-twenty she would have her eyes opened to her folly, and hate me most cordially."

Then he turned his eyes to his paper most moodily, and was soon fathoms deep in its pages, as it were, all forgetful of Jess, and the incident which had stirred his heart like wine—the clasp of those soft arms around his neck.

He had turned the second page of the *Herald*, and was running his eye leisurely down one of the columns, when an article met his eye that drove every vestige of color from his face. Like one stunned he read the caption:

"A Brilliant Marriage in High Life. Miss Queenie, the Only Daughter of Lawyer Trevalyn, of No. — Fifth Avenue, New York, Married at Noon To-day to———"

He could see no more, for a blood-red mist floated before his eyes; his hands trembled so that the sheet before him was rent in twain at the very column he had been reading, so tense was the strain of his clutch; then, like a dead one, he fell face downward under the trees, suffering from the keenest pain a human heart can know.

He was so far from the house, so far from all human sound, that the bitter cries that welled up from the depths of his anguished soul could not be heard.

And, lying there, he wept as few men weep in a lifetime. He had known that it must come; he had been watching for it; he had not missed one of the New York papers since he had been ill. He had sent for the back numbers from the day he had been stricken, and had scanned their columns with an intensity which nearly brought on a relapse when he was enabled to sit up to read them. But the article for which he searched, and dreaded so to behold, did not appear.

"Had anything occurred to break off the match between Ray Challoner and his lost Queenie?" he would ask himself over and over again. And with that thought came the glimmering hope, if that were the case, he might even yet win her, for the fortune which she craved was now his through the sale of his books.

Then he would thrust the thought from him with loathing. No! a thousand times no! He would never buy a wife. He would go unwedded to the grave first, and he hated his own weakness for still craving her love and her presence.

He had expected this intelligence, yet when the blow fell, it was as though it had killed the living, beating heart in his bosom, withered it, as lightning blights and withers a giant oak and fells it to the earth.

Queenie was married at last, and to his rival. That was the one thought that whirled through his brain, and almost drove him mad.

She was lost to him forever! Ay, as much as though she lay in the grave, and again and again such terrible waves of grief swept over him that they threatened to dethrone his reason. He did not care to live an hour longer. All that he loved on earth was lost to him.

He had loved Queenie Trevalyn as few men love in a lifetime. She had drawn him on, encouraged him by all the wiles with which a finished coquette ensnares her victims, and then had cast him off without the least compunction.

But, ah, how strange a thing is the human heart. Through it all, no matter what had befallen him at her fair, false hands, he loved her still, with a love which refused to be killed.

Although he hated himself for his weakness, he would have given all he had in the world, ay, his very prospects of Heaven! if he could have averted that marriage. Ay, given every dollar of the wealth which had come to him too late, to have been standing on the spot where he was lying now (with his face buried in the long grass, uttering bitter moans) with Queenie Trevalyn's hands clasped in his, looking down into the depths of her wondrous eyes listening to her dulcet voice, though in his innermost soul he realized that every word those sweet, rosy lips were uttering was false— false!

"I must banish such a wish or I shall, indeed, go mad!" he sobbed, dashing his hand over his eyes, as though he could shut out the picture which his memory conjured up at will.

But it was useless; he had loved too well, and the wound was too deep. If he had a revolver with him in that hour, the rest of his life story would never have been written, for he would have ended it then and there.

How long he remained there like one stunned he never knew. He took no heed of the flight of time. He was suddenly brought to a realization of his surroundings by the touch of a little hand, cool as a lily leaf, upon his burning brow, and Jess' voice saying, in alarm:

"Now I know that you are very ill, indeed, Mr. Moore, when I find you lying here where I left you hours ago, and groaning so," and the dark, curly head was bent down close to his, and Jess began to cry bitterly over him, stroking his face, and then his clenched hands, as a child might caress a loved animal lying at her feet cruelly hurt.

"Don't, Jess, little girl!" he whispered, in a choking voice. "I am not ill, as you think, believe me; and I thank you for your sweet sympathy. Surely, you are the only being on the wide earth who has the least interest in me, whether I am sick or well, or whether I live or die." And with those words, a strange resolve came to him to marry Jess, that she might have the fortune, and then make away with himself at once and end it all!

CHAPTER XXV.
"WILL YOU MARRY ME, LITTLE JESS?"

"Ne'er with laurel wreath around me,

Have I wreathed my weary brow,

Since to serve thy fame I bound me—

Bound me with a solemn vow.

Evermore in grief I languish—

All my youth in tears is spent;

And, with thoughts of bitter anguish

My too-feeling heart is rent.

"Joyous those about are playing,

All around are blest and glad,

In the paths of pleasure straying—

My poor heart alone is sad.

Spring in vain unfolds each treasure,

Filling all the earth with bliss;

Who in life can e'er take pleasure,

When is seen its dark abyss?"

Although Mr. Moore had schooled himself to meet the blow that some day, sooner or later, he should hear of the marriage of Queenie Trevalyn, when that day arrived the shock almost killed him; he was dazed, bewildered, stunned by it. All of a sudden his splendid courage and pride gave way, as did his self-control, and lying there in the long grass where he had fallen, he sobbed like a child—and it was thus that Jess had found him.

He did not try to rise as the girl bent over him; indeed, all his strength seemed suddenly to have left him. Jess' sweet pity and sympathy, as she stroked his face with her little hands, soft and cool as rose leaves, were very acceptable to him just then, in the first throb of his bitter woe.

"I am very sure you are ill, and will not let any one know," she declared. "Do let me help you to this bench, where you can sit down until you are able to come to the house. In the meantime, I will go and fetch you a glass of cold water from the old well; that will revive you very quickly."

"No," he said, clutching at her hands, "never mind going for the water. See, I—I am better now," and as he spoke he struggled to his feet, staggered over to the garden bench and sank down upon it.

"I should like you to sit down here beside me, little Jess," he whispered, hoarsely; "I have something to say to you."

For some moments he sits in utter silence, looking across the tops of the waving trees—looking, yet seeing nothing, for he is busy with his own conflicting thoughts.

Jess watches him wonderingly, trying to read the thoughts that cause his handsome, grave face to grow graver still and his lips to twitch.

"It will be better so," he ruminated. "It would be selfish of me to shuffle off this mortal coil without doing some one good deed for the benefit of some human being; and what better act could I do than marry this child, that she may, in accordance with the will, receive the great fortune which otherwise she must miss, and be thrown, penniless, upon the world? Directly after the ceremony I can explain to her that I am the John Dinsmore whom she dreaded so, and then quietly go away, waiving all of my rights to the inheritance in her favor."

"Of what are you thinking, Mr. Moore?" she asks, wistfully. "Whatever it is," she adds, slowly, "it is almost making you cry again."

"I was thinking of you, and trying to decide your future," he answers, slowly, "and it culminated into the one question I now ask you: Will you be my wife?"

"Your wife!" she gasps, wondering if she has heard aright, and believing she must be in some strange, sweet dream from which she will awaken in another instant.

He nods, dumbly. It is a great effort for him to utter the words, and his lips refuse to repeat them.

"Do you really mean it, Mr. Moore?"

Again his lips refuse to perform their service, and he nods assent, almost regretting the proposal, now that it has been uttered and is past the power of being recalled.

He does not look at her, or he would see how the warm blood has leaped into the rosebud face, and the round, dimpled cheeks have taken on a carnation hue, and the dark eyes are shining like stars. Nor does he know that those words have called her young heart from her bosom in a great, warm gush of love. He thinks more of her than she ever dreamed he did, she is telling herself, as she puts one hand over her fluttering, little heart, while the other creeps up to her blushing face.

Indeed, under the circumstances, and taking the girl's ignorance of life and the world into consideration, she should not be blamed for not realizing that there are other motives than affection which actuate men's actions at times, and that this was one of them.

His wife! He must love her well to ask her to be that, and the blood—which has been flowing so sluggishly in her veins ever since she has read in Mrs. Bryson's letter to her that on the following day her visit would be brought to a close—leaps wildly now, and her heart gives a great bound, and goes out to her companion warmed with the fire of a young girl's first love.

"What is your answer, little Jess?" he asked, with an effort. "Is it yes—or no?"

For answer, she throws herself into his arms, like the impulsive child that she is, and, clinging to him, cries:

"Oh, I am so happy—yes, I will marry you, Mr. Moore. But, oh! won't they be surprised at Blackheath Hall, for they think I am to marry that horrid Mr. John Dinsmore, whom I perfectly hate."

He holds her off at arm's length, and his keen eyes read her face scrutinizingly, as he says, slowly, anxiously:

"I hope you will never regret the action, Jess. Always remember that in asking you to marry me I was studying your best interest, as you will understand when you are old enough to realize all."

"Jess! Jess! where are you?" cries Lucy's voice, from down the path; "Jess! Jess!"

"Go to her, and say nothing of what has transpired," whispers "Mr. Moore," releasing her hands and pushing her from him. "I will see you here early to-morrow morning, and will have arranged everything by that time. Good-night, Jess!"

He made no attempt to stoop and kiss the lovely, young face turned so expectantly up to him; indeed, it never occurred to him to do so.

Another instant and the slim figure was hurrying down the path in the direction of Lucy's high-pitched voice.

"Mr. Moore" stood with folded arms, looking after her. There was no lover-like ardor in his breast; no passionate thrill of triumph filled his heart to think that he had won so lovely a young creature; only a sort of weary, stoical resignation, with the thought surging through his brain that he had sacrificed himself upon the altar of stern duty.

In fact, he pitied himself when he thought of what was before him; but it never occurred to him to pity the girl, who was far more to be pitied, in all her fresh, young bloom and trustful innocence.

Even Lucy wondered at the expression of Jess' face when she entered the house, where the bright rays of the lamp fell full upon it, for there was a glory on it that made her companion marvel.

She could not help thinking of her mother's comparison, in speaking of Jess, that she always looked like a blushing rose. Surely, she looked it to-night, with that vivid crimson bathing her cheeks and brow.

"I want to help you to pack, Jess," she said; "you forget you are to take the noon train, and there is always so much to attend to at the last moment."

"How good you are, Lucy," said Jess, laying her soft, warm cheek against her companion's. "You are tired, while I have done nothing the livelong day; I should not let you add to your weariness the packing of my trunk."

"It will be a pleasure for me to do it for you," declared Lucy. She did not add that she would not know a happy moment until Jess, with her pretty, dimpled face and starry eyes, was well away from the farm, and the presence of Mr. Moore.

In an incredible space of time the little trunk was packed by Lucy's nimble hands; then it was time to retire, and for the second time in her young life Jess was unable to sleep.

For hours she thought of the wonderful thing that had happened—Mr. Moore had asked her to be his wife, and she had said "Yes," and to-morrow morning he would tell her what his plans were regarding it.

When she did fall asleep, she dreamed of her hero as she always had done every night since she had been beneath that roof, and, strange to say, she dreamed that Mr. Moore had kissed her—a thing he had not ventured to do, in reality—and the girl was quite sorry to awaken at last and find that the bliss of the kiss she had felt upon her lips was only the vagary of an idle dream, and the impulsive child wished that the sweet dream had been a reality.

CHAPTER XXVI.
LOVE.

"From whence does he come, and whither he goes,

There is not a mortal in all the world knows.

He comes in a smile, and goes in a kiss,

He dies in the birth of a maiden's bliss;

He wakes in a tear, he lives in a sigh,

He lingers in hope, refusing to die.

But whence he does come, and whither he goes,

There is not a mortal in all the world knows."

Her wedding day! That was the first thought that entered Jess' mind, as she opened her eyes the next morning, and with a bound she was out of her couch to see from the window what fate portended in the way of a cloudy or a sunshiny day for her.

It was as yet too early to determine that, for the first gray streak of dawn had not appeared in the eastern sky, and the early mornings were always misty, and every branch and shrub and blade of grass was burdened by great drops of dew.

"I am sure the sun is going to shine," she ruminated, "and that will mean: 'Happy is the bride the sun shines on,' as the old saying goes."

Jess made all possible haste with her toilet, and hurried down as fast as she could to the grounds; but, early as she was, Mr. Moore was there before her.

He greeted her in the same grave, dignified manner habitual to him, it never occurring to him to offer her the slightest caress, even though she was his promised bride; and before the sun reached the zenith she was to be his wife.

He smiled a little as she came fluttering down the garden path, and at the eager face she raised to his in greeting.

"How early you are," she cried, putting out her little hand to him. "I did not think you would be out for hours and hours yet, and here you are before me, and it is not yet five o'clock; you are out of your nest earlier than the early birds are."

He did not think it necessary to tell her that he had not been in his nest all the long night through, but had spent the long hours between dusk, that deepened into midnight and then stretched away into early morn, in pacing up and down under the sycamore trees, looking the future in the face, and bidding farewell to the dearest hopes of his life.

Jess knew so little of the habits of lovers that his lack of eagerness or affection in greeting her passed unnoticed.

He took out his watch and glanced at it.

"There is a long walk before us, and I think we had better start at once," he said, abruptly; "we can return in at least a couple of hours, and during that time we shall not be missed.

"You are sure you are willing?" he asked again, as they reached the garden gate.

Jess looked up shyly into the grand face. She would have gone to the other end of the world with him. But she answered only a simple "Yes."

They walked on through the early morning together, side by side, and to the end of her life, ay! and in the years when she understood it better, she remembered her companion's white face, grave even to sternness, and his preoccupied air.

He did not notice the beautiful rosy dawn that flushed the eastern sky directly before them, nor the birds, as they awoke from their nests and went soaring away toward the blue dome that bent above them; nor did he see the flowers lift their sleepy heads and shake the dew from their drowsy eyelids.

Jess cast furtive glances at her companion, her heart beating and her every sense tingling deliciously at the thought that she was on her way to be married to the handsome gentleman by her side, from whom she was to be parted nevermore.

How different were the thoughts of her companion as they neared their destination, and the moments advanced in which his bonds were to be sealed for life—they seemed irksome beyond the possibility of bearing, and nothing but his strict idea that he was doing his duty restrained him from asking little Jess to release him from the marriage which had been forced upon him by his uncle's odious will.

The people of the village were all astir as they reached it; and when they made their way to the rectory which lay beyond, they found the good man who presided over it out in the little garden which surrounded the parsonage.

The handsome stranger who accompanied the young girl made known his errand as briefly as possible, asking if he could perform the marriage ceremony which would make his companion his wife at once.

The rector smiled benignly.

"As quickly as the words can be uttered, my good sir," he replied, as he invited them to step inside the house.

The little parlor, with its simple, meager furnishings; the tall, handsome man by her side, with almost the ghastliness of death on his face; and the kindly, old minister, book in hand, ever afterward seemed like a weird dream to little Jess. She did not even hear the name her bridegroom uttered in so low a voice, and he saw that she did not; and he promised himself that he would surprise her with the startling truth that he was John Dinsmore on their way home.

She heard the words which the minister uttered, and which her companion repeated after him: then she was dimly conscious of repeating the same words—though the name she uttered was John Moore—and then, as the hand of her bridegroom clasped her cold, fluttering fingers, she heard the old minister solemnly say, in a still more far-off hazy voice:

"I pronounce you man and wife; and those whom God hath joined together let no man put asunder."

Even in that supreme moment the deathly pale bridegroom made no offer to kiss the little bride who clung to him as tightly as if in affright.

The minister noticed this omission of the usual custom of newly-wedded pairs and marveled at it—the bride was so young, so sweet and so fair.

The good man was rather astounded at the amount of the bank note which the bridegroom placed in his hands.

He watched them depart, as they had come, down the high road; and over and over again he asked himself the question whether or not the handsome man loved the girl whom he had just wedded.

"It was certainly not for money he made her his bride," he ruminated, "for of the two, I should say that he had the wealth and she only her sweet youth, beauty and innocence."

Mr. Moore uttered no word until they were almost in sight of the farmhouse again, much to Jess' great wonderment.

At last he turned to her, and said, abruptly:

"Fate has had her way, her plans have been carried out to the letter, and you are now my wife, little Jess."

"Your wife!" murmured the young girl, shyly. "I—I almost imagine it a dream, it seems so—so unreal."

"Why does it seem so?" he asked, abruptly, not caring so much for her answer as for the fact that it would give him a few moments more while she was talking to nerve himself for the ordeal of talking the future over with her, and incidentally, of course, revealing his identity.

"Because all of the brides that I have ever heard of or read of went to the church to be married, and wore long, trailing dresses of white and bridal veils, and carried in their hands great bouquets of roses; and when it was over there were ever and ever so many carriages around the church door to take the bridal couple and all of the friends who had assembled to witness the ceremony to some place where a grand feast was in waiting, and then there was dancing and making merry."

"Poor child! What a contrast your own hasty marriage has been; but always remember, come what will, that I took this step for the best, for your welfare and happiness only. Promise me that you will always keep that thought before you when you look back at this day and hour," he said, huskily.

She promised, without having the least notion of what his words implied, but through it all she felt a vague feeling of disappointment, she could feel the tears rising to her eyes. Not that she was not as desperately in love as ever with the handsome man whom she had just wedded; just what it was that was weighing so heavily upon her young heart she could not have explained.

While he was thinking how he should best break the truth to her that he was John Dinsmore, the words were stayed on his lips by Jess remarking:

"Won't Mrs. Bryson and all the rest at Blackheath Hall be surprised when they hear that I am married, though? And they, hurrying up as fast as they can to get my wedding clothes ready to marry another. I am going to tell you a big secret—now that I am married to you, I must keep nothing from you, you know. If I had not met and married you, I should have had to go home and have married the other handsome fellow, who is so much in love with me, and who has just left Blackheath Hall for New Orleans to arrange matters for us to go there on the wedding trip. Won't he be disappointed, though, and won't those black eyes of his flash lightning when he hears what I have done? I half pity him, poor fellow, he was so desperately in love with me—at least, so he said, and every one else said so, too."

John Dinsmore stopped short in the daisy-studded path, his face grown even more ghastly than when he stood before the minister.

"Tell me, girl!" he cried, hoarsely, grasping her arm as in a vise, "do I understand you to say that you had another lover to whom you were preparing to be married at the time you came here?"

"Oh, what have I said, what have I done, that you are so angry at me?" cried Jess, piteously, cowering from the awful sternness that crept over his face and shone in his eyes.

"I want the whole truth, and I must have it, here and now, before we proceed one step farther," he said, slowly and harshly.

"Tell me about this man of whom you speak, when and where you first met him. Who is he? If I have understood you aright, you are as fair and false as others of your sex. While he was making preparations for a marriage with you, you have coolly jilted him by marrying another—for what purpose Heaven only knows! Probably you fancied I had more money. I know they credit me here with being enormously wealthy."

CHAPTER XXVII.
DECISIONS.

"Down deep in my heart, in its last calm sleep,

A dear, dead love lies buried deep;

I clasped it once in a long embrace,

And closed the eyes that veiled the face

I never again might see.

I breathed no word, and I shed no tear,

But the onward years looked dark and drear,

And I knew, by the throbs of mortal pain,

That a sweetness had fled which never again

Would in life come back to me."

Looking up into the face of her companion, Jess saw that it was ghastly white with horror, his lips trembled with unconcealed emotion. Anxiety and sorrow, mingled with impatience, darkened his brow. She gazed at him wonderingly, and like one fascinated.

"Tell me," he repeated, "is this thing true, that you have thrown over another, a good and true man, who is at this moment making preparations to marry you, to wed me?"

She tried to answer him, but his sternness terrified her; she had never dreamed that that handsome face could look so rigid and fierce, nor those dark eyes hold so much fire and scorn.

Her trembling lips moved, and all he could hear were the words:

"Hard and cruel."

"Hard and cruel!" repeated her husband, looking down upon her with bitter contempt; "it is you who have proven yourself to be that by doing such a cruel, unwomanly act. I could never have thought you capable of inflicting such a cruel wrong upon one who loved and trusted you—to his bitter cost!"

"Have I acted so very wrong?" cried Jess, clutching her two little hands together tightly and looking up into his eyes with a face as white as his own.

"Wrong!" he exclaimed, contemptuously, "we will waive that, Jess. You have done that which I will never pardon. Now tell me why you did it—what actuated your course?"

Still the girl was silent, fairly bewildered by his words.

"I think I can see through it all," he went on, bitterly; "but let me hear the truth from your own lips, dispelling my mad delusion that you were young and guileless as an angel, and not a fortune hunter, like others of your sex. You say you were about to wed another. When did you meet him, and where, and who is he? I repeat," he questioned, sternly.

"He is a handsome young man whom I met at Blackheath Hall," murmured the girl, as though the words were fairly wrung from her lips, and she would tell no more than was actually forced from her. "He saved my life, and—and when he asked me to marry him, and told me to think it over while he was away at New Orleans, I wrote him that I—I consented, and that the marriage should take place, as he so desired, as soon as I could get ready. While they were making my trousseau I was to spend a few weeks with a New York family, 'to get my manners polished up,' to use Mrs. Bryson's words, and—you know the rest—Fate led me here."

While she had been speaking her companion's face had grown whiter still, if that could be. He realized that he had made a fatal mistake in supposing this girl had been waiting for him—John Dinsmore, the joint heir with her to Blackheath Hall—to come down there to ask her to marry him.

In that moment of excitement it did not occur to him to press the question as to his name, since she did not seem inclined to inform him concerning it. Indeed, what did his name matter to him, he ruminated, moodily.

She loved that other fellow or she would never have consented to marry him, was the thought that passed with lightning-like rapidity through his brain. She had also believed Lucy Caldwell's report that he himself was fabulously rich, and, as that other love of his had done, thrown over the poorer suitor for the richer one.

He had been intending to tell Jess on their way back to the farmhouse that he was John Dinsmore, who had also been expected to come to her and lay his heart and fortune at her feet; now his lips were dumb. He decided to keep that fact a secret from her for the present, until he could see a path out of the dilemma in which he found himself; determining that for the present she should know him only as Mr. Moore, the man whom she had married on the impulse of the moment.

There was another decision he reached then and there, and that was, that he would lose no time in untying the knot between them which had been so hastily tied; and then, with the fortune which would be hers because the will of the elder Dinsmore had thus been complied with, she would be free to wed this lover who would be so heartbroken over her loss. For, of course, he must have been wedding her for love alone, it being well known all about where she lived that she would be penniless if she did not marry the heir of Blackheath Hall.

Yes, he would divorce Jess as soon as the law could accomplish it; that would be a shade better than to shuffle off the mortal coil to set her free, after giving her the right to the Dinsmore fortune.

In his calculations the bare possibility of another lover had never for an instant occurred to him.

All this changed his plans of the immediate future very materially.

He had been intending to announce their marriage as soon as they returned to the farmhouse, but under the present turn of affairs, he concluded that secrecy for the present was best.

"You are very angry with me!" sobbed the girl, wretchedly, and these words aroused him from the deep reverie into which he had fallen.

"You have stabbed me at my weakest point, little one," he answered, very huskily, "reopened a wound which I have been endeavoring valiantly to heal. Of all things, I cannot endure a girl who throws off one lover coolly for another. I despise of all things, of all women, I mean, a jilt!"

Ah! if Jess had but told him the exact truth at that moment what a lifetime of pain would have been spared her; had but explained to him that she was fairly forced into the betrothal with that other one by Mrs. Bryson, the old housekeeper, because that other lover represented himself to be John Dinsmore, the heir of Blackheath Hall. Ah! what investigations would have been instigated at once, and what cruel wrong averted!

But fate's thread was strangely tangled, and they were intended to play the bitter tragedy out to the end, and suffer all the sorrows that fell to their lot.

"Owing to the existence of these difficulties which have just arisen we must keep our marriage for the present a most profound secret," he said, slowly; "say that you will do this, little Jess?"

"I will do whatever you think wisest and best," murmured the girl, vainly struggling to keep the tears back from her dark, wistful eyes.

"That is right," he replied, hurriedly. "See, they are looking for you, as usual. Enter the house as though nothing unusual had transpired. You must go with Lawyer Abbot when he comes to take you away with him to—to the Trevalyns of New York; and I will communicate to you after you have reached there, in, say, a week or a fortnight at most, the course our future is to take. Until that time, adieu, little Jess."

She had no time to answer him; indeed, she could not, for her poor little heart was almost bursting with grief at the thought of parting from him.

It seemed to Jess that in leaving him she would leave all the brightness and joy of her young life behind her and go forth into rayless darkness and woe.

"Where have you two been?" cried Lucy, looking anxiously from the one to the other; "my uncle, Lawyer Abbot, is here, and he is very much afraid you will cause him to miss his train."

"I am sure the rich and elegant Mr. Moore has not been making love to her, or her face would never wear that woe-begone expression," thought the clever Lucy, and her spirits arose high at the anticipation of Jess' departure, which was now only a few moments distant, which would give her Mr. Moore all to herself, and she mentally resolved that no other pretty young girl should come visiting her while he was beneath that roof.

To the girl who had just been made a bride, and was bound by a solemn promise that the marriage should be kept secret, the parting from her handsome husband who was bidding her good-by so calmly was like tearing her living, beating heart in twain.

It was not until the carriage rolled away and the tall sycamore trees screened him from her sight as he waved an indifferent adieu to her from the porch that Jess broke down utterly, weeping as though her young heart was broken.

"Are you indeed so sorry to leave Lucy Caldwell?" asked the old lawyer, in wonderment, adding, "dear me, in what a short time young girls learn to care for each other, it would appear. Three weeks ago you did not know that there was such a girl as Lucy on the face of the globe, now you are crying your eyes out at leaving her. Brace up, little Jess, Lucy shall pay a visit to the Trevalyns along with you, if I can arrange matters. So be comforted, child, that promise will make you happy, I know."

But, despite this assurance, little Jess still continued to weep on, refusing to be comforted.

It was well for her that he did not divine the cause of her tears.

The parting to the newly wedded husband was of little consequence; he felt that he had accomplished the duty his dead uncle had imposed upon him, of marrying the girl that she might inherit the Dinsmore millions—that was all there was of it.

He would have been amazed had any one even hinted at the possibility that the girl he had just wedded cared for him, loved him with all the passionate strength of her young heart, and that it would take two to sever the bonds which bound them together.

CHAPTER XXVIII.
THE DARKENING CLOUDS.

"Ah, cruel as the grave,
Go, go, and come no more!'
But canst thou set my heart
Just where it was before?
Go, go, and come no more!
Go, leave me with my tears,
The only gift of thine
Which shall outlive the years."

The letter which Jess had received from Mrs. Bryson of Blackheath Hall on that memorable day on which she was to prepare for her journey to visit the Trevalyns—had contained another item that had troubled the young girl greatly.

It ran as follows:

"We were greatly surprised, and need I add, pleased, by an unexpected visit from your affianced husband. Mr. Dinsmore was greatly troubled, however, over the fact that you had been permitted to go away from the hall.

"'Mischief will come of it. A presentiment which I cannot shake off tells me so.' He seems so downhearted over it that——Forgive me for breaking my promise to you, Jess. I thought it wisest and best to tell him where you had gone, to visit the Trevalyn family of New York. I also told him of the little incident which had intercepted your visit, and that you were on the farm of Lawyer Abbot's brother-in-law, but were to start for New York with Lawyer Abbot the day after my letter reached you.

"Still he did not seem to be thoroughly satisfied. He walked the length of the drawing-room up and down with knitted brows, his face haggard and anxious.

"'I repeat that I fear mischief will come of it,' he declared. 'Jess is a girl who has never been away from the seclusion of Blackheath Hall. She does not know the world of men and women beyond these confines. Ten to one she will as likely as not fall in love with some farmhand there, and marry him out of hand, or elope with him, or do something equally hoydenish. You know Jess is not like other girls.'

"To appease his annoyance, we agreed that he should meet you and Lawyer Abbot at the first junction the other side of Caldwell, and finish the journey with you."

It was little wonder, after reading that, that Jess had consented at once to wed the man of her own choice when he had asked her to do so, and made no demurrer when he declared the marriage must take place without delay—that marriage that seemed now almost like a dream to Jess as the train bore her quickly away from her newly made husband.

Her thoughts were so confused she did not realize what she had said or done that he should get so angry with her on that homeward walk. It was the last drop in her cup of sorrow when he parted so coldly from her, without one good-by kiss, one tender word of farewell.

Jess had watched the tall figure out of sight, and then gave way to the bitterest, most passionate weeping that her girlish eyes had ever known.

But to return at this point to Ray Challoner, who was passing himself off so successfully as John Dinsmore, the heir prospective of Blackheath Hall.

When he had returned to the hall from his hasty trip to New Orleans, it was with the full determination of pushing the marriage forward to a climax as quickly as possible. His rage knew no bounds when he learned that fate had served him so dastardly a trick as to send Jess away on a visit.

He thanked his stars, however, that the trip north, to the home of Queenie Trevalyn, in New York, had been intercepted.

He was quick to plan, and equally quick to execute, and he determined that Jess should never get to the home of his former sweetheart, Queenie Trevalyn, if by human ingenuity he could prevent it, for it would never, never do for Jess to tell them that she was soon to marry the hero of that past summer at Newport; for, if she were to describe him, the description would be so vastly different from what they knew John Dinsmore to be, that investigations would be sure to be set on foot, and the wild plot of Raymond Challoner to win the Dinsmore millions would be frustrated—nipped, as it were, in the bud.

He remembered Queenie Trevalyn's parting words to him:

"From this hour we are bitter enemies, Mr. Challoner. Enemies to the death. You have insulted my pride, and the day will come when you will bitterly rue it!"

To lose him this heiress would be just the kind of revenge most pleasing to Queenie Trevalyn, who realized all too well his love of wealth and luxury.

No; Jess must never reach New York and hear the story of how John Dinsmore had been Queenie's admirer, and all the rest she had to tell, for no doubt, out of pique, Jess would not take him then, believing him one and the same John Dinsmore, of course.

No; he would meet Lawyer Abbot and Jess ere they reached New York, manage somehow to get the lawyer out of the way, and then marry Jess then and there, whether she would or no, and by fair means or foul.

But once again fate checkmated him. By a change in the railroad schedule, which took effect on the day she started north, Raymond Challoner missed Lawyer Abbot and Jess, and consequently they went on to New York one train in advance of him.

He raved and cursed like a madman when he reached the junction where he expected to meet them and found this to be the case. He would have to go by a train which reached New York some seven hours later, there was no help for it, and he was therefore obliged to make the best of the matter after his chagrin had worn itself out.

As the lightning express bore him along, he contented himself with laying out his plans.

Of course it would never do for him to go to the home of Queenie Trevalyn calling himself John Dinsmore, as he inquired for Jess—never in the world. He must wait and watch for the first opportunity of seeing Jess alone, and then, well, then he would carry out his deep-laid plan of marrying the girl ere she ever had the opportunity of returning to the house.

He bethought himself that the best, and the safest place for him to go, in the meantime, was his Uncle Brown's.

"Not that the old curmudgeon will be glad to see me; more than likely he will shut the door in my face; but I'll swallow down that insult, or any more that he may offer, to see if it is possible to patch up a truce with him and get into his good graces again. I am sure that he has cut me off without a shilling, as he notified me that he would do. Still, while there's life there's hope, as the old saying goes."

Upon reaching New York Raymond Challoner suited the action to the resolve, and made his way to his uncle's home at once. He took a cab until he reached within half a block of his destination, then dismissed the vehicle, knowing that it would never do for his miserly old uncle to behold him indulging in the luxury of riding.

"Hello!" muttered Challoner, rubbing his eyes in amazement as he stood before the street number he was looking for, "am I mad, or do my eyes deceive me? The place painted, and lace curtains at the windows, and an air of luxury around his miserly abode. Surely something out of the ordinary run of events has transpired. The old man has slipped off this mortal coil, or rented the house to some one who knows better than he did how to keep up a house in a first-class neighborhood—that will be a pride, instead of a disgrace and a nuisance to the people on both sides of him.

"He vowed he would live here till the day he died. Now, who knows if he changed his mind in this instance, he might do it in the affair of the will—make a new one leaving his vast possessions to me? Well, well, we shall see. If others live here now, they can probably give me some information as to where the old bundle of bones, or, rather, my dear uncle, has gone to."

He ran lightly up the steps and rang the bell, noting that even the old bell had been removed and a brand new silver one of latest design had been put in its place.

In answer to his summons a liveried servant opened the door.

The recognition was mutual.

"Master Raymond!" exclaimed the man, while that young man uttered in the same breath: "Dan! togged out in fine feathers, or do my eyes deceive me?"

Before he could answer, Raymond Challoner went on, wonderingly:

"What is the meaning of all this change, Dan? Has my uncle taken to living like a prince in his old age? I should as soon have expected to see the world suddenly come to a standstill."

"There's a mighty change in the old place, sir, I can tell you; and the reason for it is plain enough. Master Brown has taken to himself a young wife, sir," answered the man, enjoying the amazement on Raymond Challoner's face.

"My uncle married!" he gasped. "I can hardly credit the evidences of my own ears, Dan. I am dumfounded—bewildered!"

"I knew you would be, sir, when you came to hear of it," returned the old servant, watching the young man's white face, and almost pitying him, even while he did not like him, for he knew that the information he had just given him was Raymond Challoner's deathblow to the expectation of inheriting a penny from his uncle.

"Is he within, and can I see him?" asked the young man, pulling himself together by a mighty effort. "Dan, I must see him!"

The old servitor looked exceedingly uncomfortable, as he answered with hesitancy:

"I am sorry, Mr. Ray, but my orders from him were to deny you admittance if you ever came here and asked for him."

CHAPTER XXIX.
"LEAVE MY HOUSE."

"To look for thee, sigh for thee, cry for thee

Under my breath;

To clasp but a shade where thy head hath been laid,

It is death.

"To long for thee, yearn for thee, sigh for thee,

Sorrow and strife;

But to have thee, hold thee, enfold thee,

It is life—it is life."

"So he has bidden you turn me from his door in case I ever have the temerity to present myself?" repeated Challoner, dryly, his thin lips under his mustache curling into an unmistakable sneer, and a look not pleasant to see creeping into his eyes.

"Those were his precise words, sir," assented the man, quietly. "He is in, but it would do little good to tell him that you were here; he would go off into a towering rage, and you know what that means. He is worse than ever, sir, when he gets into a tantrum. It would be as much as my place was worth, Master Raymond, to tell him you were here and wished to see him."

"Let this be an inducement to you to do my bidding," said Challoner, slipping a bank note into the man's hand. "Make what excuse for my presence you deem best—that the door was left accidentally open and you found me standing in the hall—anything."

"I will act upon that suggestion, as it is a clever one, Master Raymond," and he turned and left him pacing angrily up and down the corridor.

"Married!" muttered Raymond Challoner between his clinched teeth. "That is indeed a blow to me. But even now I ought not to lose hope. Perhaps there is some way of making him jealous and casting her off. I will think up a plan to part them just as surely as my name is——"

His meditations came to an abrupt ending, for, raising his eyes, he beheld the tall, angular form of his uncle standing there before him. How long he had been standing there regarding him thus keenly, Challoner did not know. He wondered vaguely if he had been muttering any part of the thoughts aloud that had been whirling so madly through his brain. He could only hope not.

"So, you have presented yourself here after my express orders that you should never darken my door again, have you?" cried the old man, harshly, his keen gaze penetrating his unwelcome visitor like the sharp blade of a knife.

"Forgive me, uncle," replied Ray Challoner, affecting an earnestness which would have deceived any one else save the man standing before him. "I know you said that, but it was in the heat of passion. I had hoped that you would find pardon for me as time melted your heart, and reflection showed you that I could not be so bad as they had painted me with the hope of belittling me in your eyes."

"Liar, forger, thief—and—murderer!" hissed the old man, taking a step nearer him and glaring into his face. "Could anything on the catalogue of vices add to the shame as such a record as has been yours, unless I add to the true bill—libertine—which you are as well?"

A red flush crept over Challoner's face, and the dangerous look deepened in his eyes again—a fact not unnoted by the elder man.

"I washed my hands of you some time since, and so I informed you," went on the old man, harshly, adding: "Then why are you here? You have gotten into some new scrape from which you wish me to extricate you, I'll be bound. But, by the Lord Harry, I shall not do it. I will see you hanged first! You never come near me excepting when you want to wheedle money out of me. I know you like a book, Raymond Challoner, and you are a book whose pages I have closed forever and will never reopen."

"If you will give me time to speak, and will listen to me, I will tell you why I am here," retorted Challoner. "I have been in no scrape, as you term it, nor am I in need of money. I heard that you were ill and I came to your side in all haste."

The old man laughed aloud, declaring, harshly:

"In that case you came to see if you could influence me to make a new will in your favor, or, if you could get me alone, and I was too weak to resist you, to choke me into complying with your wish, eh?"

"You are hard upon me, uncle," responded Challoner, huskily, wondering if the old man had the powers of a sorcerer that he could read his thoughts so correctly, for that very thought had passed through his mind. "It seems of little use to tell you that I have mended my ways, having seen the folly of them, and that I am now giving myself up to work—hard work."

"You—work!" roared the old man, contemptuously. "Don't tell me that, for I know that you are lying. You would never put in an hour's honest work as long as money could be filched in any way from some victim or other. You are no good in the world; on the contrary, a continual injury to some one—whoever is unlucky enough to fall in with you. I will have none of you! Go from my presence! Leave my house more quickly than you entered it. Your very plausible tale about being anxious over the state of my health does not work with me, I tell you. Begone! before I call the police to remove you, or, to speak more plainly, to throw you into the street!"

Raymond Challoner drew back and looked at the man before him. They were all alone, this man who was goading him on to madness, and himself. All alone!

"Go! or I will most assuredly carry out my threat!" cried the old man, raising his voice shrilly. "You are wanted up at Saratoga for a felonious assault upon a man, which ended in his death. I knew when I read of the peculiar mark which the murdered man's temple bore, of a triangle with a large stone in the center, probably a diamond, whose hand it was that dealt the murderous blow, but because my blood flowed in your veins I made no sign—I held my peace."

"You could not prove the accusation you are daring to make," cried Challoner, trembling like a tiger ready to spring.

"There are many, I fancy, who would be only too ready to do that," retorted the old man, laconically.

Raymond Challoner's bad blood was up. He never thought of the consequence, and quick as a flash he thrust out his right hand, dealing a powerful blow at the man before him. But, quick as he was, the other was quicker. He stepped aside just in time to escape the terrific blow aimed at him. But in so doing he forgot that he had been standing so near the flight of stone steps that led to the basement below, and ere he discovered the fact, one fatal step backward sent him crashing down the entire flight!

The accident had been witnessed by two of the servants, who were just about to ascend the stairway. They had not seen the old man's antagonist strike the blow at him, for he was beyond their line of vision, but they had seen him step backward.

When he was hurriedly raised, they found that he was unconscious, and suffering from a severe scalp wound.

Raymond Challoner was equal to the occasion. In an instant he had leaped down the stone stairway and was bending over the stricken man, expressing the wildest grief for the accident.

"Carry him to the sofa in the rear parlor, and let a doctor be sent for at once," he commanded, and the servants, recognizing him as the injured man's nephew, hastened to do his bidding.

"The young wife is out driving," said Dan. "I do not know where to send for her, sir, but I expect that she may be in any moment."

"Never mind her," was the brief response. "She could do no good if she were here, but on the contrary would be in the way. All we can do is to make him as comfortable as possible until medical assistance arrives."

This was done, and the old man was placed on the sofa, with the curtains drawn back as far as possible to let in the light of the November afternoon which was fast waning.

Although it was near dusk, it was still light enough for the doctor to attend his patient without lighting the lights when he arrived, which was a very few moments after he had been summoned.

Ray Challoner stood by the improvised couch with apparently much solicitude.

The old man's head had scarcely been bandaged ere there was the sound of silken skirts in the corridor without.

"It is my lady," exclaimed old Dan, hurrying forward to acquaint her with what had transpired.

Instinctively Raymond Challoner's eyes sought the door for the first glimpse of the woman who had cheated him out of a fortune by wedding the old miser, as his uncle was called—for his gold.

He was standing in the shadow of the portières when she entered.

One glance, and he could hardly repress the cry of amazement that hovered on his lips. His eyes encountered the tall, willowy figure of Queenie Trevalyn.

Challoner hastily turned up his coat collar and pulled his felt hat down low over his eyes, that her eyes, in sweeping around the room, might not recognize him.

"Mrs. Brown, I believe," said the doctor, stepping forward and bowing profoundly to the lovely young woman who came hastily into the parlor, her costly silken robe trailing after her on the velvet carpet.

"Yes," she answered, adding in a hurried voice that somehow had a note of eager expectancy in it: "The servants tell me that my—my husband has met with an accident. I trust it is not of a serious nature."

"Yes—and no, madam," replied the doctor, bluntly. "For a younger man the accident would be nothing. Your husband's age is against him. It is all in the attention he receives whether he recovers or succumbs to it."

Was it only the doctor's fancy, or did he behold a gleam of satisfaction in the eyes of the old man's bride, as he uttered the last four words?

CHAPTER XXX.
HIS UNCLE'S BRIDE.

The shock of finding Queenie Trevalyn the bride of his aged uncle can better be imagined than described. Raymond Challoner was fairly dumfounded at it. He could almost have believed his eyes were playing him some amazing trick in tracing such a resemblance, until he heard her speak.

There was no mistaking that smooth, perfect, melodious voice that every one who heard it at Newport had likened unto the chiming of silver bells, it was so deliciously sweet.

But just now there was a harsh, jarring strain in it that revealed all too plainly the nature of her thoughts and hopes.

Glancing up at that moment she caught the eye of the young man who stood on the doctor's left, with his coat collar turned up and his hat pulled so low down over his face that his eyes only were visible.

She started confusedly. Where had she seen just such a pair of eyes as were those regarding her so fixedly? Where?

The doctor's voice recalled her to the fact that the old man who called her wife, the old man whom she had wedded for his fortune, was lying before her mortally hurt, and she must pretend great sorrow and anxiety concerning him, though she felt it not. At the first glance at the white old face lying against the pillow, her heart gave one wild leap.

What if his injuries were fatal—and he should die? Then, ah, then she would be free to recall John Dinsmore, the man she had found out to her bitter cost that she really loved—and marry him.

No wonder she started guiltily at the bare notion that the stranger with the piercing eyes was reading her very heart thoughts. She made an effort to answer the doctor's remark with seeming agitation, caused by grief.

Pressing her dainty point-lace handkerchief to her eyes she murmured behind its folds: "If his recovery depends on his being carefully nursed, you may be sure that we will have him up and about as quickly as it can be accomplished."

"I am sure of it, madam," replied the doctor, with a low bow. "I shall send a trained nurse to you immediately," he went on briskly, "and in the meantime, I would ask that you administer the powders which I shall leave you, every fifteen minutes. Failure to do this would be fatal."

"I will attend to it myself, until the nurse you speak of arrives," she murmured.

Promising to return in the course of an hour or two at the very latest, the doctor took his leave.

Glancing furtively about, Queenie did not see the stranger who had stood beside the doctor, and she concluded that he must have been an assistant, and that he left with the doctor. Still, the lurid gaze of those eyes haunted her—she could not tell why.

"Ah! I have it!" she cried fiercely, at length, after she had dismissed the servants, telling them that she would watch beside her husband's couch, and that she would call upon them when she needed them. "Yes; I know now where I have seen just such eyes. They looked out at me from the face of false, fickle Raymond Challoner, that never-to-be-forgotten day at Newport, when he stood before me and told me that our betrothal which had lasted just one day, would have to be broken if I had been so unfortunate as to lose the vast fortune which I was credited with having.

"It was in that bitter hour that I learned the worth of a true love, such as John Dinsmore's, which I had flung away for the idle fancy of such a creature as Raymond Challoner.

"Raymond Challoner, you who ruined my life, where are you now, I wonder? If we ever meet again, just as surely as I live, I will take a horrible vengeance upon you.

"I have wealth now," she went on, wearily, "and will be one of the wealthiest women in the great metropolis. But, ah, what is it worth to the love of one true heart that I could love in return?"

And the beautiful woman sank back in the cushions of the velvet chair, and something very like a tear glistened in the proud, dark eyes.

Then she suddenly pressed her hand to her heart, muttering:

"There may be happiness in store for me yet, but it will be after he dies and leaves me freedom and his wealth," and she gazed intently at the white face which seemed to grow whiter still under the softened rays of the gas jets with their opaline shades.

The little French clock on the mantel struck the hour.

Queenie started to her feet.

"It is time for the first dose of powders which the doctor left," she muttered, reaching her jeweled hand toward the table for them.

Then suddenly her hand dropped to her side and she glanced furtively about the luxurious room.

"If I did not follow the doctor's instructions in regard to giving him the powder, who is to know?" she whispered under her breath.

For an instant she stood motionless, with the contents of the little white paper containing the life-giving powder clutched tightly in her hand.

The little clock on the mantel ticked on and on. One, two, three, four, five minutes passed, and she stood thus like a statue carved in marble. Another five minutes, and with a shudder she hastily crossed the room and emptied the contents of the little white paper into the depths of the silver cuspidor.

"Among the cigar ashes contained in this, it will never be traced," she whispered, fearfully.

She was not an adept in crime. This was her first offense against the laws of God and man. It was little wonder that she trembled so violently as she crept up to the couch and watched breathlessly the effect of the emission of the powder.

"In an hour from now, when the doctor returns, his patient will be beyond all mortal aid," she muttered, hoarsely.

Twice the sufferer stirred on his pillow and moaned faintly as he murmured piteously:

"Oh, for youth, and health, and strength, that you might love me, my beauteous young bride. They say that December should not wed with May—that it is against nature's laws—but I have tried to convince myself that the rule did not always hold good; that my case was an exception; that Queenie loved me for my old and battered self, not for my gold."

The bride who stands beside the couch recoils from him with a gesture of loathing.

Love that pitiable wreck of manhood, who is seventy if he is a day. How dare he expect it? What madness to imagine it.

"Kiss me, Queenie," he moaned. "Lay your soft cheek against mine, that the swift current of youth's warm blood may chase the death dew that is gathering on my brow. For your sake I will overcome the deadly faintness that is stealing over me. I will live—live—live!"

"To make my days one ceaseless round of annoyance—ay, torture," muttered the girl, bending over him, noting that though he is fighting the fiercest battle man ever fought to overcome the grim destroyer, death, which is hovering over him, his convulsive throes grow weaker and weaker, and his face takes slowly on that yellowish hue that there is no mistaking.

The second quarter of an hour has been gathered into the past, and the contents of the second paper have been consigned to the silver cuspidor, the third quarter is well-nigh spent, but the beautiful woman who watches seems to pay no heed to time.

One convulsive gasp, another, and the man whom she calls husband falls back motionless on his pillow.

"He is dead!" she whispers, half aloud.

"Yes, he is dead," answers a deep voice close by her elbow, "and you, my dear madam, are his—— Well, the word I would use is an ugly one, and I will substitute in its place—you are responsible for it."

"It is false!" Queenie tries to gasp as she reels backward in horror, too awful for words, and glares with dilated eyes at the intruder who has suddenly loomed up before her. But the words die away in her throat in a spasmodic, deathlike gurgle.

Before her she sees standing the man with the bright, piercing eyes, whom she had believed to be the doctor's assistant, and whom she fancied had left the house with him.

His coat collar was still turned up, and his hat pulled down over his face, revealing only those black, malicious eyes.

"You have not been alone, as you fancied yourself to be, madam," he went on, in that voice which seemed strangely familiar to her. "I remained behind, to see that you carried out the doctor's instructions, upon which the life of the man now lying dead before you hung. I seated myself in that armchair in the bay window, which the lace draperies conceal, but from my position I could see all that took place. In fact, being scarcely ten feet from you, I could not help overhearing every word that fell from your lips."

"No, no, no!" shrieked Queenie, falling on her knees at his feet.

"Hush!" he commanded, quickly, placing his hand over her mouth, "don't you know that you will arouse every servant in the house, and that they will be flocking to the scene? I have much to say to you ere the alarm that your husband is dead is given out. There, don't be alarmed; I want to be your friend if you will allow me to be so. It is not my intention, at least not my present intention, to betray your crime to the world. You did a very rash thing, to be sure, but, then, I intend to be your friend for the reason that it is for my interest to be so."

"Who are you?" gasped Queenie, leaning heavily back against the casement. "I seem to know you—and yet I do not. My God!" she exclaimed in the same breath, "am I mad or dreaming, or do my eyes deceive me? You are Raymond Challoner!"

CHAPTER XXXI.
IN HIS POWER.

"O'er her brow a change has passed;

In the darkness of her eyes,

Deep and still a mystery lies;

In her voice there thrills a tone

Never in her girlhood known."

For one full moment the two who had parted from each other in such bitter wrath on that never-to-be-forgotten morning at Newport stood once again, face to face, looking into each other's eyes.

It was Queenie who broke the dead silence that reigned in that awful chamber of death.

"Raymond Challoner!" she repeated, falteringly, and he could see that she was almost on the verge of utter collapse.

"Yes, Raymond Challoner, at your service," he responded, cynically.

"What are you doing here?" she cried, hoarsely, still wondering if she were not laboring under some horrible nightmare.

"What to you seems now so astounding can be most easily explained," he answered. "I am the nephew of the man you have wedded; the one who should have been his heir, and whom he discarded."

That this information was astounding to Queenie he could readily see, and because of that he readily conjectured that her husband had not mentioned him to his bride, for which he was now truly thankful.

It took but an instant for Queenie to recover herself. The color rushed back to her deathly white face, and the cold, harsh expression her features had worn of late came suddenly back to them as the thought crossed her mind that at last she was revenged upon Raymond Challoner, for had she not every dollar of the wealth that would have been his at that moment but for her? But in the next instant she realized that her hour of triumph over him had not yet come, for she was in his power; one word from his lips would send her——

She did not follow out the rest of the sentence; she dared not. "Come," he said, touching her on the arm, and placing her with a firm, masterful hand into an armchair close by, "you must not give way to your emotions. You will need all your self-control."

In a few words he explained his presence in that room; that he had come to call on his uncle; the bitter quarrel that ensued, ending in apoplexy which had caused the accident; his call for a doctor, and volunteering to remain by his uncle's side until the return of his wife, and of his intense amazement to learn who that wife was—his own sweetheart of other days—and how he had retired behind the heavy draperies of the windows for the purpose of making known his presence to her when he should find her alone, fearing that some sort of a scene might ensue.

"Why did you not make your presence known at once, as soon as the servants had left the room?" she gasped.

"I was conning over in my mind whether it was really best to acquaint you with my presence beneath your roof, or to wait until morning and go quietly away without revealing myself to you. In the face of what has occurred, I knew that the best thing to do was to apprise you of my presence."

"What do you intend to do?" she queried, hoarsely, her hands trembling like aspen leaves as they clutched the arm of the chair for support.

"I intend to be your friend if you will allow me to be so," he replied, suavely.

"Impossible!" cried Queenie. "It is against nature for you to wish to be my friend when I come between you and a fortune."

"It is neither the time nor the place to tell you all that is in my thoughts," he responded, "but I may as well drop you a slight hint as to their trend. What would be easier than for you in the near future to reimburse me with the fortune which you are the means of taking from me?"

"You mean for me to one day marry you?" she gasped.

"I see you have divined my thoughts most accurately, my fair Queenie," he answered.

She shrank from him in loathing too great for words, crying:

"Not for this whole world would I marry you, Raymond Challoner. I would sooner die."

"Do not decide too hastily, my fair enemy," he returned, mockingly. "Remember, 'discretion is the better part of valor,' as the old saw goes. I shall leave you now, for it would never do for us to be found here together. I will see you early on the morrow."

Before she was aware of what he was about to do, he had raised her jeweled hand to his lips, kissed and dropped it, and the door was closing softly after him.

When the doctor arrived, and the servants ushered him into the sick room, they found the beautiful young bride lying prone upon her face in a dead faint by the side of the still, stark form lying in his last sleep upon the couch.

"Dead!" exclaimed the doctor briefly, at the first glance at the old millionaire's rigid features. Then he turned his attention at once to the grief-stricken woman, who had apparently swooned ere she could summon help in her dying husband's last moments. Neither the doctor nor the servants would have pitied her so deeply could they have seen her when she returned to consciousness in her own boudoir an hour or so later.

She dismissed the maid who was watching over her; then sprang from the couch and paced the floor up and down like a veritable demon in woman's form.

"Was it for that that I dared and accomplished so terrible a crime?" she whispered, clutching her hands tightly over her heart. "No, a thousand times no, for I hate Raymond Challoner with all the strength of my heart and soul. I only wanted to be free from the shackles of iron which bound me, that I might recall the only man I have ever loved—John Dinsmore. And now, when success dawns for me, another cloud, more formidable than the one which has just been dissipated, gathers over me.

"I shall never marry Raymond Challoner, that he may share the wealth which will be mine, while we both know in our secret hearts that we detest each other. Let come what will, I will defy him to do his worst, and in the meantime I will recall him whom I sent from me." And through her brain rang the fateful words:

"And when your love has conquered pride and anger,

I know that you will call me back again."

Her riotous reverie was suddenly cut short by the entrance of her mother.

"Oh, my darling, my precious Queenie! We have just heard through one of the servants, who came hurrying to us with the awful intelligence, of his death, and I could scarcely credit the news until I came and saw for myself."

The mother and daughter looked steadily at each other, each reading the other's thoughts.

"You are now a wealthy widow, my dear child," murmured Mrs. Trevalyn, dropping her voice to a low whisper, and adding in the same breath, "you want your mourning made up in the most becoming manner, for there are no women so attractive as young and beautiful widows. The first six months you will want all black crape; at the end of the second six months you can introduce a little white or lavender here and there, and———"

"For Heaven's sake, hush, mamma," cried Queenie. "I cannot endure it. I am thinking of something else, I assure you."

"Dear me!" cried Mrs. Trevalyn, in a very injured tone of voice. "One would think that you had just lost a very dear and loving husband, of whom you were foolishly fond, instead of an old man whom, you and I both know, you wedded for his money, and whom we cordially hated personally. Isn't his death what you have been longing for ever since you turned away from the altar with him, I should like to know?"

"Of course," whispered Queenie; "but—well, to tell you the truth, I was thinking of John Dinsmore, and wondering how he would take the news when he heard that I am free again. He did not fancy widows. You remember how many there were at Newport, and all setting their caps for him."

"An old love who has become a widow is quite another matter," declared Mrs. Trevalyn, energetically. "As soon as he hears of your bereavement, he will make that an excellent excuse to call upon you or write you, offering his condolence; that will pave the way for other sympathetic calls, and in a year from now, if you play your cards well, you can land the man you have always wanted, John Dinsmore."

"And whose wife I would have been to-day, had you not kept dinning continually into my ears that I must marry for wealth, and that love was not to be considered."

"My dear child, I thought you were sensible on such matters; do not grow sentimental at this late date. When you jilted handsome Mr. Dinsmore, he was not worth a penny, so consequently he was not to be considered in a matrimonial light; but now that his fortunes have changed and he is wealthy, why that puts a different face upon his prospects of winning a very lovely and brilliant girl like yourself."

For answer Queenie burst into a paroxysm of tears, crying, wildly:

"But it can never be now, mamma—never, never! the Fates forbid!—and my future will be horrible to contemplate."

"Do not talk wildly and unreasonably, my child. Why should fate forbid your marrying John Dinsmore, should he come wooing a second time, which he is sure to do, he was so much in love with you?"

For a moment Queenie was tempted to tell her mother all of her awful story, but on second thoughts she concluded that it would be safer to keep the horrible truth locked carefully in her own breast. An idea had come to her—perhaps she could buy Ray Challoner off by dividing the millions with him which she was sure to inherit as his uncle's widow.

CHAPTER XXXII.
WHAT MIGHT HAVE BEEN.

"Strong in my heart old memories wake

To-night.

Live on my lips dead kisses burn;

Hot to my eyes wept tears return;

Forgotten throbs my pulses shake,

To-night.

"Love is avenged—my buried love—

To-night.

The weakling present slips away;

The giant past alone has sway,

Potential as the gods above,

To-night."

"I do not understand you in the least, my dear," exclaimed Mrs. Trevalyn, as Queenie still continued to wring her hands, weeping bitterly the while. "Your eyes will be in the back of your head if you keep on wailing and weeping in this way," she added in annoyance, "and a pretty sight you will present then. Always remember to keep your face looking beautiful, no matter what else goes amiss."

Thus admonished, Queenie dried her eyes, but she could not keep back the heavy sighs that arose to her lips at the very thought of Raymond Challoner and his hint that she must marry him.

"I had forgotten to tell you an interesting piece of news mother," said Queenie, "and that is that I hear Raymond Challoner is the discarded nephew of—of my—my late husband."

This was indeed news to Mrs. Trevalyn, and she said so, adding in the next breath:

"He broke his betrothal to you, Queenie, because your father had lost his fortune. I should not be a particle surprised if he were to attempt to renew his suit when he finds that you have money, my dear, but you can afford to whistle him down the wind. Why, my dear child, what is the matter? You look so woefully pale, quite as though you were going to swoon. Your nerves are overwrought, and no wonder. I must go now, for I never can bear to be about when there are such grewsome things going on as making arrangements for a funeral. I had almost forgotten to tell you a little piece of news which I was going to run over anyway to-day to tell you about."

Queenie never raised her face from her hands, and her mother went on:

"The young girl whom old Lawyer Abbot wrote us about, asking that we receive her to visit you for a few weeks, arrived late yesterday afternoon. Her surprise was great to learn that you had married and left us, and were living in another part of the city.

"'Then I shall have to go straight back to Blackheath Hall!'" she said, disappointedly.

"'By no means, my dear!' I answered. 'Remain in the home our dear Queenie's absence makes so desolate as long as you like. I am sure we will be only too glad to have you here. I shall take you to see Queenie as soon as you are thoroughly rested from your long trip!' Of course she stayed.

"You will be surprised when you see her, Queenie," Mrs. Trevalyn went on. "She is the most beautiful creature my eyes ever rested on, and quite the strangest girl imaginable. It was well old Brown did not see her, beauty worshiper that the old fellow was, or he would have made her the wealthy widow instead of you, I fear."

"Is she so much fairer than I?" exclaimed Queenie, in intense pique, bridling up in an instant.

Her mother laughed softly, saying: "I fancied that remark would arouse you from the lethargy into which you are falling; that was my purpose in saying it. Pretty? Yes, the girl is more than pretty, but you are beautiful, my peerless Queenie; you must not forget that."

The very next day occurred the reading of the will, and then—the thunderbolt from an apparently cloudless sky burst.

It was found that the so-called reputed millionaire was a bankrupt. There was scarcely enough money left after his just debts were paid to insure him a decent burial.

"I cannot, I will not believe that I have been cheated thus!" cried Queenie, springing to her feet and tearing the trappings of heavy crape from her and trampling them under foot.

Even the lawyer, who was reading the last word of the will, paused in wonderment at this heartless exhibition of rage, and in the very presence, too, of the dead. He almost feared that the enraged beauty, who had wedded the old man for his wealth, would hurl the casket to the floor.

It was Raymond Challoner who led her from the room.

"My disappointment is as great as yours," he said, grimly, "but I seem able to control myself better. We are both paupers, it seems," he went on, in the same whisper, "and we should sympathize with each other."

"Of course," he added, "marriage is for a second time not to be thought of in connection with you or me, but even though I will not be obliged to shield you with my name, you can yet be of use to me, and I to you, in keeping the secret of the true cause of my uncle's death."

Queenie was crushed, humiliated to the very earth. She made no comment. As though in a glass darkly, she was trying to outline her future. As a wealthy young widow, her place in society would have been one to be envied.

With her father a bankrupt, and the man she had married a bankrupt as well, she saw nothing before her save seeking employment for her daily bread.

Could she ever hope to win John Dinsmore then? She would belong to one world and he to another, and those words lay as far apart as heaven and earth.

Her companion, who was still clasping her arm tightly as he led her along, broke into her reverie by saying:

"Let us step into the music-room for a few words more, Queenie. I have something of importance to say to you still. Consent to aid me and I will make it worth your while; you shall have a fortune at least half as great as the one which you have just lost, if I can win what I am aiming for. Will you spare me a few moments of your time, and give me your undivided attention?"

She laughed a low, harsh laugh. "My time is not so valuable now as—well, if you have any plan to offer by which I may have the hope of retrieving my fallen fortunes, why should I not listen to your plans—and eagerly?"

"Now you are speaking very sensibly," he rejoined, leading her into the music-room and closing the door carefully after them, to insure their not being overheard by any of the servants.

Queenie was so thoroughly in his power that he knew he need have no hesitancy in telling her his plans from beginning to end, without fear of her daring to expose him; on the contrary, he would force her to aid him in his determination to win the Dinsmore millions.

He began at the beginning, telling her of much that she did not know, of that duel on the sands at Newport, on her account, in which he had, as he believed, mortally wounded his adversary, John Dinsmore.

He saw her start, and turn deadly pale, but he went on, hurriedly:

"He lingered for some weeks, but in the end succumbed to his injuries."

"Murderer!" gasped Queenie. "Oh, God! he is dead, then! dead!"

Raymond Challoner looked at her coolly, as he replied:

"We do not call affairs of honor by such a hard name as that which just now passed your lips, my dear madam. We took our chances, one against the other; that was fair play. He was as liable to shoot me as I was to shoot him. It was not like willfully planning in secret and carrying out a deliberate murder."

Queenie fell back in her seat, powerless to reply. She knew but too well the meaning he would convey by those words.

She made no further attempt to interrupt him, and he related the tale, which sounded to her ears like some weird romance, of how he was *en route* to the races at New Orleans, and the accident which necessitated his remaining over at the crossroads for the next train, which would not come along for some hours; of the interesting story the old landlord had told him of the death of some man in England who was worth many millions, and the extraordinary will he had left behind him, namely, that half of his estate should go to his nephew, John Dinsmore, and the other half to a young girl who had been brought up as a foundling upon the estate, provided these two should marry.

"The young girl," he went on, "resided upon an estate known as Blackheath Hall, in the vicinity where I was at that time. The man was your one-time lover, Dinsmore, whom you considerately threw over for me."

Again Queenie's lips moved, but no sound came from them. He could see that she was vitally interested in his narrative—indeed, she scarcely moved or breathed even, during the recital; her eyes were riveted upon his face, as though spellbound.

"You will wonder how all this is of interest to you, Queenie. I am fast nearing that point. I must tell you all, that you may better understand the exact situation.

"Well, to cut the story as short as possible, knowing that Dinsmore had passed in his checks, I conceived the daring scheme of passing myself off for him, marrying the girl, and inheriting the Dinsmore fortune, which I would lose no time in putting into cash. I knew that I would have little trouble in proving the identity, as I could get hold of the private papers he left behind him through the doctor who attended him, who was a sworn friend of mine. Dinsmore had once visited that part of the country when he was a child, but I counted on the people not remembering his childish features.

"Well, the daring scheme worked like a charm even beyond my wildest hopes. I succeeded in establishing my identity as John Dinsmore, and in becoming betrothed to the co-heiress. That girl is now in New York, visiting at your old home. Her name is Jess. I rely upon you to aid me in marrying her, for to tell you the truth, she detests me, and wants to back out. Accomplish this, and you shall be a rich woman for life, Queenie."

CHAPTER XXXIII.
TO WRECK A YOUNG GIRL'S LIFE.

"Dreams, we have spent full many a lingering hour

Of heaven-sweet rest

Together. Wrapped in your most secret bower,

With vision blest,

I've seen the budding of Love's fairy flower

Within my breast;

How long is it, dear love, since we were face to face,

Full many years;

Look deep into my heart—there you will trace

Your myriad tears."

For some moments after he had ceased speaking, Queenie still sat there, regarding him with that same intensity of gaze that made him feel a trifle uneasy.

"Why do you not answer me?" he queried, impatiently. "Are you with me in my valiant scheme for a fortune—I was going to add, or are you against me? but I know you would not dare thwart me in my desires. You are in my power, and my will henceforth shall be your law."

The cold eyes meeting his gaze so steadily did not flinch, nor did the marble face grow one whit whiter at this open declaration, reminding her of the precipice on which she stood and would stand for all time to come, unless fate should sweep this man from her path. Indeed, her face could grow no whiter.

She had lived through two terrible shocks; first, that the man whom she loved better than her own life was dead, and, secondly, that had he lived he would, in all probability, have wedded another.

"It was a most unaccountable turn of fate's wheel that this girl should have come North to visit you, of all people, Queenie," he resumed, thoughtfully, "and I expected no end of difficulties in the matter. It would have been natural for her to confide to you that she was soon to wed, and I could imagine your amazement when she told you that the man she was to marry was John Dinsmore.

"Of course, in the interchange of girlish confidences, you would have told her that he was, once upon a time, and not so very many moons ago, your admirer.

"If descriptions of him were entered into, then I would be detected, I well knew. I would not have dared present myself at your home under that name, of course, and I could see no way out of the labyrinth, or rather, dilemma, but to watch and wait for her visit to you to terminate, and return to her home.

"I could illy brook the length of time this would consume, for I am in sore straits and need the money, which I can gain possession of, thanks to the trustfulness in human nature of that old imbecile, Lawyer Abbot, just as soon as the marriage between myself and the lovely Jess is consummated.

"I repeat, the girl distrusts, and even dislikes me, and has, furthermore, written me that the marriage can never take place now, and a lot more of that kind of nonsense, which I, of course, pay no attention whatever to.

"You must urge my cause for me, Queenie, and induce this girl to marry me as quickly as possible, presenting me, of course, in the character which I assume of John Dinsmore.

"I would not dare call upon her at your father's home, for no doubt he has met the real John Dinsmore, and the whole trick would be exploded there and then. I would lose a fortune, and you would lose one likewise, by not being able to aid me in carrying out my daring scheme.

"You must send for the girl to take a little trip with you to some nearby resort, and while there I will come and press my suit."

"What a clever schemer you are!" burst out Queenie, recoiling from him as though he had been a cobra.

"I am, unfortunately, obliged to live by my wits since my dear uncle cut me off so summarily. I had been used to gratifying my luxurious tastes, and that took money. I fell naturally into scheming for it. But that is neither here nor there. The question is: Will you aid me to secure the Dinsmore millions for the consideration which I have offered you—a stipulated sum, paid down in cash in the hour the marriage between myself and this Jess takes place?"

He was prepared for her answer, "Yes," knowing that she dared not refuse whatever he might ask.

"I will leave you now," he resumed, "and will call again to-morrow."

Queenie was glad when he bowed himself out of her presence. She shuddered, as with a sudden chill, for the memory of his cynical, mocking smile, as he turned away, she knew would follow her as long as she lived.

Challoner had barely opened the street door ere a coach stopped just in front of the house, and three young men sprang from it, dashing up the marble steps to where he stood, three steps at a time.

"I beg your pardon, sir," said the foremost of the newcomers, "for waylaying you in this brusque fashion. Permit me to explain that we are reporters for an evening paper. We have been sent to you, if you are one of the family of the dead man, whose will has just created such a furore, on the announcement that the supposed millionaire was discovered to be a bankrupt, for a correct statement, if you will kindly accord it to us."

Ray Challoner's brows gathered into a frown.

"I am the nephew of the man who has just died," he assented, "but I want to keep it out of the papers; it's not a thing to comment on, don't you know."

"It's sure to get into the papers," said the spokesman of the party. "We will have to write up something. It is much the best way to give us a correct account of it."

He turned to his companions for affirmation of this sentiment, and they both nodded assent, pulling their writing pads and pencils from their pockets as they did so.

Challoner gave them an account to suit himself. It was just as well for the dear public at large not to know the exact truth as to know how matters actually stood.

"That is all there is to tell," he said, when he had finished, moving away from them down the steps.

Hailing a passing hansom cab, Challoner hastily entered it, leaving the trio on the steps, still comparing notes.

One of them, however, was staring after him with a strange expression upon his face, which had suddenly grown very white.

"Boys," he said, huskily, "ever since we have been talking to that fellow, I have been cudgeling my brain as to where I had seen him before, but my memory seemed determined to baffle me. I have it now; he is the despicable cur that engaged in that duel in Newport with John Dinsmore, fatally wounding the finest gentleman that ever lived.

"You see, I only saw this Challoner—that's his name—by dim moonlight, and on that one occasion only, so it was little wonder that I was a trifle mixed as to his identity. I was Dinsmore's second, if you remember."

"Yes, we remember," assented his companions, and one of them asked:

"Can you tell us whatever became of John Dinsmore?"

Jerry Gaines—for it was he—heaved a deep sigh that came from the very depths of his heart.

"He was wounded in that accursed duel, as I have said," he went on, slowly. "For some weeks his life was despaired of, and when he began to convalesce, he decided to take a trip South, partly to regain his health and strength, and partly to attend to another little matter which meant much to him in a pecuniary way. Well, he never lived to reach the end of his journey. There was a terrible railway accident; the train went over a high bridge, rolling down an embankment of something like a hundred feet or more, and all of the coaches caught fire. It happened at night, and when morning dawned, it was found that but a mass of charred timber, bones and ashes remained to tell the pitiful story. Dinsmore was not among the few rescued. That was his fate, boys, and Ballou and I have mourned for him like brothers from that day to this. We are the Trinity, the inseparable three, you know."

Brushing a tear from his eye, Jerry Gaines went on:

"Poor John Dinsmore never knew of the brilliant honors that awaited him in the success of the book which has just been published, nor the money which would have been his from its sale. Nor how the papers printed his picture and the praise that was accorded him.

"Boys," he added, with a sudden energy and a darkening of his fine brows, "I am going to reopen that quarrel which laid Dinsmore low, and cause that despicable cur of a Challoner to answer to me for it."

"Let bygones be bygones, Jerry," advised his brother reporters. "You cannot bring back your friend John Dinsmore, and there is little use in letting him spill your blood, too."

"No matter what you say, my friends, there will be a reckoning between me and Challoner at no distant day. I will hound his footsteps night and day, until I find an opportunity which suits my purpose, and then—well, John Dinsmore's difference with that man will be avenged. It will be either Raymond Challoner's life or mine."

"I, too, imagine that I have seen his face somewhere before," said one of the other reporters, slowly, "but, like you, Gaines, my memory baffles me, for the time being, to place him, but it will assuredly come to me sooner or later."

Raymond Challoner had not been talking to the trio five minutes before it suddenly dawned upon him who two of them were—the one, John Dinsmore's second in that midnight duel on the sands of Newport; and the other one—well, that reporter had been on hand when he had been arrested for a crime which would have landed him on the gallows if he had not made his escape in a manner challenging the daring of Claude Duval himself.

He had made haste to leave them the instant their identity had dawned upon him, and he felt reasonably sure that they had failed to recognize him—a fact for which he thanked his stars.

"Now for pretty Jess and a speedy marriage with her," he ruminated, as the carriage rolled down the avenue. "I see I must hurry matters and shake the dust of New York off my feet speedily."

CHAPTER XXXIV.
UNDER THE MASK OF FRIENDSHIP.

"I know not now, nor never knew,
Why lives so linked were rent apart!
But this I know, that only you,
Can claim a place within my heart;
It may be that you do forget,
And think it is the same with me,
That olden love is dead, and yet
We once both said it could ne'er be!"

When Queenie found herself alone, after the departure of Raymond Challoner, she gave full vent to the bitter grief she had kept pent up in her breast, upon learning from him of the death of the only man whom she had ever loved, though the knowledge of that love had come to her too late.

She could hardly bring herself to believe he was really dead, lying a mass of charred remains, he who had been such a strong, active, handsome man but a few short weeks ago. How could fate have severed the golden cord of his noble existence at the very height of his success and glorious fame!

She brushed at length the burning tear drops from her eyes, muttering:

"If he is indeed dead, then my past and my future are dead—there is no hope of happiness for me hereafter."

But even in the midst of her grief she realized that the worst possible thing that she could do would be to give way to it so utterly.

All at once every hope upon which she had built her expectation of a roseate future lay in ruins at her feet. She was not even the wealthy widow that she had expected to be.

Then she fell to thinking of all that Raymond Challoner had promised if she would aid him in his schemes of urging this girl Jess to a speedy marriage, in order that he might gain the Dinsmore millions.

Queenie's curiosity over the girl made her forget her sorrow for the time being, in realizing the fact, that even had John Dinsmore lived, this was the girl whom he would have been in duty bound to wed. This was the girl who would have lived in the sunshine of his presence.

"He would never have loved her, for his love was mine—all mine!" she cried, clutching both of her hands convulsively over her heart. "Such a man loves once in a lifetime—no more!"

She lost no time in sending for Jess to come to her, and she was agreeably surprised to see the girl return with the messenger.

Queenie had expected to see a shy little Southern rosebud; instead, she beheld a glorious young creature of such rare beauty that for a moment she held her breath in astonishment as she gazed upon her; and even in that moment the thought ran through Queenie's mind:

"Despite John Dinsmore's assurances that he would never love any one else but me, he would have been hardly human not to have fallen in love with this peerless little Jess at first sight had he but seen her."

Queenie's reverie was cut short by the girl advancing with outstretched hands toward her, saying:

"I am Jess—and you are Queenie Trevalyn! I—I beg your pardon, Mrs. Brown. Dear me, how funny the thought of your being even married, let alone being a—widow—seems," she rattled on, breathlessly. "I love you already, you are so sweet. Won't you let me kiss you, and won't you say: 'Welcome, Jess?'"

"I was just about to say that, and offer not one, but as many kisses as you like," said Queenie, opening out her arms to the graceful little figure that bounded into them.

That was the beginning of the friendship which was to end so disastrously for poor Jess.

Queenie was a thorough woman of the world, versed in its arts, its deceits, while Jess was but a child of nature, with a heart as open as the day, and free from guile or knowledge of falsity; therefore it was little wonder that she quite believed her welcome genuine.

In a week's time, "the two girls," as Queenie's mother persisted in calling them, were as inseparable as though they had known each other from childhood up.

"I am so glad that you came to me just when you did, dear Jess," murmured Queenie, "for I was feeling my grief so keenly that I thought my poor heart would surely break."

Jess crossed the room and stood in front of the picture of the late departed Mr. Brown, studying the wrinkled face it represented; the bald head, smooth as a billiard ball; the shrunken mouth and chin, and almost sightless eyes, and her thoughts broke into words, and quite before she considered what she was about to utter, she said, impulsively:

"How could you ever have loved so old and withered a human being, Queenie, let alone marrying him; and you so young and fair? I thought when I first saw the picture hanging here that he was your great-grandfather."

A flush stained Queenie's face from neck to brow for a moment, and her heart gave a great strangling throb. It was fully a moment ere she replied, then she said slowly:

"I will not tell you an untruth, Jess; it was not because I loved my husband that I married him. He saved my father from financial ruin, and I married him because he demanded my hand as the price of it. There was no question of love between us."

"I should never marry a man I could not love, no matter what the consequences of my refusing were," declared Jess.

"You have never been placed in such a position; you can hardly tell what you would do or would not do, dear," murmured Queenie, thinking that that remark was a fine opening for Jess to make a confidant of her in regard to the lover who was to have been forced upon her by the Dinsmore will.

In this surmise she was quite correct. Jess wheeled about from the picture, and flinging herself on a hassock at Queenie's feet, she buried her young face in her false friend's lap, exclaiming:

"Ah! but I have had a most thrilling experience, I assure you, Queenie. May I tell you all about it?"

"If you like, dear," was the answer, and she lowered her white lids over her eyes that Jess might not see the hard, steely glitter in them should she chance to look up suddenly.

"I did throw over a lover and a fortune into the bargain, because I could not like, let alone love the man whom I would have had to wed to gain the money, though the loss of it made me—a pauper!"

"What a romance!" cried Queenie. "Do tell me all about it, dear—who would have ever dreamed that you, who look so much like a child, had ever contemplated marriage, let alone decided so important a step."

"It is romantic," said Jess, slowly. "I doubt if any other young girl in the whole wide world ever had such a strange experience as mine has been."

And, glad enough to find so attentive and sympathetic a listener, Jess, with the confiding innocence of youth, proceeded to narrate to her new-found friend the story of her life; how, from the first recollection she had had, she had been a part and parcel of Blackheath Hall, yet had lived a life wholly apart from its inmates.

If Queenie had not conceived, down deep in her heart, a deadly hatred of this girl whom fate had decreed for John Dinsmore, the man she loved, she would have been moved to pity by Jess' recital.

"I have no recollection of a home, or a mother," continued Jess, resting her dimpled chin on her pink palms, her elbows on Queenie's knee, and her large, dark, soulful eyes gazing up into the wine-dusk eyes looking down into her own. "The knowledge of that was my earliest grief. I seemed to be like Topsy—'just growed there, nobody knowed how,' as that waif and stray expressed it.

"I was there on sufferance, as it were. I belonged to nobody, and nobody belonged to, or took the least interest, in me. I roamed where I would, as neglected a specimen of humanity as one would wish to see. I had no friends save the birds in the deep woods, and the wild animals I had trained and made comrades of.

"My one passion was reading. I scarcely know how I ever managed to learn how to decipher the stories that I was so fond of. One of the old colored mammies about the plantation had learned to read and write, and taught me as much as she knew—my education ended there. Once a year the cast-off clothing of the housekeeper was made over for me—that was all the interest ever exhibited in me. Nobody ever took the trouble to ask if I were sick or well, satisfied with my strange lot, or lonely, if I had a heart within my bosom that longed for companionship and sympathy, or how I even existed.

"No one knew how I would throw myself down in the long grass in the depths of the silent wood, for the birds never told my secret, and cry out to the pitying skies to send me from heaven just one wish, grant me one prayer, and that was for some human being to love, some one who would love me in return; for some one to hold my hands, and ask me in a kind and gentle voice if I were weary, and if I were, to pillow my head on a kindly breast and soothe me while I wept out my woe there. The young girls I read of had happy homes, tender mothers, kind fathers, sisters dear, brothers, and—lovers; why, then, was this height of human happiness beyond my reach? I longed for companionship, and girl friends."

"Had you no thought of—a lover?" queried Queenie, ever so softly.

"Yes," whispered Jess, almost shyly. "I had my ideal of the kind of a man who would captivate my heart; a girl who reads much has her ideal, you know. I often said to myself: 'If there is a Prince Charming in this world for me, he must be tall, and grave, and handsome, with blue eyes, and chestnut hair waving above a broad, white brow, and——' Why, what in the world is the matter, Queenie? You look as though you were dying."

CHAPTER XXXV.
HIS STORY.

The girl sprang to her feet, looking at Queenie in great affright.

"You were about to faint. You are ill?" cried Jess, in alarm.

"It was only a momentary faintness, dear," murmured Queenie.

But the truth of the matter was that Jess had described John Dinsmore so accurately, just as she had seen him when she had parted from him on the golden sands at Newport, that never-to-be-forgotten evening when she had flung from her the heart and the love in it that she would have afterward given worlds, had she possessed them, to recall.

She wondered if Jess could by any possible means have ever met the real John Dinsmore; but in the next breath she told herself that it could not have been; the girl was just conjuring up this mental photograph of the hero who could win her heart purely from her imagination, never dreaming that there had been a man in existence who had fitted that description exactly.

Thus, assured that Queenie's indisposition was but momentary, and that she really cared for her to go on with her narrative, Jess continued:

"My life might have gone on for long years more in just that dreary fashion, had not a singular event happened. A lawyer—your parent's friend, Lawyer Abbot, suddenly appeared at the plantation one day, and asked for the housekeeper of Blackheath Hall. I overheard the conversation between them, and his mission there, which was to tell her that the master of Blackheath Hall had just died abroad, and to inform her as to the conditions of his will, which was, that the girl Jess (meaning me) who was then on the plantation, and who had made it her home there, for many years, was to receive half of his entire fortune, providing she married, within the ensuing twelve months, his heir, and nephew, John Dinsmore.

"To cut a long story short, Queenie, this John Dinsmore soon came down to Blackheath Hall for the purpose of 'looking me over,' as he wrote the housekeeper that he would do. From the first moment we met, I took a most terrible dislike to him, although he was the greatest dandy imaginable.

"There was something about him which seemed to warn me not to trust him, and to fly from him—I cannot explain what it was. As was expected of him, he asked me to marry him; and by dint of persuasion from the housekeeper, I, at length, reluctantly consented, although every throb of my heart seemed to speak and tell me that if I married him I would rue it—rue it—rue it! I felt so terribly about it that it seemed to me I must get away amidst new scenes to get up courage to take the fatal plunge into the turbulent sea of matrimony.

"For a wonder, Mrs. Bryson, the old housekeeper of Blackheath Hall, did not oppose my strange notion, as she termed it; instead, she consulted with Lawyer Abbot, and the result was that they concluded to send me to visit you in New York."

At this point in her narrative Jess stopped confusedly, turning from red to white, her heart throbbing so tumultuously that Queenie could not help hearing it.

"Go on, my dear," she said, sweetly. "You cannot tell how interested I am; it is better than reading a love story from a novel."

"You would think so if you knew what happened next," thought Jess, but she dared not put that thought into speech. She said, instead:

"As you may have heard, my visit to you was intercepted on the very morning I was to take the train in company with Lawyer Abbot, for New York, by a telegram informing us that you were away, and would not return for a few weeks.

"My disappointment was so keen that, to assuage my great grief and dry my tears, Lawyer Abbot proposed that I should go somewhere, now that I was all ready to go, and proposed sending me to a relative of his, on a farm.

"I hailed this eagerly—anything to get away from Blackheath Hall. Well, I was kindly received by the good farmer, and his wife and daughter, and there I spent the happiest days that I had ever known. I was loath to tear myself away from the place even when I received a letter from Lawyer Abbot, stating that you were now at home, in New York, and that he was coming to conduct me there at once. Ah, Queenie, when I left that farm, I left all the happiness that I had ever known behind me. I wrote to the man to whom I had betrothed myself that I wished to break the engagement; that it was impossible to ever marry him now, for I found that we were as wide apart as though we had never met, and that I had never had any love for him, and that he was to consider the matter irrevocably settled.

"That is all my story, Queenie," she concluded, and the girl that bent over her never dreamed that the most thrilling chapter in little Jess' life history had been omitted from the tale. No one in the wide world would have guessed that little Jess had left—a husband on that lonely farm whom she had learned to love with all the strength of her young heart.

She had obeyed his instructions to the letter, not to let any human being know of her marriage until he gave her permission to do so.

"So there little Jess' romance seems to end," murmured Queenie. The girl nodded and hid her face, painful with rosy blushes, upon the shoulder of her false friend.

"Now I am going to tell you a little romance which will no doubt surprise you very much, Jess," declared Queenie, "and I will begin with the statement that I know John—John Dinsmore, the lover whom you have so foolishly discarded—very well."

"You know him?" gasped Jess, opening her great, dark, velvety eyes very wide and wonderingly.

Queenie nodded assent, adding: "I knew all about his courtship, for he made a confidant of me, writing me all about it, as we were such very old friends."

Before Jess could speak she went on hurriedly: "You are making the greatest mistake of your life, dear, in attempting to break your engagement with him, for he loves you so passionately that he can never live without you—he said that in his letter to me—that if anything happened to part you, that he would shoot himself, and put an end to his sorrow and despair."

"I am greatly surprised that you know him, and like him so well," cried Jess, impatiently.

"I like him so well I have asked him to visit us at my country seat to which I am going next week, bearing you with me. He was more than surprised to hear that you were coming to New York to visit me, of all people, and accepted the invitation by return mail.

"I suppose I am telling tales out of school when I also tell you that the dear fellow was well-nigh heartbroken because you had bound those whom you left behind you with a solemn promise not to divulge to him your destination. Strange how he found it out, wasn't it?"

Jess had sprung to her feet trembling like a leaf. "I cannot see him, indeed I cannot, Queenie," she cried in an agitated voice, "and I assure you, oh, so earnestly, that the marriage can never, never take place!"

"Fie, fie!" cried Queenie, "I will not listen to anything like that. You have taken an aversion to him, but that is certain to wear off when you know him better. You know, dear, that there is a whole world of truth in the old saying that 'the course of true love never does run smooth.' You are sure to have your little differences at first—love tiffs, as some call them—but it will all come out all right in the end. I am sure you are too sensible a girl, Jess, to want to back out now, after your *fiancé* has made every arrangement for his wedding with you. It would be the height of impropriety, dear."

"Will you believe me that I can never, never marry him now, Queenie?" whispered the girl, earnestly. "Do not let him come. I do not want to see him. I will not see him."

"Do not be so willful, Jess," exclaimed her friend, gathering her arched brows into a decided frown. "I have asked him to come, and I cannot recall the invitation without hurting my old friend and playfellow to the very depths of his honest, loving heart. I could not be so cruel when you have no just cause to offer as to why you do not wish to meet him again, save a prejudice which should not exist. Surely you cannot find so much fault with him for loving you so devotedly; that is a trait to recommend, not one to blame. As you go through life, Jess, you will learn one of its greatest lessons, and that is, never to despise an honest, true love, for indeed there is little enough of it to be met with."

"All that you say is true from your point of view, Queenie," returned the girl, in a distressed, husky voice, "but I repeat, I can never marry him now—never!"

"You would rather see a splendid fortune flung to the winds!" said Queenie, impatiently, and with something very like a covert sneer in her voice. "Remember, if you throw him over, you make not only a beggar of yourself for life, but a beggar of him, and that you have no right to do.

"He has always looked upon himself as his uncle's heir, and you, by your action, would change that, willfully and pitilessly. You would wreck him for life, not only in his heart's affection, but in his worldly prospects. And last, but by no means least, you would defy the will and the wish of the man who gave you shelter at Blackheath Hall all these years, instead of having you sent to some foundling's home. Surely your gratitude to him deserves compliance with his wise decree."

Queenie had used all her weapons of argument, and she stopped short, looking at Jess to see the effect of her words upon her. Jess was as pale as a snowdrop, and great tears trembled on her long, curling lashes.

"It can never be," she reiterated in a trembling voice. "I beg of you to say no more about it, Queenie. Only let me have my way in not seeing him, if you would be kind to me."

"I refuse to wound the man who loves you so dearly by giving him such a cruel message," replied Queenie, coldly and harshly.

CHAPTER XXXVI.
THE WEB OF FATE.

"If fate should let us meet, what should we do?

Would each our hearts their olden love renew?

Or would the clouds that o'er us loom

Remain unmoved, with all their gloom,

If we should meet—if we should meet?"

At this juncture of our story, it is most imperative that we should return to John Dinsmore, whom we left standing, cold and taciturn, on the porch, waving his child-bride good-by as she went from him in company with Lawyer Abbot.

He did not go into the house, as Lucy Caldwell ardently hoped he would do, but instead started off at a swinging pace toward the orchard.

He wanted to be alone, where he could have the luxury of undisturbed thoughts, and where he could get away from the presence of Lucy Caldwell and her love-lit glances and blushing face, all of which were most annoying to him, as they disclosed the fact that the girl was learning to care for him, a fact which troubled him, as he had given her no encouragement to become infatuated with himself; on the contrary, had taken every possible means on every occasion to discourage it, and dissipate any hopes which she might be indulging in.

His long strides soon brought him to the orchard. Walking to the farthest end of it, he flung himself down under one of the gnarled old trees, and gave himself up to grim reflections. Had he done a wise action in marrying the girl from whom he had just parted in such cold, angry pride?

Over and over again he asked himself that question, and tried to answer it satisfactorily to his troubled mind.

He acknowledged most freely to himself that he did not love her, and never could; that he had wedded her through a principle of honor which urged him to give the girl his name that she might inherit the wealth that his uncle had intended for her, and that he had lost every atom of respect that he had entertained toward her at the acknowledgment from her lips that she had been betrothed to another, and had thrown that other lover over—to marry himself.

"Had she confessed that before the marriage took place, I would have cut my right hand off sooner than have married her," he muttered, grimly.

The lesson he had received at the hands of the one girl he had loved, in this regard, had taught him to despise a jilt as he would the deadliest of cobras.

Before he had met Queenie Trevalyn, he had believed in women much as he believed in angels—that they were incapable of deceit, or treachery, and could do nothing wrong.

And now his experience with Jess strengthened the conviction that his theory concerning the fair sex had been radically wrong. Now he believed from the very depths of his heart that they were incapable of feeling a true affection, and were ready to jilt one lover, at the very altar if need be, if they found some one else more eligible—that they were mercenary to the heart's core.

He did his best to dislike little Jess, but, do what he would, his heart seemed to warm to her in spite of himself.

"She is young, and has had no one to tell her, no one to warn her, of the sin of trifling with an honest man's affections, and breaking his heart," he ruminated, passing his hand thoughtfully over his brow.

"There is only one thing to be done, and that is, to set her free as soon as it can be lawfully accomplished, that she may wed the man who held her plighted troth at the time she came here three weeks ago."

All that would take time. He felt sorry for the poor fellow, whoever he might be, because of that. He would see that Jess was free from the bonds that bound her to himself at the earliest possible day; that was the best he could do for his unknown rival.

John Dinsmore thus settled the matter in his own mind, and tried to feel duly happy over the result of his decision, but somehow he felt a vague regret, he could not have told why.

He had promised Jess that she should hear from him in the course of a week, or two weeks at the most. Now, after much reflection, he concluded to go to New York, and see her there, and tell her plainly the course he proposed to adopt.

She could certainly find no fault with his action when he revealed to her the astonishing information that he, whom she had wedded as plain Mr. Moore, was in reality John Dinsmore, co-heir with her to all the Dinsmore millions.

Her marriage with him had entitled her to her half of the vast estate, and he was willing to sign over the balance of it. He cared nothing for wealth, although it had poured in upon him from the sale of his famous book.

True, he had not communicated with his publishers since the day he left Newport to go South, and had met with the accident which laid him up at Caldwell farm; but for all that, he knew the money had accumulated, and was ready for him whenever he chose to call for it.

And once again he told himself bitterly that fame and fortune had come to him too late.

Had he possessed it in that bitter hour upon the Newport sands, when he laid his heart at the dainty feet of the proud Queenie Trevalyn, she might have accepted, and married him, and his blood ran riot for an instant through his veins at the bare thought of it. But he put her away from his thoughts most resolutely, telling himself that he must not allow his mind to dwell upon her for an instant, for she was now, of course, the bride of Raymond Challoner.

He had no thought that she would be in New York; indeed, he fancied that she would be spending her honeymoon abroad.

"Why should I yearn for you still, my queen?" he murmured hoarsely, stretching out his arms toward empty space with a great, tearless sob that he strangled fiercely in his throat rather than give it utterance. "God only knows; and I add: God help me!"

He had gained his self-possession, and was his usual calm self when at length he retraced his steps to the farmhouse. He went directly to the low-roofed kitchen, where he was sure of finding Lucy and her mother preparing the midday meal.

The girl looked up brightly and shyly as the long shadow that fell across the floor told her that he was near. Indeed, some subtle instinct would have told her of his near presence, even had there been no sunshine, no light, and the darkness of Erebus had shrouded the earth.

"I am making something you like, Mr. Moore," she said, holding up a great dish of golden-brown crullers before him. "And mother has made an apple pie, and you are also to have Johnny-cake and honey."

"You and your mother are very thoughtful, and very considerate of my likes—regarding the good things you are preparing—but I fear I will not be able to enjoy them for the reason that I am come to tell you that I am going to take the next train that leaves for New York, which will leave me scarcely more than time to get from here down to the depot in the village."

Glancing carelessly enough from the mother to the daughter, he saw the laughter die from Lucy's face, and the light from her eyes. She laid down the dish of golden-brown crullers on the table, still looking at him piteously, it almost seemed to him. He did not understand the expression of her face. It was as one who awaits a sentence of life or death.

"What is the matter, Lucy; are you ill?" cried Mrs. Caldwell in alarm, seeing how white her daughter's face had grown, but before she could reach her side, Lucy had fallen in a dead swoon to the kitchen floor.

For an instant the young man standing in the doorway was dazed with amazement, but in the next he sprang forward to raise the girl.

"Do not go near my Lucy! Do not touch her!" cried the unhappy mother, distractedly. "This is all your work, sir—all your work!"

John Dinsmore drew back in much distress. Never by word, act or deed, had he given the girl encouragement to bestow her affections upon himself. He was touched deeply. He remembered his own hopeless love for Queenie Trevalyn, and could sympathize from the very bottom of his heart with any human being who loved in vain.

His eyes filled with tears; he who had been drawn on by dimpling smiles and coquettish glances until his whole heart had been drawn from his bosom, only to be ruthlessly cast aside when he acknowledged, while he pleaded for the heart of the girl he loved, that he had not wealth to offer her.

"You will at least allow me to carry her into the other room and place her on the settee for you?" he asked, gently, noting that the slender form, light as the burden was, would certainly be beyond the strength of the mother's arms.

Again she waved him away.

"Living or dead, you shall not lay a finger on my child," she said, bitterly, adding, with a burst of grief: "I am sorry, sorry that you ever darkened the farmhouse door; but I never dreamed you would lure my girl's heart from her, and then coolly inform us that you were going away."

He made the irate mother no answer; indeed, of what use would it be to defend his actions? Nothing that he would say would mend matters. He must go at once. It was very sad; very pitiful; but all the same he must go.

He said good-by to Mrs. Caldwell, and turned sorrowfully away, when she turned stolidly in another direction, refusing to take any notice of him. It was better that he should go ere Lucy returned to consciousness.

An hour later he was speeding on toward New York, leaving the farm and its occupants far behind him, to see them never again. He meant to see Jess at once, and have the parting over with her without unnecessary delay, and after that—well, it mattered little enough to him what became of him.

CHAPTER XXXVII.
A GREAT SURPRISE.

"Like some lone bird, without a mate,

My weary heart is desolate;

I look around, and cannot trace

One friendly smile, one welcoming face;

And e'en in crowds, I'm still alone,

Because—I cannot love—but one."

John Dinsmore experienced quite a change of climate when he reached New York from that which he had just left behind him in the sunny South. A violent snowstorm was raging, and it was bitter cold.

Busy as the streets of the great metropolis always were there seemed to be more than the usual throng surging to and fro, and then John Dinsmore remembered what he came very near forgetting, that it was Thanksgiving Eve.

How happy were the faces of all who passed him, as though there were no such things in the world as sorrow, desolation, and heartaches. He smiled a bitter smile, telling himself that he had little enough to give thanks for, in the way of happiness. He hesitated a moment on the corner of Broadway, wondering if it were best to go to a hotel, or to the room of his old friends, Jerry Gaines and Ballou.

"I do not feel equal to seeing and talking with even the Trinity to-night," he muttered. "They would want an account of all that transpired since I saw them last, and I am not equal to it just yet. How surprised they will be, and pleased to know that I escaped the wreck under which the papers had me buried, and still more pleased to learn that I married the girl that Uncle Dinsmore selected for me; but they will do their best to argue me out of my firm resolve to divorce the girl. But nothing that they can say or do will shake me in my purpose. I will set the girl free in the shortest possible time, that she may wed the man to whom she was engaged when I came upon the scene and married her, never dreaming she was in love with another, and that the reports of my wealth had tempted her to prove false to him. I know but too well what the poor fellow must have suffered."

Finding himself in the vicinity of the home of the Trevalyns, that is, the address Queenie had given him when they were at Newport, he concluded that there was no time like the present to discharge the unpleasant task. He therefore turned his steps in that direction at once.

A brisk walk of scarcely three minutes brought him to the number he was in search of, No. — Fifth Avenue.

The obsequious servant who answered the summons at the door bowed low to the tall, distinguished-looking gentleman whom he found there.

It was then that John Dinsmore made the fatal mistake of his life. He called for Miss Trevalyn, instead of Mrs. Trevalyn.

"Evidently the gentleman doesn't know that our young lady is married," thought the servant, and he answered with a smile:

"The lady has changed her address, sir. You will find her at No. — Fifty-second Street."

The man would have given him additional information in the next breath, but at that instant John Dinsmore turned swiftly, and with a courteous bow descended the steps.

"Probably an old beau of our young lady's," thought the servant, gazing thoughtfully after the tall, commanding form. "I should say also that he is not a New Yorker, or he would have known all about Miss Queenie's marriage to the old millionaire, who turned out on his death to be almost a pauper. That ought to be a warning to all young girls who would marry old men for their supposed wealth."

Meanwhile John Dinsmore was making his way with long, swinging strides to the address given, which he knew could be scarcely more than a couple of blocks or so away.

He could not see much of the exterior of the house, for, although scarcely five in the afternoon, it was already dark.

Once again he asked for Miss Trevalyn, instead of inquiring for Mrs. Trevalyn, his thoughts were, alas! so full of the girl he had loved so madly, so deeply—and lost so cruelly.

The servant stared for an instant blankly, but in the next he remembered that that was the name of his young mistress before her marriage, and with a low bow invited the gentleman to enter, throwing open the drawing-room door for him.

John Dinsmore knew that she would recognize the name his card bore at the first glance.

After much consideration he had thought it best to acquaint Mrs. Trevalyn with the true state of affairs before seeing Jess—she being the girl's hostess, and the one whom she would seek advice from—after he had had his interview with her.

He seated himself in the nearest chair and awaited her coming.

He had scarcely seated himself ere his eyes fell upon a picture of Queenie, a life-size painting, hanging upon the opposite wall. His heart was in his eyes as he gazed.

The old sorrow that he thought he had strangled to death by main force of indomitable will seemed to have sprung instantly into new life. The old sorrow was crying aloud. What vain, wild passion; what deep regret, there was still in his heart! He tried to withdraw his eyes from the fatal beauty of that pictured face, which was, ah! so lifelike, but it seemed impossible for him to do so.

A mad desire which he could not repress seemed to draw him toward it, and mechanically he allowed himself to cross the room and stand before it. And he could hardly keep from falling on his knees before it, touching the little hands that seemed so lifelike; and, God help him, to restrain himself from kissing passionately the beautiful lips that he had hungered so to caress from the first moment that he and Queenie Trevalyn had met.

The temptation mastered him. "Just once; no one in the wide world will ever know," he muttered, hoarsely, "and what can it matter; it can do no harm to the soulless canvas," and, raising his feverish face, he kissed passionately the lips of the picture, not once, but many times. Then he turned away with his heart on fire, and flung himself down into the depths of the great armchair again, burying his face in his trembling hands.

"A love such as mine can never die," he groaned, and he wondered how he should ever be able to meet Queenie face to face, and live through it, if it was such an effort to gain anything like composure when he came suddenly upon her picture in her mother's drawing-room.

He thought of the few happy weeks in which he had sunned himself in the presence of his idol without a care or a thought of how it was to end, although he should have realized the great gulf more clearly that lay between them at that time—she being rich, and he poor as it is the fate of most authors to be.

And lines of his own composing, lines which appeared in his book, came to his mind:

"'Tis no easy matter, as most authors know,

To coin pleasant thoughts from the mind's full mint;

And then, after all, he must ask no pay,

But be satisfied merely to see it in print."

He wished with all his heart that the girl he loved so well had married some man more worthy of her than Raymond Challoner, the libertine and gambler.

He turned the chair around. He had always imagined himself a brave man; now he knew that he had not the control over himself that he had imagined.

"Fool that I am, I would give ten years of my life to live those three blissful weeks at Newport over again," he muttered sadly and hoarsely. "I feel so unnerved that I almost wish that I could find some excuse for leaving this house without seeing Jess; but that cannot be, I suppose, for that must be Mrs. Trevalyn's step which I hear in the corridor."

With a heavy sigh he crushed back the unhappiness that had swept over his heart, and summoned by a mighty effort the calm expression which had become habitual to his face, and the coldness to his eyes.

It was not an instant too soon, however, for at that moment the portières before the door were swept back by a white, jeweled hand.

CHAPTER XXXVIII.
AT HIS FEET.

"Can I behold thee, and not speak my love?
E'en now, thus sadly, as thou standst before me,
Thus desolate, dejected, and forlorn,
Thy softness steals upon my yielding senses,
Until my soul is faint from grief and pain."

—ROWE.

When the servant took Mr. John Dinsmore's card to his mistress, he found that lady sitting moodily alone before the sea-coal fire which burned brightly in the grate.

"A caller, on such a day, and at such an hour," she muttered quite below her breath, as she took the card from the silver tray.

One glance at the superscription which the bit of pasteboard bore, and she fell back in her chair, almost fainting from sheer terror.

The question of the servant, who was regarding her critically, aroused her to her senses. He was saying:

"Are you out, or in, my lady?"

The color rushed back to her face, and the lifeblood to her heart.

"What a fool I am," she told herself, a frown gathering upon her face. "It is Raymond Challoner, of course, as he is now masquerading under the name. Of course I might have expected this, but, nevertheless, it shocked me.' But aloud she said:

"I will see the gentleman."

When the man had departed she arose slowly to her feet, ruminating: "As he is impatient, I will not keep him waiting; but he will not relish the message which I bring him from the obstinate little Jess, that she positively refuses to see him, despite all my pleading with her. Raymond Challoner is not quite the lady-killer that he imagines himself to be."

Despite the fact that she prided herself upon her beauty, and always looking her best on every occasion, she did not even glance at the long French mirror as she swept past it.

She walked slowly down the stairway and along the broad corridor, pausing before the door of the drawing-room, which was ajar.

She swept back the heavy velvet portières with her white, jeweled hand, pausing on the threshold for an instant.

One glance at the tall, commanding figure of the gentleman who had arisen hastily from his seat, and a low cry, half terror, and half joy, broke from her lips.

Great God! Was her brain turning? Was she mad? Or did her eyes deceive her? Instead of the slender, dapper form of Raymond Challoner, she beheld the tall form that she had mourned over as having long since mingled with the dust. John Dinsmore it was, standing, alive and well, before her, in the flesh, surely—not a ghost, a phantom, a delusion.

John Dinsmore reeled back as though some one had struck him a heavy blow, and one word fell from his white lips—"Queenie!"

With an impetuous cry she sprang forward, holding out both of her hands, sobbing:

"John, have you found it in your heart to forgive me? Surely it must be so, or—or you would not be here, you, whom I mourned as dead, believing the newspaper accounts which described the terrible wreck of the train on which you were a passenger."

She advanced to his side and touched his hand, murmuring in the old, sweet voice which had haunted him both night and day for long, weary months:

"John, speak to me. Surely you are here to tell me that you forgive me." And before he could divine her intention, she had flung herself on her knees before him.

For half an instant he almost believed that he was the victim of a mad, wild nightmare. The woman he loved so madly, the woman who so cruelly deceived him, the woman whom he had tried in his heart to scorn, to hate, kneeling before him, asking his forgiveness! He almost fancied that he did not hear, or see aright.

His first impulse is to gather her in his arms and rain all the passionate love that has been locked up in his almost broken heart upon her, but, just in the nick of time, he remembers that they are no longer lovers—that a barrier is between them. His face flushes, and his arms, that had stretched forth involuntarily to clasp her, fall heavily to his side.

His teeth shut tightly together. He is angry with himself for showing his weakness.

A hot flush mantles his brow. He folds his arms tightly over his chest and looks down at the beautiful girl kneeling before him, wondering vaguely where Raymond Challoner, her husband, is.

At that moment he catches sight of her dress, which he had not noticed before—black crape, the emblem of widowhood—and his heart gives a spasmodic twitch.

"Rise, madam," he says, hoarsely. "Why should you kneel to me?"

"Here I shall remain until you tell me that you forgive me," she answers, beginning to weep bitterly, and going on through her sobs: "Listen to me, John. I will die if I cannot speak and tell you all. Do not look at me with those eyes of scorn. If you knew all you would pity instead of scorn me. They made me marry him—my parents, I mean—because of his wealth."

John Dinsmore's lips twitch. He essays to speak, but the words he would utter refuse to come from his lips. He is like one suddenly stricken dumb.

"John," she goes on in that same sweet, piteous voice that reaches down through his heart to the farthest depths of his soul, "you loved me with all the strength of your nature once, but that you had the power to cast me so utterly from your thoughts, from the moment you discovered my unworthiness, I never for a moment doubted. Oh, Heaven! it was the thought that you had utterly forgotten me, while I, bound to another, loved you more than ever, that caused me so much misery. Bound to a man I hated, and loving you, alas, too late! with all the strength of my heart! Think of it, John Dinsmore, and if a heart still beats in your bosom, you cannot withhold your forgiveness. When my husband died I—I felt as though I had begun a new life, with the fetters thus removed from me."

"Your husband is dead, Queenie?" gasps John Dinsmore.

She flushes deeply, and answers with deep agitation:

"You might have known my—my—husband was dead, or I would never have made the confession to you which I have just now made."

"I had not heard of Raymond Challoner's death," he answered, trying in vain to steady his voice.

"You are in grave error if you think I married Raymond Challoner," answered Queenie, quietly. "I—I married his uncle—an old man of three score years and ten—at the urgent request of my parents, who would give me no peace day or night. I—I married him to save my father from financial ruin, believing him to be a millionaire. When he died, a few days ago, I learned that he was on the verge of bankruptcy. It is a just punishment to me—a just punishment. But I have gained more than the wealth of the world could purchase—my freedom. Oh, my love of other days, do you understand that I am free now to be wooed and wed? Surely you still care for me, John Dinsmore. You are only trying my love not to tell me this and set my heart at rest."

As she utters the words she clasps both of her hands tightly about his arm and looks up into his face, which has grown strangely pale.

"Hush! hush!" he whispers, tearing himself free from the light hold of those lovely white hands. "I cannot suffer you to utter another word, madam. I will forget what you have said, for I ought not to have listened to it. It is my turn to ask you now to listen, and what I would say is this: There is an impassable barrier between you and me, Queenie."

"A barrier!" she gasped. "Surely there is nothing in this world that can separate us two a second time."

"It is you who are mistaken," he said in a very unsteady voice. "There is an impassable barrier between us, I repeat, in the shape of—my wife. I am now married."

Queenie's eyes almost start from their sockets, the shock and the horror of his words affect her so terribly. He is married! She wonders that those words did not strike her dead. She stands for a moment looking at him like one bidding a last farewell to life, hope, and the world.

"You are married?" she gasps again. "Oh, my God! my punishment is more than I can bear!" and she sinks on the floor at his feet with a piteous moan, burying her face in her hands and weeping as women seldom weep in a lifetime.

It was not in human nature to see the woman whom he still loved so madly lying there weeping for love of him, without his heart being stirred to its utmost, and John Dinsmore was human enough to feel the warm blood dashing madly through his veins and his heart, beating violently with all the old love reawakening.

He turns and walks excitedly up and down the length of the long drawing-room, his arms folded tightly over his heaving chest.

"Then, if you did not come here to see me, and did not know I was now a widow, why are you here?" cried Queenie, at length, standing before him with a death-white face, a strange suspicion dawning in her breast.

"I am here to see my wife, who is beneath this roof," he answered, huskily. "My wife is little Jess, but as she was bound to secrecy concerning it, I can see that she has not told you."

CHAPTER XXXIX.
A TEST OF LOVE.

"Let no one say that there is need

Of time for love to grow.

Ah, no, the love that kills, indeed,

Dispatches at a blow."

"Jess is your wife!" repeated Queenie, in a voice so hollow and deathlike that it might have come from the tomb.

John Dinsmore bowed his head in assent, and as he did so, his companion detected a shadow of bitterness in his eyes, and a whitening of his face.

"What to you seems so strange can be explained in a very few words, if you care to hear that explanation," he said, slowly.

Queenie bowed her head eagerly. Like him, words seemed to fail her. She sank into the nearest chair, pointing to one opposite her, but he declined the proffered seat, remarking that, "with her permission, he would prefer standing."

For some moments he stood leaning against the marble mantel ere he could control himself sufficiently to tell his story.

Then he began almost abruptly:

"When you knew me at Newport, I told you that I was simply John Dinsmore, Author, Bohemian. I did not add that I was the last of kin of a wealthy uncle who had always told me that I should be his heir, for I despise men who live in expectancy of falling into dead men's shoes, and getting the good out of fortunes which other men have toiled for. I depended upon myself and my own achievements for getting along in the world.

"Well, to make a long narrative brief, scarcely two days had passed after you and I had parted that night on the sands, ere the intelligence was brought to me that my uncle had just died abroad, and that I was his heir. But there was a condition to it, however, in the shape of a codicil, declaring, that in order to inherit this fortune, I was to become the husband of a maiden whom he had selected for me, to wit: a young girl named Jess, who lived on his plantation, Blackheath Hall, down in Louisiana. The will also added, should I fail to do this, the girl, Jess, like myself, would be disinherited."

"And you, whom I thought the soul of honor, beyond the power of being bought by sordid gold, wedded this girl for the Dinsmore millions!" cried Queenie, bitterly.

He looked at her reproachfully, and his firm lips quivered ever so slightly. The accusation was galling to him.

"No," he said, sharply; "not so. Fate, if there indeed be such a condition, forged link after link of the chain, and I was"—he was going to add—"drawn into it," but he bit his lip savagely, keeping back the words. But Queenie's quick wit supplied just what he withheld.

After a brief pause he continued:

"I was on my way down South to tell the girl that the wedding could never take place, when that railway accident occurred which held me prisoner, as it were, at the farm of the Caldwells for many weeks. Not wishing the information to get into the newspapers, I gave those good people the name of Moore. Imagine my amazement when fate, as I call it again, brought the girl, Jess, to that very farmhouse."

"And you fell in love with her and married her out of hand?" broke in Queenie again, trembling with agitation.

"Again you are in error," he retorted, with a deep-drawn sigh. "Looking on the girl, I pitied her, for the reason that my failure to fall in love with and wed her would cost her one-half of the Dinsmore fortune, just as it would cost me the other half. My action would make her homeless, penniless. The more I brooded over that the more I pitied her, and one day a path out of the dilemma seemed to suddenly open out before me. Something seemed to say to me: 'Why not marry the girl, and thus secure the fortune to her which should be hers?'

"At first my heart rebelled at the notion, but the more I turned it over in my mind, the more it seemed my solemn duty to do so. I put the plan into execution at once, lest my resolution should fail me, and still calling myself Mr. Moore, I asked Jess to marry me, and her answer was 'yes.'

"I meant to tell her who I was after the marriage ceremony, and add 'now that I have secured to you the fortune that is yours through my uncle's desire, I leave it with you to fulfill your marriage vows, or bid me depart,' and to also tell her that I intended to make over my share of the Dinsmore millions to her.

"Before we reached the farmhouse again, after the marriage, which I need scarcely add was a secret one, I exacted a promise from the lips of Jess that she would not reveal what had taken place until I gave her permission to do so.

"She left with Lawyer Abbot for New York within the hour, I promising to write her within a fortnight after she had arrived here. Instead, I concluded that it was best to come in person, see her, reveal my identity, and leave my future and my fate in her hands. That is my story. I did not know I should find you in this house, Queenie, Heaven knows I did not. I was informed that your parents now resided here. I thought you were wedded to Raymond Challoner, and away in Europe on your bridal trip."

"Instead you find me a widow," murmured Queenie, looking up into his face with eager shining eyes and her breath coming and going swiftly with every palpitation of her heaving bosom.

"Too late, too late!" he muttered in a low voice almost under his breath, but not so low but what his companion caught the words.

"No, no!" she cried, vehemently, "it is not too late, John Dinsmore. This girl is nothing to you, less than nothing since you do not love her. Give her half of the Dinsmore millions, since it must be hers, and divorce her, as you had planned, and then—then——"

"Good Heavens! What are you saying, Mrs.——"

John Dinsmore stops short, and Queenie knows that he cannot call her by that name—that it sticks in his throat.

Queenie has the grace to blush, and then she covers her crimson face with her hands! Surely he must understand what she has left unsaid—and he does, and gives a great start of surprise. Hitherto Queenie has occupied a pedestal high as an angel in his heart. Is this the girl whom he has worshiped so madly, this girl who is coolly counseling him to divorce the girl who is his wedded wife? All in an instant of time the mad, passionate love he has had for Queenie dies a tragic death.

It was his intention to divorce little Jess, but now that it is proposed to him by another—oh, strange perversity of human nature!—he seems to recoil from it, he knows not why.

Queenie's quick intuition tells her that she has lost ground with John Dinsmore in making such a cool, calculating, unwomanly proposition, but before she can utter another word to mend matters, in his opinion, she hears the voice of Jess calling to her from the corridor outside:

"Queenie, Queenie, where in the world can you be? I have looked everywhere for you."

Another instant and she will reach the drawing-room.

Queenie darts to the door to intercept her. She must not enter that room in which her husband is standing.

But as Queenie flies from the apartment by one door, Jess enters it by another.

For one instant she stands fairly transfixed, as her gaze encounters the tall, commanding figure standing there.

In the next she has reached his side with such a cry of intense delight that in spite of himself it has gone straight to his heart.

"My husband! oh, my husband!" And almost before he is aware of what is happening, two soft, white arms have been flung about his neck and a pair of rosy lips is pressed to his, and a world of ardent kisses is showered upon him, in a way which fairly takes his breath away.

"How delightful of you to come and take me by surprise like this," Jess was crying, breathlessly and delightedly. "I was thinking of you just this minute, and that I would give anything in this world to see you."

He feels that he must make some retort, but he is at a loss for words, and he can only articulate:

"Are you so very glad to see me again, little girl? Why is it—why?"

"Why?" echoes Jess, with a melodious little laugh like liquid sunshine. "Why, because I love you so. I have loved you more and more every hour and day that we have been apart, until I felt that I could not stand being away from you much longer, and now you are here, and I am so glad—so glad!"

"Little Jess," exclaims John Dinsmore, holding the girl off at arm's length, "child, do you know what you are saying?" And his face grows deathly white as he looked down into the fair, dimpled, flushed young face gazing so fondly up at him.

"Of course I know what I'm saying!" laughed the girl, joyously. "I am telling how dearly I love you—love you better than all the wide world besides, and how happy I am now that you have come for me to claim me, and take me away with you. I shall never leave you again, never, never, never! I have thought of nothing but you night and day since you sent me from you, and counted the hours until I should behold you again; but that is all past now. Oh, how good of you to come for me before the two weeks were up."

"My God!" bursts from John Dinsmore's lips, as Jess reiterates her love for him over again in impulsive, childish fashion. "I never dreamed of this!"

"You have forgotten to kiss me, and say that you are as glad to see me as I am to see you," she goes on, breathlessly, in a headlong fashion, as she falls to kissing him in her impulsive way over and over again, fairly smothering him with the intense love she is showering upon him—a love that he knows wells up from the very depths of her young heart—a love which she is too innocent to attempt to try to conceal from him. No wonder he looks at her askance—wondering how in the world he is ever to utter the words that he has come to tell her—that he is there to bid her an eternal farewell!

CHAPTER XL.
THE FIRST LOVE.

"Oh, Love, poor Love, avail

Thee nothing now thy faiths, thy braveries?

There is no sun, no bloom; a cold wind strips

The bitter foam from off the wave where dips

No more thy prow; thy eyes are hostile eyes;

The gold is hidden; vain thy tears and cries;

Oh, Love, poor Love, why didst thou burn thy ships?"

John Dinsmore holds the girl off at arm's length and looks down into the sweet, innocent young face with troubled eyes.

"You love me!" he repeated, as though he were not quite sure that he heard aright.

Jess pushes back the soft black curls from her face and laughs gayly, and the sound of her voice is like the music of silver bells. She does not answer his question in words, but nods her dark, curly head emphatically.

His hands fall from her; he turns abruptly and takes one or two turns up and down the length of the long drawing-room.

How shall he utter the words to her which he has come here to say? How shall he tell her that he is there to say good-by to her forever?

"Do you know what I have been thinking ever since I came to this house?" she asked, as he paused an instant by her side, with the deep, troubled look on his face which so mystified her.

"No," he answered, hoarsely, glad that she was about to say something, for it would give him a moment or two longer in which to come to a conclusion.

"I was thinking how very stupid I am, and how wonderful it was that you married a little simpleton like me."

That was the very opening he needed, to utter that which was weighing heavily on his mind; but without giving him the opportunity, although his lips had opened to speak, she went on, blithely:

"I am going to study hard and become very wise, like the lady I am visiting here. But, oh, I forgot; you do not know Queenie—Mrs. Brown, I mean; but, dear me, it seems so odd to call her Mrs. anybody, she is so much more like an unmarried girl. Oh, she is so lovely, and graceful, and sweet. Do you know, it occurred to me only yesterday that had you seen her first, even though she is a widow, you might have fallen in love with her instead of me."

This was becoming almost unendurable. Who knew better than he the charms of Queenie?

"I am going to be stately and dignified like she is, and I am going to be wise and womanly. Do you think you will love me quite as much then as you do now?"

He could safely answer "Yes," for he did not love her at all.

"Thank you so much for assuring me of it," she murmured, seizing his white hands and covering them with kisses. "Now I shall begin with a will."

The girl did not seem to notice the shadow that was growing each moment still deeper on his face, and the look of despair that was gathering in his troubled eyes, and the gravity, almost to sternness, that had settled about his mouth.

Each moment this bright, gay child, who loved him so dearly, and was telling him so in every word, act and deed, was making the task before him but the harder.

How would she take it when he told her that she need make no sacrifices, or study, on his account, for he never intended to see her again?

"You do not know how much I have thought about you since I left you that day on the farm," she went on. "When you faded from my sight in the distance, though I strained my eyes hard to look back at you, standing there on the old porch, I bowed my head and wept so piteously that poor old Lawyer Abbot was in great fear lest my heart should break. I never knew until then what love, that they talk about, really was.

"All in a moment it seemed to take a deeper root in my heart—my life seemed to merge into yours—and I lived with but one thought in my mind, of the time when you should come for me, and I should never have to leave you again——never, never, never! And every moment since my heart has longed for you, cried out for you. You were the last thought I had when I closed my eyes in sleep; and then I dreamed of you; and my first thought on awakening was of you—always of you. Is not that the kind of love which the poets tell about, and which you feel toward me?"

This is the opportunity which he has been waiting for, and he attempts to grasp it, and get the disagreeable task over. It is the golden chance he has been so eager for.

Slowly he puts his hands on both of the girl's shoulders, and looks down into her beaming, dimpled, happy face, and in a low, trembling voice he says:

"My little wife"—it is the first time he has called her wife. He has never before addressed her by an endearing term. It has always been "Child," or "little Jess," before, and every fiber of the young wife's being responds to that sweetest of names—"My little wife."

As John Dinsmore utters these words he sinks down in the chair opposite her, but the words he is trying to speak rise in his throat and choke him.

In an instant two soft, plump arms are around his neck, a pair of soft, warm lips are kissing his death-cold cheek, and a pair of little hands are caressing him. His child-wife has flung herself into his lap, exclaiming:

"That is the first time you ever called me wife, and, oh, how sweet it sounded to my ears."

John Dinsmore's heart smote him. He could not utter the words which would hurl her down from heaven to the darkest of despair just then.

"Let her live in the Paradise of her own creating at least another day," he ruminated; and then a still brighter thought occurred to him, to write to Jess, telling her all. If she wept then, or fainted, or went mad from grief, he would not be there to witness it. He was not brave enough to give her her death wound, with the cruel words that they must part, while she was clinging to him in such rapturous bliss, covering his face with kisses.

And that was the sight that met Queenie's gaze as she returned to the drawing-room a few moments later.

Jess in her husband's lap, her face pressed close to his.

For a moment Queenie stood as though rooted to the threshold. She had purposely remained out of the apartment, seeing Jess enter, until he had time enough to tell her his errand there, and the picture that met her startled eyes went through her heart like the sharp thrust of a sword.

"My God! is it possible that he has changed his mind about parting from her? Does he love her?" was Queenie's mental cry.

At the sight of the beautiful vision in the doorway, John Dinsmore springs to his feet, putting his young wife hastily from him.

Jess is blushing like a full-blown rose in June.

"Oh, Mrs. Brown—Queenie—don't be so terribly shocked, please," she cries, dancing to her side and flinging her arms around her. "I am going to explain something about this gentleman which will surprise you dreadfully. He is my husband!" And as she utters the words triumphantly, she steps back and looks at Queenie, cresting her pretty head sideways, like a young robin.

It is a most embarrassing moment for Dinsmore. He stands pale and silent, between them, wondering if ever mortal man was placed in such a wretched predicament. On one side stands the girl he loves, the girl he wooed and lost on that never-to-be-forgotten summer by the murmuring sea, and on the other side the girl who loves him, the girl to whom he is bound fast by marriage bonds, and to whom he owes loyalty and protection. From deathlike paleness his face flushed hotly.

He longed to seize his hat and rush from the house. In his dilemma fate favored him. There is a ring at the bell, and the next instant callers are announced in the sonorous voice of the servant.

John Dinsmore seized this opportunity to make his adieus. He never afterward remembered just how it was accomplished, or what he said. He only remembered telling Jess that she should hear from him on the morrow. The next instant the cold air of the street was blowing on his face.

He had gone without kissing the quivering mouth of his young girl-bride. He had not even seen that it was held up to him for a parting caress.

Queenie noted that fact in triumph.

"It would not take so long to get a divorce from her, and then—— Ah, Heaven! the one longing of her life would be granted. She would be his wife."

Queenie was so carried away with her own thoughts and anticipations that she was barely conscious that the girl-wife's arms were once more thrown about her, and Jess was whispering in her ear:

"Now you know why I could not marry the other one, and did not wish to see him again. I was already a wife. What do you think of my—my husband? Is he not adorable?"

CHAPTER XLI.
"WAS IT ALL A DREAM?"

"Mine is an unchanging love,

Higher than the heights above,

Deeper than depths beneath,

Free and faithful, strong as death."

Many a long hour, while the great city was sleeping that night, Queenie paced the floor of her boudoir, deeply absorbed in her own turbulent thoughts.

It had been an exciting day to her, being brought face to face with her old lover whom she had mourned as dead, and more exciting still to learn of the barrier which fate had raised between them in the shape of John Dinsmore's bride—Jess, the girl who had been living under her own roof as her guest.

What would Raymond Challoner do, and say, she wondered, when she informed him that the real John Dinsmore was alive, and more astounding still, was wedded to the girl whom he was laying his plans to win, because of her fortune?

What vengeance would the arch-plotter take when he found his grand scheme for millions lying in ruins at his feet? Queenie feared that he would not lose an instant in putting John Dinsmore out of the way most securely, and still have the effrontery to attempt to carry out his scheme, should it become known to him that the little bride, Jess, did not know the real identity of the man whom she had wedded. Should she tell him that John Dinsmore lived, and that Jess was his wife, or not? That was the troublous question she asked herself over and over again.

"He must not harm one hair of John Dinsmore's head," she muttered fiercely. "For he will be mine as soon as he can free himself from the ties which now bind him."

Then her thoughts took another turn. A scheme came to her worthy of the arch-fiend himself. Yes, it was feasible, and it should be carried out.

It was almost dawn when Queenie threw herself upon her couch. She fell into a deep sleep, and it was almost noon when she awoke the next day, tired still, and unrefreshed.

"Was it all a dream?" she muttered, as she rubbed her eyes and gazed at Jess, who stood by the window in her room, patiently waiting for her to awaken—Jess, with the happiest smile she had ever seen on that dimpled young face, a smile as bright as the morning itself.

"You lazy, beautiful queen!" cried the girl, springing to her side, "how long you are sleeping to-day, and I longing to talk with you. I felt like awakening you with a shower of kisses."

Queenie drew back from her embrace with repellent coldness.

Down in the depths of her heart she hated with a deadly hatred this girl who had the right to kiss the face of the man whom she loved, and who bore his name.

"What is the matter, Queenie? Are you not well?" exclaimed Jess, with earnest solicitude. "Why, your hands are like ice; even your lips are cold."

"I have a headache. If you don't mind, I'd rather be alone for a little while," she replied, abruptly.

Without another word Jess turned slowly and quitted the boudoir, wondering greatly at the change of manner of her new-found friend, and wondering if she had possibly done anything to offend her.

But upon reaching her own room Jess forgot very quickly all about Queenie and her grievance, in giving herself up to her delicious daydreams of the future that awaited her with the reappearance of her handsome, dignified husband.

"Oh, how I love him," the girl murmured, resting her dimpled cheek against her pink palms. "It seems as though I had only just commenced to live to-day. He ought to be here soon now. He said he would come on the morrow, and then——"

Her thoughts were rudely interrupted by the entrance of Queenie, who came direct to the window where she sat, and laid a white hand lightly on the girl's arm.

"You are come to tell that he—my husband—is here!" cried Jess, tremulously, her face flushing with unconcealed delight.

Queenie bent over and raised the dimpled chin in her hand, looking searchingly down into the fair, happy young face, and then she answered, slowly:

"I wish to Heaven I could tell you so, my poor dear."

"Why, what can you mean, Queenie?" cried Jess, springing to her feet, a premonition of coming evil rushing over her heart.

"Can you bear a great shock, my love?" murmured Queenie, in a low voice, tightening her hold of the girl's arm. "Are you brave enough to hear something that will be a great blow, a great sorrow to you?"

Jess looked at her in affright. Her two little hands clutch at Queenie's skirts, while her eyes, like two burning flames, seem to devour the face of the false friend.

"If it is something about my—husband, tell me quick!" she breathes hoarsely, "for the suspense is killing me."

"I would to Heaven that it was not my lot to break the pitiful news to you, Jess, but perhaps I can do it better than any one else."

"Yes, yes; go on, go on. I am sure it is something about my husband," whispers Jess in intense excitement.

Queenie nods, and clasps the two ice-cold hands of Jess in her own, while she prepares to utter the death-warrant to the girl standing so innocent and so helpless before her—at her mercy.

"Little Jess, I pity you with all my heart," she begins, "and my heart bleeds for you. I cannot keep the truth back from you an instant longer. Something has happened to your husband."

"He is hurt!" shrieked Jess, wildly, clutching at her heart as she gulps out the choking words.

"He met with an accident as he was leaving here, and he is—dead!" whispers Queenie.

The words have scarcely left her lips ere Jess falls like a log at her feet.

Dead! Queenie thinks at first, but as she bends over her, she finds to her disappointment that is but a swoon.

For a moment she stands gazing down at her evil work with a fiendish smile curling her lips.

"This is the first step I have taken in the plot to part this girl most effectually from the man I love, and have set myself to win," she muttered in a hard voice, adding: "Why should I not? For he loves me—not her."

She hears the maid's step along the corridor, and hurries to the door to intercept her.

"The same gentleman who called yesterday," thought the maid under her breath, as she presented Mr. John Dinsmore's card to her mistress, saying aloud: "The gentleman asked to see Miss Jess."

"Very well," returned the beautiful young widow, her hand trembling in spite of her apparent calmness, as she took the bit of pasteboard.

"She will lie there, in just that condition until long after my interview with him is ended," she muttered. "Still it is always wise to take every possible precaution."

So saying, as she glided from the apartment, she turned and locked the door noiselessly, and slipped the key into her pocket.

On her way down to the drawing-room she paused long enough in her own apartment to secure a letter which she had spent long hours the night before in writing.

In the drawing-room below John Dinsmore was pacing up and down impatiently enough at the delay, for he was sure his little wife would fairly fly down to his arms upon learning he was there.

Jess' reception of him the day before, and her acknowledgment of her love for himself, had fairly carried his heart by storm. He could not doubt but that other love affair had been brought about by a mistaken fancy on the girl's part, and that her affection for himself was true love, the first and only time she had really loved.

The peep he had had into her heart had been a revelation to him, and then, and then only, he realized an amazing truth, that his own heart answered that love—responded to it with an intenseness that startled him with its power.

"Thank Heaven that I did not tell her yesterday that the object of my visit was to inform her that we must part; that I intended to divorce her. Great God! I must have been mad to think of flinging aside so ruthlessly a heart of such pure gold," he ruminated. "I am thankful, indeed, that I knew my own heart in time. Instead of telling her that we must part, I will tell her that I am come to take her away with me, and that we shall never be parted more, and that I love her even more fondly than she loves me, and that henceforth our lives shall be one long, sweet dream of bliss, that her happiness shall be my care, and a lifetime of fond devotion shall repay her for giving her sweet, bright self to my keeping."

Would she never come to him? Oh, how the moments seemed to drag, he longed so to clasp Jess in his arms, and give her the first kiss of love, burning, passionate love, that he had ever pressed upon her lips—and she his bride.

He almost believed that his love had developed into idolatry for Jess, his sweet girl-bride.

CHAPTER XLII.
THE PLOT THICKENS.

"I believe love, pure and true

Is to the soul a sweet, immortal dew

That gem life's petals in its hours of dusk.

The waiting angels see and recognize

The rich crown-jewels, love, of Paradise,

When life falls from us like a withered husk."

As John Dinsmore instinctively turned toward the door, the silk portières were swept aside with a white, jeweled hand, but his disappointment was great, for, instead of beholding Jess, he saw Queenie, in her long, trailing robes of black, standing on the threshold.

He greeted her constrainedly, for he noticed the heightened color that flashed into her face, crimsoning it from brow to chin, and the dazzling smile of welcome on her lips.

Queenie swept into the room and up to his side with the graceful, gliding motion peculiar to her, and which he had always admired so greatly.

Then he noticed that she held something in her hand—a letter.

"You expected to see your wife," she began, and then hesitated as though at a loss how to proceed.

"Yes," he answered, and she saw him give a sudden start and turn pale, as he quickly asked:

"Is she not—well?"

A sudden fire leaped into Queenie's eyes at his solicitude over Jess, and it hardened her heart toward him for being so interested in any human being save herself. She felt no remorse for what she was about to do; no sorrow for the blow her hand was about to inflict.

No one would have dreamed that the sympathy she assumed in the expression of her face as she looked up at him was far from being the real state of her feelings. No one would ever have imagined that beneath her calm demeanor her heart was rent with a war of dark, angry passions, the outcome of a love which she realized was hopeless, by the cold, distant greeting he had given her. She felt within her heart and soul that he was there to claim Jess and take her away with him to happiness and love, instead of being there to inform her that he wished to part from her. Queenie's keen intuition, her knowledge of men and the world, told her that.

Slowly she held up her white, jeweled hand with the letter in it, saying, gently:

"The bearers of unwelcome messages often share the fate of the messages they bring. Do not let me be so unfortunate, Joh—Mr. Dinsmore."

Still he did not answer; his eyes were riveted on the letter she held, which he could see bore his name.

"This is for you," she said, gently, "but ere you open it, let me say a few words to you."

Again he bowed his fine, handsome head, wondering what she could have to say to him, and also what Jess could have written to him about, for he believed he recognized the handwriting upon the envelope, and his heart was on fire to tear it open and devour its sweet contents.

"Last evening Jess had a caller—a gentleman," began Queenie, slowly, pretending not to notice the violent start John Dinsmore gave. "He remained an hour or more, and after he left, and Jess had returned to her own room, which is opposite mine, I saw that she was strangely agitated, and yet extremely jubilant—hilariously so.

"She did not come into my boudoir to chat, as has been her custom since she has been my guest here, saying she had a letter to write. That was the last I saw of her, as I kissed her good-night and left her.

"This morning one of the servants handed me this letter, saying that Miss Jess, as they called her, had given this to them the night before at a late hour, requesting that it should be given to me to place in your hands when you should come to-day. I will retire into the library while you read it at your leisure."

The next moment John Dinsmore found himself standing alone in the luxurious drawing-room with Jess' letter in his hand.

"Why should his little bride write to him, instead of telling him anything she had to say in person?" he wondered, vaguely, and with the letter still held unopened in his hand he asked himself who Jess' caller of the previous evening could have been. But quite as soon as the thought shaped itself in his mind, he came to the conclusion that it must have been Lawyer Abbot. No doubt the letter was to inform him that she had confessed her marriage to the old lawyer, and begged him to send her word that he was not so very angry, ere she ventured to come to him.

He broke the seal and drew forth the letter. He had seen but one of Jess' letters before, the one which had reached him when he was lying sick unto death from the outcome of the duel at Newport, consequently he could not recollect the chirography very clearly, save that it was in an unformed, straggling, girlish hand—the same as this appeared to be.

As John Dinsmore's eyes ran rapidly over the first few lines, the blood in his veins turned as cold as ice, and a blood-red mist seemed to sweep across his vision.

The letter ran as follows:

"My Husband: When you are reading what I am now writing, I shall be flying far away from you. I will tell you now by the medium of pen and paper what I was too much of a coward to tell you yesterday in person, and that is, that our marriage was a terrible mistake, and I am rueing it most bitterly, especially since last evening.

"At that time some one came to call upon me. I might just as well tell you frankly who that some one was—the lover with whom I broke faith when I so thoughtlessly, on the spur of the moment, sealed a bitter fate for myself by marrying you. We had quarreled, and I, well, to be truthful, I married you just to make him suffer, but the words were scarcely uttered which bound me to you ere I rued it most bitterly, though I did not betray my grief to you by word or act.

"Well, my old lover came, and I—I do not ask your pity for my weakness, for I realize fully that I do not deserve it. I knew that I could not live my life out if he went from me again, though I knew I was bound to you. Well, he felt the same toward me that I felt toward him, and we both agreed to brave the world for love—and each other.

"I gathered my few articles together, and—as I have said, by the time you are reading these lines I will be far away with the man I love.

"I should not blame you if you were to get a divorce from me at once. I realize that this admission from me gives you the proper grounds for it. Indeed, I should be thankful if you would, for then I shall be free to marry the man who already has my heart. I hope you will find forgiveness for me in that big, noble heart of yours.

"Forget me, and that I ever came into your life, and be happy, as I feel sure you will be, in some other girl's love.

"I have nothing more to say, except that I hope you will not search for me, for it will be useless. You can never, never find me. All that I ask from you is to be let alone. I have followed the dictates of my own heart, and that must be my reason for the step I am to take.

"Again I urge that you make no attempt to discover my whereabouts. Thanking you in advance for complying with my earnest request in this respect, I sign myself for the first and last time.

"YOUR WIFE JESS."

For some moments after he had finished this cruel epistle, John Dinsmore sat staring at it like one suddenly bereft of reason. Little Jess gone! eloped with a former lover! He could scarcely believe that he had read the written lines aright. He told himself that he must be laboring under some mad delusion.

Over and over again he read the fatal words, until every line was burned in letters of fire indelibly into his brain.

He passed his cold, trembling hands over his brow. Great beads of perspiration were standing out on it, and his veins were like knotted whipcords.

Little Jess, who only yesterday had clung to him with loving words and kisses, awakening all the love that had lain dormant in his heart and soul, had fled from him. He could almost as easily have looked for the world to come suddenly to an end, and all time, light, hope and life to be suddenly blighted and turned into chaos and darkness!

In that moment of bitter pain he thought of lines he had read only the day before in a book which he had seen on the drawing-room table, while he was awaiting the coming of Jess. They recurred to him now with crushing force:

"I met a kindred heart, and that heart to me said: 'Come;'

Mine went out to meet it, but was lost in sudden gloom.

Whither wander all these fair things, to some land beyond life's sea?

Is there nothing glad and lasting in this weary world for me?"

Never until that moment did John Dinsmore realize how deeply he had learned to love the girlish bride who had just fled from him, crushing his heart and wrecking his life so cruelly.

For the second time in his life he had been ruthlessly hurt by the woman to whom he had allowed his honest heart to go out in abounding love.

He heard a rustle beside him, and raising his death-white face quickly, he saw Queenie standing before him.

"I know all, John—Mr. Dinsmore," she murmured, "and I pity you from the depths of my heart. If I could give my life to bring her back to you, if you love her, I would gladly do it. And yet, she's not worthy of such terrible grief as you are enduring."

Alas! in that hour of his bitter woe, how sweet was Queenie's sympathy, which was indeed balm to his wounded, bleeding heart.

CHAPTER XLIII.
THE LOVE THAT WILL NOT DIE.

"Oh, answer, love, my pleading!
The precious moments pass;
And I long these waters o'er
May come no more, alas!
Ah, while to-night is left us,
It should not fly in vain.
Come forth this once, lest fate decrees
We never meet again!
I wait, my heart's adored one,
Beneath the moon's bright beams.
Come—come, it is the hour that brings
The time for lovers' dreams!"

In after years, when John Dinsmore looked back at that moment, it always seemed like a memory of a hideous nightmare, standing there with Jess' letter in his shaking hand; the letter in which she told him that she, his wife, had eloped with a former lover. In that hour the sympathy of Queenie seemed like balm to his bleeding heart.

"Mr. Dinsmore," she said, in that sweet, smooth, silvery voice of hers, that had always had the power to thrill him to the heart's core, "my heart is bleeding for you. What can I say, what can I do to comfort you?"

He sank into the nearest seat, covering his face with his shaking hands. Queenie advanced a step nearer, and her soft, white hands, cool and white as lily leaves, fell on his bowed head lightly.

"I know, I can understand how deeply your pride is wounded," she went on, hurriedly. "But instead of wasting one thought over her, you should be rejoicing at getting rid of her so easily—remembering that her action sets you free from the bond which galled you, leaves you free to woo and wed one whom you can love. Do you not realize it?

"She was never a fit companion for you," continued Queenie, eagerly; "you knew that. You should never have expected anything else from a girl such as she was—a wild, gypsyish creature, without even a name to face the world with. Of course she came from a source where her parents dared not own her, and one should not be surprised that she has developed evil tendencies; it is easy to surmise that they are bred in the bone, and she acted upon them at the first opportunity which presented. I predict that she will reach the lowest level that such a low-born creature——"

The sentence never was finished. With a bound John Dinsmore sprang to his feet, his face white as death, his eyes blazing like coals of fire.

"Stop, madam!" he cried, in a hoarse voice. "Not another word, I command you. Remember it is my wife whom you are reviling so cruelly!" and he towered before her, the incarnation of cold, stern, haughty anger.

For a moment only Queenie loses her self-possession, the next instant her face is wreathed in a cruel sneer, as she answers, defiantly:

"Am I mad, or do my ears deceive me? Are you really championing the cause of the girl who has betrayed you so shamefully? made your name, of which you were so proud, a byword for the sensational press when they learn what has happened? Most men would resent her action with all the pride in their natures, and despise her accordingly; being glad to be rid of such a——"

"Again I cry hold!" cut in John Dinsmore, in ringing, sonorous tones. "I will not hear another disparaging word of the girl who bears my name!"

"I suppose that you will search for her, and when you have found her, you will forgive her freak of mad folly, take her back to your heart and home, and be happy ever afterward, as the story-books say."

"That is precisely my intention," announced John Dinsmore, coolly, and in a determined voice. "The fault was mine. I alone am to blame for what has transpired. I wedded her, and instead of cherishing the impulsive child as I should have done, I sent her from me—cast her out a prey to just such vipers as the one who has crossed her path, and led her from the right path. She was young, and craved and needed love and protection, neither of which she received from me; the lesson I have learned is a most bitter one. I will spend my life in trying to find my little Jess, and when I have found her, I will atone to her for my fatal mistake in sending her from me."

As Queenie listened, all in a moment the realization that he meant that he would never be anything to herself swept with full force over her heart.

"John Dinsmore," she cried, pantingly, "you must not search for her; let her go where she will!" and with a flame of crimson rushing over her face from chin to brow, she whispered: "If you will you shall have me—and my love! Fate parted us two, who were intended for each other, once before; let us not let her part us a second time!"

"I am sorry to speak harshly to a lady," he returned; "but you force the words from my lips, and therefore you must hear them; and not only hear, but heed them.

"You can never be any more to me than you are at the present moment, madam. I acknowledge that there was a time when such words as you have just uttered would have filled me with the keenest rapture; but that time has long since passed; for you no longer fill the remotest niche in my heart. My love died for you long ago, and to-night my respect goes with it; for the woman who would counsel me to turn from my wedded wife, no matter what she has done, and find consolation with her, is one whom I do not desire even to know."

As he uttered these words he strode from the room, leaving Queenie staring after him, the very picture of a fiend incarnate, with her eyes blazing like two coals of yellow fire, and her face and lips bloodless.

"Foiled!" she shrieked. "Foiled! and I had set my heart and soul upon winning him, and the way seemed so easy!"

But one thought occurred to her; if it was indeed so, she would take a terrible vengeance upon him, a vengeance that he would never forget, or get over to his dying day.

She made up her mind that she would strike at his heart through Jess, for whom he was going to search the wide world over.

"You may search, but you will never find her, John Dinsmore!" she cried, hoarsely, beating her breast fiercely with her clinched hands. "I will look to that. You are parted as truly as though the grave yawned between you!"

When she reached her boudoir, and a little later looked in at Jess, she found her still lying in the same dead faint upon the floor.

She bent over the girl, gazing long and bitterly at the lovely, upturned young face, her eyes glowing luridly as she noted how perfect was the loveliness of her every feature.

"Yes, he has learned that he loves you, when it is too late!" she muttered, catching her breath hard. "I will strike his heart through you!"

She was not long in maturing her plans; she set to work to revive the girl without calling any of the servants to assist her in the operation, believing what they did not know they could never repeat to any one.

Her labors were soon rewarded by seeing Jess open her large, dark eyes slowly.

"What is it, Queenie?" she murmured, vaguely; then, in the next breath, before her companion could vouchsafe a reply, she cried bitterly: "Oh, Father in Heaven, I remember all now—the awful intelligence you brought me, that my darling husband, to whom I was to go to-morrow, is dead—killed by an awful accident! Oh, God pity me, how can I ever bear it? I had loved him so well, with all the strength of my heart and soul!"

To an enemy less relentless than the beautiful fiend who bent over her, the ghastly change in the lovely young face, looking so appealingly up into her own, would have drawn forth pity.

If she had had her own way, she would have let the girl die then and there of a broken heart; but that was not a part of the programme she had laid out for herself. It seemed that she was not to win John Dinsmore and his fortune, and her funds were running terribly low; the only way that she knew of to gain a share of the Dinsmore millions, which had slipped by her, was to aid Raymond Challoner to wed this girl, Jess, just as soon as her grief was sufficiently assuaged to allow her to be talked—even coerced—into it.

What the outcome of the affair would be she did not know or care. They would have a lively time recovering her share of the wealth, if the nefarious scheme ever came to light.

She resolved that it would never do to tell Raymond Challoner that John Dinsmore was alive, and had been in New York; and, furthermore, to acquaint him with the startling information that Jess had met and wedded John Dinsmore under the name of Mr. Moore.

She would keep all that from Raymond Challoner; what he did not know would not worry him.

And last, but by no means least, as soon as Jess was in a fit condition to be prevailed upon by argument, or persuasion, to keep the past a profound secret, and marry the man to whom she was engaged, to secure the Dinsmore millions from going to waste, it should be accomplished.

Queenie determined that if she could not wed John Dinsmore and secure his fortune one way, it should be done in another manner.

CHAPTER XLIV.
THE WAYS OF PROVIDENCE.

There was another thing of which Queenie was equally convinced, and that was that the safest place for Jess, for the present, was beneath her own roof. John Dinsmore would, of course, never dream of looking for her there.

She knew full well that he would not come near her home, therefore, she did not fear a meeting between Raymond Challoner and him.

Queenie was not surprised when Raymond Challoner presented himself at her home the following afternoon, impatient to know what progress she was making with her arguments to induce Jess to reconsider her dismissal of himself and his suit; and very anxious to have an interview with the girl.

"That will be impossible for the present," declared Queenie; "for she has worked herself up into a state bordering almost on hysteria; indeed, she is so bad that I was obliged to call in a doctor to attend her, and his instructions were that she must be kept perfectly quiet; nothing whatever of an exciting nature must disturb her, or the result would be a serious case of brain fever."

Raymond Challoner bit his lip with the most intense vexation.

"By the eternal, luck seems to be working dead against me!" he cried. "I am almost strapped as to cash—I must marry that confounded contrary girl, and without delay, too, to secure that fortune. You know delays are dangerous!"

"Am I not equally as anxious? I am in the same position financially as yourself; my funds are horribly low, and your marrying this girl, and securing the Dinsmore fortune, which you have promised to divide with me as compensation for my services, is everything I have to depend upon; so why should I not expedite matters to the fullest extent of my power?" she demanded.

"With your woman's wit, you ought to be able to arrange matters somehow," he persisted, doggedly.

"I will do the very best I can; that is all that I can say," she responded, and he was obliged to let matters rest in that way. He took a reluctant leave, with the understanding that he was not to call again until he was sent for, which Queenie declared should be the first moment in which she had Jess' promise that she would see him.

And Queenie meant what she said. For decency's sake she allowed a week to pass since she had informed Jess of her husband's tragic death, ere she put her scheme in motion.

At the end of that week Queenie took the girl in hand.

"This will never do, my dear," she said. "You must take the punishment which has been meted out to you meekly."

"Punishment!" echoed Jess, putting her dark curls back from her tear-stained face with her little, trembling hands. "What have I ever done to offend Heaven, that I should deserve punishment? That is the wrong word for it, you meant affliction."

"I meant exactly what I said, my dear," returned Queenie, softly. "It is my firm belief that the Lord meant to punish you for flinging aside so ruthlessly the solemn wishes of the dead!" she added, solemnly and impressively.

Jess looked up into her face with bewildered, tear-stained eyes, murmuring faintly:

"Still I do not comprehend."

"You certainly ought not to need me to refresh your memory in regard to the fact that you were in solemn duty bound to wed him whom the man who thought enough of you to leave half of his fortune to desired you to marry."

"But I did not love him, Queenie," sobbed the girl, piteously, "and I did love the man whom I married.

"Go where I would, his face was always before me; it smiled up at me from the hearts of the flowers over which I bent, it looked at me from the dancing waves of the rippling brook. I saw it framed in the fleecy clouds when I looked up at the blue sky, and from the golden stars when the night fell, shrouding the world in impenetrable darkness.

"Oh, Queenie, I often wonder if any other girl in this whole wide world has ever loved as fondly and as dearly as I loved the handsome, noble gentleman to whom God seemed to consecrate me when I became his bride. Ah, why should God punish me, and desire me to marry another when I loved my husband as devotedly as that?"

"God's motives are not for us to question; it seems that He did," replied Queenie, tersely, adding, after a seemingly thoughtful pause: "Do you know that I think His anger can only be assuaged by your carrying out His design yet?"

She knew by the bewildered look in Jess' eyes that she did not in the least comprehend the hint she had just given her.

"I consider it my duty to speak plainly to you, Jess," she said. "I am quite sure that your husband was removed for the purpose of your carrying out yet the provisions of that will."

"Oh, no, no, no!" cried the girl, wildly. "I would not marry the best man that ever walked the earth; for me there is but one love, and therefore but one husband!"

"There is another matter to be considered," said Queenie. "Do you want to go out into the world penniless, and earn your own living, which you surely must do if you persist in refusing the rich gifts the gods offer you? It is a question which you must not decide rashly."

"I do not care for the Dinsmore millions!" sobbed the girl. "I can get along without them. Please do not say any more to me on the subject, Queenie, my poor heart is so sore."

"There is just one thing more that I must call your attention to, which you seem to have forgotten entirely," Queenie went on, pitilessly; "and that is, even if you are perfectly indifferent in the matter, you still should remember that in pursuing the course you persist in adopting, you are not only injuring your own prospects, but you are consigning to a life of misery and toil another, the man whom the elder Mr. Dinsmore intended should enjoy half of his great fortune.

"Think long and seriously, Jess, ere you consign one whose only fault is loving you too well to a life of poverty and misery. It would be better far to give your life up to the noble purpose of making another happy, even though your heart is not in what you do.

"In a fortnight he will come here to see you, and will ask for your final answer. I repeat, think long and earnestly ere you say him nay. He need never know what took place while you were at the farm those few weeks. In fact, I would counsel that you keep it carefully from his knowledge. Let that part of your book of life be a sealed chapter, which no human eyes may scan. Why tell him, and make him miserable, when silence is wisest and best, since it tends to his contentment and peace of mind for all time?

"I leave you to think it over carefully, Jess. Surely you are too noble to consign the one who loves you so well to the bitterest of poverty. He does not know how to cope with it; he has always looked upon the Dinsmore fortune as his, some day; therefore he is not equipped to fight for his daily bread during the remainder of his life. If life and love are all over for you, consecrate your future to doing good deeds, and surely this is one."

So saying, she left the girl to her own pitiful reflections. Can it be wondered at, by dint of constantly holding this aspect of the case up before the girl's troubled eyes, that slowly but surely she began to influence the girl, who was scarcely more than a child in her ideas, that it was her duty to sacrifice herself to save the man who was co-heir to Blackheath Hall from a life of poverty.

It was with many bitter tears that at length Jess sobbed out that she would do exactly what Queenie advised. Life, hope and love were all over for her, it did not matter much what her future was.

"Your lover of the old days will be here to-morrow," announced Queenie, at length, "and shall I make his heart glad by telling him that you relent, and that matters will be between you as they were when you were down on the plantation in Louisiana; that you will meet him as your affianced husband?"

Jess covered her face with her two little hands, which shook like aspen leaves, and nodded dumbly. She could not have said "yes" to have saved her life; she tried to utter the word, but it stuck in her throat and choked her.

CHAPTER XLV.
NAMING THE DAY.

Raymond Challoner lost no time in acting upon Queenie's advice. The very next afternoon he presented himself at her home, and Queenie herself went to fetch Jess at once.

"How shall I ever go down to the drawing-room to see him!" cried Jess, distractedly, as she clung to her false friend with death-cold hands; "if he speaks to me of love, or marriage, I am sure I shall fall in a swoon at his feet."

"That is not being brave," retorted Queenie, impatiently, "you promised me faithfully that you would put the past from you, and try to believe that it was but a dream; this is not carrying out your word."

Jess straightened herself up with apparent difficulty, the awful pallor still upon her face. How she made her way down the stairway, she never afterward quite remembered, so strong was the feeling within her that she would swoon with each step.

Raymond Challoner advanced to greet her in his jaunty, inimitable, graceful manner.

"Little Jess!" he cried, holding out both hands in greeting, "words fail to express to you how glad I am to see you."

Her white lips parted, and her large, dark, startled eyes looked away from the eager blue ones in much trepidation. She murmured some faint words which he could not quite catch.

"Why, how changed you are, little Jess!" he cried, holding her off at arm's length and looking in puzzled wonder down at her fair, marvelously beautiful face. "New York and the society of our mutual friend Queenie seem to have metamorphosed you completely. You left me a romp of a girl, I find you a woman; there is something in your eyes, in your face, that I have never seen there before, and I am puzzled to know what it is."

He saw her flush and then turn deadly pale under his keen, searching scrutiny.

"You are a thousand times more beautiful, and therefore more lovable than when we last met," he cried, enthusiastically. "I regretted from the bottom of my heart that they had let you slip off to New York without my knowledge, or approval, but I am obliged to confess that it has done wonders for you, my Jess—wonders."

"How could you leave me in that reckless fashion?" he went on, reproachfully. "You struck a cruel blow at my heart by doing so, and a still more cruel blow when you wrote me that you intended to break our engagement. Why, little girl, I was sick for weeks from the effects of it, praying to die, I fought bitterly against allowing them to cure me; that will show you how completely I was wrapped up in your sweet self.

"The bitterest drop in my cup of woe was that they would not tell me where you had gone, in accordance with some foolish promise given. It seemed like a stroke of fate that I should come to New York, and in coming to visit an old friend stumble directly into the house where you were visiting. Do you not agree with me that it was indeed fate? If it had not been intended that we should be reunited, I would not have been able to discover where my pearl had hidden herself.

"But, dear me, come and sit down in this sunshiny bay window, my little Jess, that I may have a better look at my newly recovered treasure; you are now so royally, regally beautiful, that I can scarcely believe you are one and the same little Jess whom I met in the wilds of Louisiana that eventful September morning, which seems long months ago, though it is in reality not so very long ago."

During the call, which seemed long and tedious to Jess, who was wondering if he would never, never go, her companion did all the talking, the girl barely answering in monosyllables, but he attributed this to bashfulness, though that was a trait in her character that he had not discovered during his brief sojourn at Blackheath Hall.

"With your permission, Jess," he said at length, "I should like to talk about our wedding; when shall it take place, my own love?"

"Oh, I don't know!" cried the girl, distractedly, "do not mention it to me—until the very last moment—and let it be as far off as you possibly can."

His brow darkened.

"That is not a very kind speech, Jess," he remarked, with considerable pique, "and does not speak very well for the depths of love you shall bear the man to whom you have plighted your troth."

She looked up at him appealingly. It seemed to her if he uttered another word on the subject she would go mad. How could she listen to words of love or marriage from another's lips when her heart lay buried in the grave of the man she had loved so passionately, with all the strength of her nature?

But she knew if she made the sacrifice which Queenie had impressed upon her was her solemn duty, she must make no outcry, utter no word of protestation against the marriage, or when it was to take place.

"I know that you spoke in jest, my sweetheart," Ray Challoner went on, smoothly, "to think otherwise would be to drive me mad, my heart is so entirely yours."

"Forgive me," answered Jess, bravely, choking down a great sob that threatened to break forth and betray the state of her feelings.

She listened like one in a far-off troubled dream while he talked to her of his plans for the future, and ended by praying her to name the day when he should claim her as his own.

"I—do not know," murmured the girl, wearily; "I—I will leave everything to you, Mr. Dinsmore," and if he had not been so jubilant over the victory and the fortune so near his grasp, he would have noticed the suspicion of tears in her lovely, dark, mournful, despairing eyes.

"Then I say, let it take place at once, my own," he declared, "the sooner the better, say a week from to-day!"

Jess shuddered, as with a sudden chill, but she kept control of her nerves by a great effort. He must not see how obnoxious the very thought of marriage with him was to her.

She wondered vaguely how she was to pass the rest of her life with him when she found a few hours so intolerable as to almost drive her mad.

"Your silence gives sweet consent, my own charming little bride to be," he cried, exultantly, and it was with difficulty that he restrained himself from embracing her then and there.

He took his leave soon after with that matter settled completely to his satisfaction, the ceremony was to be performed just a week from that day. He would have named the morrow, but that he was sure Jess would be suspicious that there was something wrong in his intense eagerness to claim her. Of all things he must avoid raising her suspicions.

He was anxious to get away from her, and celebrate his victory over the outcome of his desperate and daring plan for a fortune, by indulging in as much champagne as he could stand, for once in his life; for there would soon be an end to reckless indulgence, at least for a time. Until the Dinsmore fortune was within his grasp, and he had turned it into cash, he would be obliged to play the part of a model husband.

"She is a thousand times more beautiful than ever," he muttered, as he walked briskly down the avenue, "but her every action shows me that she abhors me, simply that and nothing else. And because of that, I feel the demon that is in me rising to the surface. I hate her for her coldness toward me and her pride, which will ever be an insurmountable barrier between us. I will marry you, my proud, haughty Jess, and after the knot is tied which makes me your lord and master, I will set my heel upon your white neck, crush that heart of yours, without mercy, and make life itself a torture to you. I will take a glorious revenge upon you for all the indignities you have heaped upon me, I promise you that."

Finding himself opposite a fashionable café he entered it, and soon finished the bottle of champagne they brought him, another bottle was as quickly dispatched; and in the best of humor with himself and the world, he began to look about him, as to who made up the fashionable throng filing into the place, in hopes that he might discover some boon companion of other days, who would share with him another bottle of the shining, sparkling beverage which had already gone to his brain.

He was getting jovial, and that was the danger signal which should have warned Raymond Challoner to desist then and there from indulging in any more of his dearest foe—sparkling champagne. Already he had begun to see two waiters filling his glass instead of one.

"Not a soul I know in the entire room," he muttered, staring around disconsolately, "now that is annoying; I would like some one to keep me company."

Suddenly his attention was drawn to a gentleman who, with two companions, was watching him furtively from a convenient point across the room.

"Wonder where I have seen that face!" muttered Challoner, "can't think to save my neck."

His memory refused to aid him.

The gentleman was—John Dinsmore.

CHAPTER XLVI.
OLD FRIENDS MEET.

When John Dinsmore had left the home of Queenie, after learning of the supposed flight of Jess, his bride, his avowed intention was to shake the dust of New York from his feet forever, and to wander on the face of the earth until he should find her whom he had learned, all too late, was dearer to him than his very heart's blood.

So intent was he upon his own bitter, despairing thoughts, he failed to notice the two young men who had stopped short at sight of him, astonishment and delight depicted on their faces. He would have passed them by unheeded, they both saw, and with one accord, each sprang forward, laying a detaining hand on his shoulders, which brought him to an unceremonious standstill.

"John Dinsmore, and in the flesh, by all that is wonderful!" they cried, simultaneously.

With an exclamation of joy Dinsmore drew back and looked into the faces of his two devoted friends, Jerry Gaines and Ballou, the artist. And John was certainly as much overjoyed to see them as they were to once more behold him.

"I almost imagine I shall wake up on the morrow and find this encounter but a wild delusion of the overwrought brain, as you novelists put it," laughed Gaines, with tears in his blue eyes as he still continued to wring John's hand, "but come into this restaurant around the corner, and we will have a rousing reunion, and you shall tell us what you have been doing with yourself, and why you allowed your tried and true old friends to spend so much grief over you, mourning you as dead."

"Yes," said Ballou; "you must come, John; it is not possible that you are contemplating refusing Jerry's request. We must get somewhere out of the teeth of this howling storm. I don't possess fur-lined garments, consequently it is going through me like a knife. Are you with us?"

"As you will, boys," replied John Dinsmore, and they proceeded at once to the place designated, a restaurant where the "Trinity" had been in the habit of dining in the past, and where Gaines and Ballou still came to get the most for their spare change.

"It is my turn to pay the bill to-night," said John, the first smile that his face had known for months lighting up his grave face. "You remember the day I left New York last—it would have been my turn to put up for the spread."

"Not so, my boy," laughed Gaines. "I have had a streak of luck to-day, and I insist upon paying the bill. If you feel so very liberal, you shall do the pretty act to-morrow night."

It was during the meal that John Dinsmore recounted to his two old friends all that had taken place since the memorable day they packed his valise for him, and sent him South, from Newport, with the double object of regaining his health and looking at the little Louisiana heiress at Blackheath Hall.

"Why, your meeting the little Jess, after all, and marrying her out of hand, without going near Blackheath Hall, and she not dreaming of your real identity, sounds like a chapter from a novel. By George! what a capital story it would make!"

"The climax to it is quite unsavory, though," replied John Dinsmore, and in answer to the looks of astonishment on his companions' faces, he drew forth the letter from his breast pocket, into which he had crushed it, and in a low, husky voice read its contents slowly aloud to them.

"Eloped with an old lover!" echoed Ballou, amazedly, while Jerry Gaines asked in a tone which he strove not to appear excited: "What was the address you read, of the house where she was visiting, John?"

He re-read the address, giving the street and number.

Both Gaines and Ballou turned and looked at each other fixedly.

"Isn't that the address of the young widow who married the supposedly rich old miser Brown for his millions, and got beautifully left for her pains—finding herself next door to a pauper on the reading of the will?"

"It appears so," replied Gaines, knitting his brows in deep thought, then suddenly he leaned over and touched Ballou on the arm, saying:

"Do you know I have a very odd idea? You remember the young fellow whom we afterward recognized as he was coming out of that house, just as we were about to enter to learn the particulars of that will, and get a chance to talk with and sketch the beautiful young widow?"

"Yes; I have every reason to remember him," nodded Ballou, in a peculiar voice, adding: "Well, what of him?"

"I believe that he is the infernal scoundrel who has eloped with John's little bride—for the reason that I went past the place the following afternoon, and saw him at the drawing-room window talking to just such a young girl as I now remember little Jess to be from the picture she sent to John while he lay ill at Newport, and which we saw."

"You know the villain!" exclaimed John, springing from his seat trembling with excitement. "For Heaven's sake tell me, and quickly, who he is, that I may follow him and shoot him down like the cur that he is, or rather pit my life against his to wipe out this stain with which he has dared to smirch the honor of my name."

"Give me until to-morrow this time to locate him and find whether I am right or wrong, John," asked Jerry Gaines. "This is a matter into which no man can rush headlong. I will find out beyond a doubt if my suspicions be true. If they are, you shall be put on his track, and when you meet him, you shall deal with him as you see best. Is that satisfactory?"

"I suppose it must be, if you say so," replied John Dinsmore, sinking back into his chair, his face ghastly pale, every nerve in his entire body quivering with the deep agitation he was undergoing.

His two friends prevailed upon him to remain in New York a week at least, pending their investigation, and to go to the old humble room which he used to share with them in the days when money was at a premium with him.

The next morning his two tried and true friends parted early from him, arranging to meet him at the same hour, and at the same restaurant, suggesting that they might have something of importance to communicate.

To John Dinsmore it seemed as though six o'clock, the hour appointed, would never come; he spent the time in walking up and down the streets, vainly searching for Jess, even in the face of the fact that her letter had said that she intended going far away from the metropolis.

Never before had he realized how intensely he loved little Jess, and what a blank his life would be without her.

And then and there it occurred to him how utterly devoid of good judgment he must have been in those days to allow himself to be carried away with so shallow and utterly false and heartless a creature as Queenie Trevalyn, whom he now abhorred, and whom he knew as she really was—at last.

He said to himself that sometimes God blesses us in denying us that which we believe our greatest good, but which would only have turned out to be our greatest misfortune.

All that day the two friends, spurred on by John Dinsmore's recital, worked zealously over the plan which they had mapped out for themselves to discover the whereabouts of Jess, the fair young bride.

On the occasion of their former visit to the house of the old miser's widow, the young artist had made quite a favorable impression upon one of the maids of the household; they decided to make use of that state of affairs now. And under pretext that the paper wanted another statement of the facts, they again presented themselves at the home of young Mrs. Brown.

To their relief that lady was out; but that did not prevent them from lingering and having nearly an hour's chat with the loquacious maid.

A few ingenious remarks led the conversation around to the beautiful young girl, who had until so lately been a guest beneath that roof, as they phrased it.

"Gone from here!" echoed the girl. "Why, it is strange that I did not hear something of it; still, it may be, as I have been away—calling upon a sick relative—since late yesterday afternoon. I just came back less than ten minutes before you came. I had not even had time to take my bonnet upstairs when you rang the bell."

Jerry Gaines was for not prolonging the interview, though they had gleaned many startling facts from this casual conversation, but something seemed to impel the young artist to question her still further on the subject of the beautiful stranger guest of young Mrs. Brown—if she had a lover, and if he ever called, and how often?

It was then that a remark fell from the maid's lips that caused both of them to start violently, and to exchange covert glances of dismay with each other, taking great care that the maid should not notice this secret telegraphing between them.

When there was absolutely nothing more to learn, they took their leave, promising to call again soon; but the next time it should not be upon business, but upon her fair self.

When the two friends got around the first corner they stopped short—gazing long and fixedly into each other's eyes.

"It will never do to disclose what we have learned to John Dinsmore tonight," said Jerry Gaines, huskily, and in this opinion Ballou heartily concurred.

"No, it will be best to await developments on the morrow," he declared.

CHAPTER XLVII.
A MOMENT OF TERROR.

The first question that John Dinsmore asked of them, when they met at the restaurant an hour later, was what success they had met with, adding that he could hardly contain himself and control his nerves, his anxiety was so intense.

"Rome was not built in a day, my dear fellow," responded Ballou, adding: "By this time to-morrow we hope to answer you more satisfactorily."

"You mean to say that you have found trace of her?" cried John Dinsmore. "Do not keep me in suspense, tell me at once."

"On or before this time to-morrow, we hope to bring you face to face with your little Jess—mind, I use the word 'hope.' That must suffice for the present, my boy," repeated Ballou.

Just as Dinsmore was about to make a response, his attention was attracted by a young man who had just entered, and who had deposited himself in a seat at an opposite table.

One glance at his face, and John Dinsmore recognized him instantly as Raymond Challoner, his foe of those other days, when they had fought that duel for the favor of fair, false, fickle Queenie Trevalyn.

As Challoner's eyes met his own, John Dinsmore saw there was no gleam of recognition in them. Raymond Challoner did not know him, and he was quite as well satisfied with this turn of affairs.

Following the direction of their friend's earnest gaze, both the artist and the reporter beheld Raymond Challoner at the selfsame moment.

"It must be that fate is playing directly into our hands!" whispered Jerry Gaines to Ballou, when John Dinsmore's attention was directed in another direction.

John had noticed that his two friends recognized Challoner; but, save a meaning half smile, he took no other notice of the other's near presence, and was glad that they seemed to ignore him.

Underneath their nonchalant manner, both Jerry Gaines and Ballou were intensely excited; and when Raymond Challoner arose to quit the place, some half an hour or so later, Gaines made a hurried excuse to leave his two friends, and passed out hurriedly in Challoner's wake; and Ballou was thankful that John Dinsmore had not the slightest suspicion that there was anything on foot in that direction.

At that selfsame hour, little Jess was sobbing her heart out in Queenie's boudoir.

She had promised to wed the man who represented himself to her to be John Dinsmore on the morrow—ay, had promised to link her fate for weal or for woe with a man whom she detested more and more each time she saw him.

"If it were not a sin for which God would never, never forgive me, I would end it all by taking my life here and now!" she moaned, clinching her hands together so tightly that the pink nails cut the tender flesh; but the pain in her heart was so severe, she never even felt the pain of the self-inflicted wound.

Queenie was purposely keeping out of her way, for she did not care to go over the ground that the marriage-to-be was all wrong—"all wrong and terrible," as Jess would pitifully express it. She had given her consent, that was enough for Queenie; she never stopped to ask herself how it was to end.

By this marriage, Raymond Challoner, masquerading under the name of John Dinsmore, would gain possession of the Dinsmore millions, would turn them into cash within a week's time, and hand her over her share of the cash for her share in bringing the marvelously daring scheme about. Further than this she did not care to look.

Of course, there would be a terrible reckoning between the real and the false heir, when the former turned up; but Queenie was content to let them fight it out as they saw fit, as long as she had her share of the money. She would go abroad, and in the mad whirl of Parisian life would try to drown her fatal love for John Dinsmore, who had flung her proffered love back into her face with such scorn.

By parting him effectually from the girl he loved, and bringing the girl within prison walls on the grave charge of bigamy, when at last he should find her, was revenge enough for even as sinister an arch plotter as herself.

She realized that there would be a stormy scene between Challoner and herself on account of her not telling him of the sudden appearance of John Dinsmore, whom he confidently believed dead, and therefore out of his way; and, most of all, that he had a legal claim upon the little heiress of Blackheath Hall.

She had not even a spark of pity in her hardened heart for the wretched young girl who was weeping her eyes out in her boudoir upstairs. She gloated, rather, over the misery of the girl who had won the love of the only man on earth whom she would ever care for.

"Let her cry!" muttered Queenie, hoarsely, as she paced up and down; "all the grief she could know in a lifetime could not equal the poignant misery I endured in the one moment John Dinsmore spurned me from him, declaring that he would not divorce that girl and wed me for all the wealth of the Indies—ay, to save his life, even, if it came to that. Some day he shall learn that it was my hand that shaped this affair, and brought the matter to a climax, and then he may, perhaps, recall the lines of the poet who has said—and, ah, how truly:

"'Hell hath no fury like a woman scorned!'"

Queenie did not seek her boudoir until a late hour, feeling sure that Jess would not be there by that time, a surmise which proved to be quite correct. The poor child had gone slowly to her own apartment, feeling wretched beyond words, and yet the morrow would usher in her wedding day.

She threw herself upon her couch, just as she was, and thus she passed the dreariest hours she had ever known. She wished that the morrow would never dawn, and then, worn out with intense grief, she finally fell into a deep and troubled sleep.

She dreamed she was roaming through the meadows fragrant with odorous blossoms, by the side of him whom she loved; she stepped across a tiny thread of a purling brook to gather blossoms which grew upon the other side of it, when suddenly the little stream widened between them, becoming a mighty cataract of water, a roaring river, which no one could ford; and they were driven farther and farther asunder by the oncoming waters, until they were lost to each other's sight in the darkness of the night which fell about them.

And, holding out her arms, and calling upon his name with mighty, piercing cries, which should have rent the very vault of heaven which bent above her, Jess awoke, to find the maid standing beside her couch, with uplifted hands and an expression of horror on her face.

"What! seek your couch like this!" the girl was exclaiming, in amazement. "Oh, miss, why did you not call me to aid you, if you were too tired to disrobe? And this your wedding day! Why, you look worn out! Let me fetch you a cup of coffee, and help you to arrange your toilet. Why, your hands are as cold as the snow outside! Are you ill?"

Jess looked up at her with her great, dark, troubled eyes.

"Yes—no!" she muttered, incoherently.

"Do let me help you, miss!" entreated the maid. "Do not send me from you; you actually look as though you were going to have a spell of sickness. It is time to dress for the ceremony—that is the message of my mistress sent me to tell you. You will have barely time to eat your breakfast and get into your wedding gown ere the bridegroom and the coach will be at the door."

"I wish it were for the grave that I am about to robe myself," thought Jess; but she said no more to the maid, who insisted on remaining with her and assisting her.

Jess pushed away the tempting little repast of bird on toast, fresh rolls, fruit and fragrant coffee which was set before her; she could not eat a morsel, or swallow a drop had her very life depended upon it.

"Take it away, Marie," she said. "It seems as though I could never eat anything again."

"What a wonderful thing love is, when it makes a girl feel like that—nervous and all broken up—on her wedding day," mused the maid, wondering when the handsome young artist and his pleasant companion would make good their promise to call. One thing she had noticed and thought long and earnestly about, and that was that they only cared to linger while she was talking to them about her mistress' guest, Miss Jess; when she persisted in changing the conversation, they had taken sudden leave.

"Everybody who sees her goes wild over her beauty," mused the maid, gazing at the girl sitting before her, with eyes that were certainly jealous ones, "and, somehow, I shall be very glad when she marries and goes away from here. Who knows but what my two new friends were enamored of her, too? The more I come to look back over their questions and words, the more it looks like that to me."

She had little time to follow up the train of her reflections, however, for time was fleeting. It wanted but fifteen minutes now to the time when the handsome, fair-haired gentleman whom Jess was to wed would come for her.

"Ah, here he is now!" she exclaimed, as the sound of a peal at the front doorbell fell upon her ear.

An instant later Jess recognized the voice of her bridegroom-to-be in the lower corridor, and at that instant Queenie, gowned and bonneted, fluttered into the room, exclaiming:

"All is in readiness, Jess, except yourself. Hurry, my love. It is unlucky to delay the marriage ceremony a moment beyond the appointed time."

CHAPTER XLVIII.
WHAT IS TO BE WILL BE.

Jess looked helplessly at her false friend.

"If the wedding must take place, I—I am ready!" she answered, in a low voice, which threatened to break into sobs ere she finished the sentence.

"Come along, then, my dear," returned Queenie, ignoring the first part of the remark. "Your bridegroom-to-be is most impatient; I can hear him pacing up and down the drawing-room."

Jess allowed Queenie to wrap the long fur cloak about her, and lead her down to the corridor below.

"Do not let him come near me, or touch my hand, or I shall surely faint!" whispered Jess, hoarsely, as she shrank behind Queenie.

The latter bit her lips fiercely, to keep back the sneering retort that sprang to them. She concluded, however, that discretion was the better part of valor, and that it would not do to seem to go against her, lest Jess should refuse to allow the marriage to take place at all, and thus upset all of their well-laid plans and her own hope of getting a good slice of the Dinsmore inheritance.

Low as Jess had uttered the words, Raymond Challoner's quick ear had caught the words distinctly, and he crushed back an imprecation most fierce behind his white teeth.

"Ye gods! how the girl detests me!" he thought; "and by the Eternal, I'll give her good cause to do so before I am through with her. She is expecting me to rush up and embrace her, while I feel more like making her ears tingle with a thorough boxing. I have no patience whatever with that kind of a girl—they arouse all the hatred and antagonism in my nature. When we turn from the altar, I will show her who is lord and master, confound her!"

But the suave, graceful manner in which he came forward, with his inimitable bow and smile, gave no warning of what was passing in his treacherous heart.

"Jess," he murmured, making not the slightest attempt to offer her a caress, but simply offering her his arm, "this is the happiest day of my life. Come, the carriage is in waiting."

Out into the bitter cold air he led her, and adown the marble steps, from which every vestige of the snow had been brushed away.

The drive to the church seemed like a dream to the girl. Queenie sat beside her, and the man whom she was to wed sat opposite. No attempt was made to keep up a conversation. Raymond Challoner was congratulating himself that he had reached the point where it was quite unnecessary.

The church was quickly reached, and the bridal party hastily entered.

"How bitter cold it is in here!" exclaimed the bridegroom-to-be, in an angry tone of voice, addressing the remark to Queenie, whom he had intrusted with the making of the hurried arrangements. "They might have had some semblance of a fire, heating up this old barn of a place. And then, again, there are half a score of people sitting about, while I ordered it to be strictly private."

"No doubt they are the caretakers; you cannot prevent them from entering if they choose," returned Queenie, indifferently.

It did not attract the particular attention of the bridegroom-to-be that all of the men present wore their coats turned high up around their necks, and their hats pulled well down over their faces, for he would have considered it only the usual precaution to fortify themselves against the bitter cold which permeated the edifice in great draughts.

They need have little fear of being recognized, for the light that flickered in through the stained-glass windows was unusually dim on this day, which had been ushered in so dark and dismal, with leaden skies, over which black, ominous stormclouds scudded.

"There isn't even the sign of a minister to greet us! I hope there is to be no hitch over this affair," he remarked to Queenie, his brows darkening perceptibly.

"He is in the pulpit, awaiting our coming; he has just entered by the side door yonder," Queenie replied.

Jess uttered no word; she was trembling like a veritable aspen leaf; whether it was from cold, or fear, or both, Raymond Challoner could not determine, nor did he trouble himself to inquire.

It ever afterward seemed like a weird dream to Jess, whether she walked or was carried down the long, dark, cold aisle, until at length she found herself in front of the altar, where the minister stood, with his open book in his hand.

She felt as though she must turn and fly from the place, her fear was so great; but this, she feared, would be hard to accomplish, with her bridegroom on one side of her and Queenie on the other. In that moment it struck her as an evil omen that Queenie should have accompanied her to the altar, draped in crape and mourning attire.

She had little time to think of this, however, for the marriage ceremony had already begun, and the man beside her was repeating after the minister:

"I, John Dinsmore, do take thee, Jess, to be my lawful, wedded wife, to have and to hold, to cherish———"

The sentence never was finished. Up from a nearby pew sprang a tall form, and with swinging strides he came down the aisle toward the altar, crying, in a deep, sonorous voice, that struck terror to two of those hearts before the altar:

"Hold! Let not this ceremony proceed! I forbid the banns!"

As he spoke, he threw back the collar of his coat, and took off his hat.

There was a piercing cry of joy, and in an instant Jess had sprung from the side of the man at the altar and into the arms of the tall stranger.

"What is the meaning of this, sir?" cried the good minister, staring in bewildered amazement from the one to the other.

"It looks, parson, as though the game were up, and that the marriage is off, and that a more formidable game is on!" exclaimed Ray, hoarsely, as he beheld a brace of officers making for the spot where he stood, while as many more guarded each aisle, cutting off every avenue of escape.

"I did not have quite time enough to carry out my ingenious scheme," he added, quickly, "or I should have been far away from here by this time; anyhow, I shall not give the real John Dinsmore, as he is waiting to proclaim himself, the joy and the fortune he is looking forward to. He shall take a trip with me!"

As he spoke, ere any one could spring forward to prevent the action, he pulled a small, silver-mounted revolver from his breast pocket, and pointing it at John Dinsmore, fired quickly. A second shot followed in less time than it takes to record it, and the second time the instrument of death was pointed against his own heart.

For the next few moments all was confusion: in the *mêlée* Jess had fainted, and Queenie, taking in all the situation at a glance, fled ignominiously from the scene, no one attempting to bar her exit, as it was understood by all present that this would probably be the course she would pursue.

When the smoke had cleared away, it was found that John Dinsmore was uninjured; for once the practiced hand of Raymond Challoner had fired wide of its mark. In Challoner's own case, the result was fatal. He had met death instantly, with that sneering laugh yet lingering on his lips.

To the bewildered minister they explained all in a few words—the dastardly scheme the dead man and the woman who had just left the edifice had planned and almost executed, to rob the gentleman who stood, pale and anxiously bending over Jess, of name, wife and fortune; how his tried and true two friends had learned, through the young widow's maid, of the marriage which was about to take place at that hour between her mistress' pretty, young guest and the young man whom they had met emerging from the house on a former visit, and that his name was John Dinsmore. Of how fate played into their hands, when they began their search for him, by meeting in the restaurant, after which they had not lost sight of him for a moment. And, furthermore, that his death brought to an untimely end the business of the officers of the law, who had trailed him down by the triangular diamond ring he wore; and who were there to arrest him for a murder done at Saratoga some months before, and for which he would have had to pay the penalty with his life, for his guilt was assured.

Ere Jess returned to consciousness, John Dinsmore had her conveyed to a nearby hotel, and here she found herself when her thoughts became clear and her dark eyes opened to life again. She almost believed it to be a wild, delusive dream to behold him whom she loved so well—not dead, but kneeling beside her, holding her hands, and calling upon her name by every sweet word in love's vocabulary.

One instant more and she was in his arms, her head pillowed on John Dinsmore's sturdy breast. That was their joyful reunion; and clasped thus, heart to heart, mutual explanations followed. And to Jess, the most amazing of them all was that fate had had her own way, in spite of her willfulness, in wedding her to John Dinsmore, the co-heir of Blackheath Hall, after all.

Her husband would not allow her to talk of that scene at the church. All he would say was:

"Raymond Challoner—that was his real name—is dead; you must forget that you ever knew him, and you must also forget that false friend, Queenie, who would have lured you to a fate worse than death if I had not come in the nick of time to frustrate her designs. She kept from me the knowledge that Raymond Challoner was attempting to palm himself off for me and gain the Dinsmore fortune by marrying you."

He was even more amazed at her crafty villainy when Jess whispered to him that she had made a confidant of Queenie, telling her of her former marriage, and how Queenie had informed her of her husband's death through an accident, which she was too ignorant of the world's ways to inquire into.

"Let us think of the arch plotters no more, my darling!" declared John Dinsmore, fondly clasping his beautiful, little bride the more closely in his arms, and covering her lovely, blushing, dimpled face with passionate kisses, while her white arms clung more tightly around his neck.

Never were two men more happy than were Jerry Gaines and Hazard Ballou over the happy ending of John Dinsmore's trials and tribulations, and the joy he entered into at last, in being reunited with the bride he loved better than his own life.

"I shall never know how to do enough for you hereafter, boys!" he exclaimed that evening, holding the hands of each, while tears which were no disgrace to his noble manhood stood in his eyes.

"I am going to make you both acknowledge my true friendship in a very practical way. When I receive my share of the Dinsmore millions I am going to buy out a New York paper, and take you both in as equal partners."

"Do you mean as artist and reporter, as we have been for years?" laughed Ballou.

"As equal partners in the enterprise," repeated John, slowly and emphatically; and the day came, soon after, in which he kept his word; and to-day "The Trinity," as they are still called, own and publish one of the most successful of all the great dailies in the great metropolis.

They are both constant visitors at John's happy home, and at the end of John's first happy year of married life, when the twin boys came, he named them after his tried and true friends, Jerry Gaines Dinsmore and Hazard Ballou Dinsmore, much to their delight. The handsome artist is still a bachelor, but at the end of the first year after John married, Jerry Gaines took to himself a bride. Guess who she was, reader mine? No less a person than Lucy Caldwell, the farmer's daughter, whom he met while she was on a visit to Jess.

Queenie, the dashing, young widow, soon after wedded another aged man for his wealth, but she was not a happy woman, because, as she often said to herself, through her fickleness she had missed the one joy that makes life worth living—love.

She lived and died envying Jess, and the great love her husband lavished upon her, to the end of her life. And the only time her proud eyes ever shed a tear was when the thought crossed her mind:

"It might have been!"

THE END.